D0847239

109123

PN       Salaman, Ester P
452         The great confession:
.S2      from Aksakov and De
         Quincey to ...
                        109123

UNIVERSITY LIBRARY
Governors State University
Park Forest South, Il. 60466

*By the same author*

TWO SILVER ROUBLES

THE FERTILE PLAIN

POEMS FROM THE RUSSIAN
(with Frances Cornford)

A COLLECTION OF MOMENTS

ESTHER SALAMAN

# THE GREAT CONFESSION

*From Aksakov and De Quincey
to Tolstoy and Proust*

ALLEN LANE THE PENGUIN PRESS

UNIVERSITY LIBRARY
GOVERNORS STATE UNIVERSITY
PARK FOREST SOUTH, ILL.

Copyright © Esther Salaman, 1973

First published 1973

Allen Lane The Penguin Press
74 Grosvenor Street, London W.1

ISBN 0 582 12598 7

Printed in Great Britain by
Ebenezer Baylis and Son Limited
The Trinity Press
Worcester, and London

PN
452
.52

To M.H.S. and P.T.S.C.

THE MIDWIFE AND THE GODFATHER OF THIS BOOK

# CONTENTS

# AUTHOR'S NOTE

I TRANSLATE from the Russian whenever I can come closer than well-known translations to the original. When quoting from *A la Recherche du Temps Perdu* I give references to both the French and English editions, in that order: I use the standard Pléiade edition of the original French text in three volumes and am grateful to both Chatto and Windus and Random House for permission to quote from Proust *Remembrance of Things Past* Vols 1–11 translated by Charles Scott Moncrieff and Vol 12 translated by Andreas Mayor. I am grateful to Mrs Cyril King for her comments and proof reading.

I have not thought it necessary to give a list of references to Aksakov, De Quincey, or Tolstoy. With the help of information given in the text there will be no difficulty in tracing the passages quoted. My purpose in giving a reference list to Proust is not scholarly but practical: to help a reader to appreciate him. Whenever his story is consecutive, as in *Swann in Love*, for instance, the reader can find his way as easily as he can in Tolstoy. But when Proust adds another and yet another stone in building a character, often separated by gaps of many hundreds of pages, I feel that the reader must be helped to find the passage. I cannot quote Proust as fully as I should like, and it is often desirable that the reader should see the quotation in its context. Those who know Proust or Tolstoy well will, I hope, be interested to compare their views with mine, and the same applies to the other writers I have dealt with. Those who have read these writers only once I can assure that whenever I returned to them, with many vivid memories in my mind, I yet found sights quite new to me. As for those who have never

1*

read any, or only part of their writings, I hope my book will generate in them the urge to read more. I confess that I have myself, throughout life, read many second and third rate writers, but in the end it was only timeless art I could live by.

'Everything of mine is a fragment of a great confession'

GOETHE: *Dichtung ünd Wahrheit* Part II Book 7

'They [my children] think my writing is one thing and I another. But every inch of me is in what I write'

TOLSTOY (in a letter to his wife, in 1885)

'This book, more laborious to decipher than any other, is also the only one which has been dictated to us by reality'.

PROUST: *Time Regained*

# INTRODUCTION

PROUST began to ponder the nature of impressions and memories already in childhood. We can follow this theme in *Jean Santeuil*, a thinly disguised autobiography written in his twenties. It was greatly expanded in *A la Recherche du Temps Perdu*. He wrote in one of his memoranda for that book: 'I must not forget that there is a recurrent motif in my life, more important than that of my love for Albertine . . . and that is the motif of recollection which is no less than the raw material of the artist's calling.'

Marcel, in a late volume of the novel, speaking of his memories of Albertine after she had died, states that she had never been more alive, though only 'in a succession of momentary flashes': 'A person', he says, 'has never been able to furnish me with more than one aspect of himself at a time, to present us with more than a single photograph of himself.' He concludes that a person consists 'merely in a collection of moments', admitting that this is 'a great weakness', but 'a great strength also: it is dependent upon memory, and our memory of a moment is not informed of everything that has happened since: this moment which it has registered endures still, lives still, and with it the person whose form is outlined in it'. And he continues: 'It was not Albertine alone that was simply a series of moments, it was also myself.'

Proust expressed these ideas in *The Sweet Cheat Gone*, on which he was working till his death: they spring from a long experience of working on his memories, recapturing them as an artist and studying their nature as a scientist. The truth of many of his conclusions can be easily verified by reading the masterpieces of autobiography: those of Rousseau, Stendhal, Aksakov, De Quincey, Harriet Martineau, and many others, and primarily the chapters on childhood which are written from memory only, late in life, at a great distance in time. Absolute factual truth is not one of their claims; what they do claim is the truth of their feelings.

I made a study of the nature of memories, based on a long preoccupation with my own and those of other writers. I studied the difference between memories of moments and memory of the background, the routine of our lives. Some of the memories of moments were fragments, some were fully recaptured. In *A Collection of Moments* I gave many examples, perhaps the most paradigmatic of which are to be found in Edwin Muir's *Autobiography*.* He had two memories of when he was three years old, one of a gold and scarlet suit, the other of a sailor suit and a canary yellow wooden whistle. He remembered the colour, the scent, the feel of the wooden whistle, but his memory was not fixed in space or time, and he himself called it a fragment. The gold and scarlet suit is part of two fully recaptured moments; in one he is walking to the school, where he is going to be baptized, dressed in the suit, with his mother holding one hand and his father the other; in the second moment he has arrived at the school, he sees the people, he sees the clergyman who is not a stranger to him, he is lifted up and then, when the cold water touches his face, he gets a terrible shock. A whole memory, that is a fully recovered one, of a particular moment which is fixed in its own sensations, space, and time, usually contains a disturbance; sometimes no more than an alert, sometimes a fright, sometimes a bad shock. I was glad to find this conclusion confirmed by psycho-analysis, though I had been unwilling to dabble in that tremendous study. Of my other generalizations and conclusions I will mention only one: when a past moment comes back involuntarily it becomes a now, and the actuality of the experience is overwhelming. This is not confined to great writers, not even to writers only; it is universal.

Working on memories over a long period – some ten years – continually opened new doors. Studying the memories of inventive writers I was fascinated by the relationship between their real memories and what they did with them in works of

* *The Story and the Fable*, 1940; reissued as *Autobiography*, 1954.

art. The view of some critics that we cannot legitimately call upon the writer's experience to question his art does not concern me. I am not intimidated by talk of the autonomy of a work of art.

It happens that I am dealing with very great novelists – Tolstoy and Proust – and if I sometimes say, or even exclaim, how wonderful, how felicitous, how great is this or that passage, I am only letting off steam. Christopher Ricks, reviewing John Bayley's book *Tolstoy and the Novel*, says that a new book on Tolstoy 'needs to convince us that it is not mere mountaineering – climbing Tolstoy because he is there'. He would probably have said the same of a new book on Proust. I am neither a literary critic nor a biographer, but I am making a new ascent. I will show, for example, that a study of Tolstoy's real memories reveals that in creating *War and Peace* he was dominated by his vision of childhood (which ended, according to him, at fourteen), and that is why it is a joyful and innocent book. (This is equally true of *Pickwick Papers*.) *Anna Karenina* is not an innocent book (as Dostoyevsky said) and no wonder: it is entirely rooted in Tolstoy's adult experiences.

I begin with Aksakov and De Quincey, who wrote masterpieces without any gift of invention or, to use Proust's term, the gift of 'translating' their real experiences into fiction. I claim that their accounts of childhood and boyhood are works of art unsurpassed by those works of the imagination, Tolstoy's *Childhood* and Proust's *Combray*. They were impersonal about their early years, but they could not be about their adult lives. This will shed light on the achievement of great novelists which is beyond that of the artist autobiographer. According to Proust: 'The book, more laborious to decipher than any other, is also the only one which has been dictated to us by reality, the only one of which "the impression" has been printed in us by reality itself.'* Most of the deciphering can only be done by the inventive imagination, and 'there is always less egoism in pure imagination than in recollection'† as Proust said. I hope to show by what means the artist autobiographer achieves impersonality when writing about his years of growing, and the

* *A la Recherche*, 12.241; 3.880.
† ibid. 7.216; 2.754.

different though related means used by the novelist to the same
end. Goethe wrote in *Dichtung ünd Wahrheit*: 'And so that
tendency started from which I have not been able to deviate my
whole life long – to transform everything that gladdened or
tormented me, or that preoccupied me in some other way, into
an image, a poem, and thus to come to terms with myself,
both correcting my ideas of external things and inwardly
quieting myself about them. . . . Thus everything of mine
that is known is a fragment of a great confession.'

In translating, transforming, the writer often feels quite
free to make an experience of childhood into one of an adult.
Consider in *War and Peace* the experience of Prince Andrey
when he visits Bald Hills on his retreat with his regiment. A
tragic moment: Napoleon has overrun Russia, and Andrey's
proud old father and his sister have left Bald Hills, that 'nest
of nobles'. He sees two little girls running out of the hothouse
where they have picked some plums: he does not want them to
see that they are being observed. Watching these frightened
little girls, 'a new sensation of comfort and relief came over
him': he realizes the existence of other human interests, which
have nothing to do with him and are just as legitimate. Compare this with the experience of Nikolenka, the Narrator of
*Boyhood*, written years earlier. The mother has died, and the
two children, Nikolenka and Katenka, the daughter of the
governess, are sitting together in a *brichka* on their way to
Moscow. They are very sensitive to each other's feelings, and
Nikolenka realizes that she is not the same as she was not long
before and asks 'Why are you so depressed?' and 'why have you
become so strange?' Finally he gets her to admit, 'Well, we
shan't always be living together . . . we shall part some day;
you are rich . . . Mamma hasn't anything.' Nikolenka does not
understand what difference that makes. I do not want to spoil
this wonderful experience of the two children by shortening it:
Katenka ends by saying that she will go into a convent, and
begins to cry. The Narrator concludes that he can date the
beginning of his boyhood from that moment: 'For the first time
the clear thought came into my head that not we alone –
namely-our family alone – lived in the world, that not all
interest centred on us, but that another life existed – of people

who had nothing in common with us, people who did not trouble about us, and even had no conception of our existence.'

*Boyhood* is closer to autobiography than *Childhood*, as I will show later, but still Tolstoy gives himself the freedom to alter facts and use more than one model for a character; in short *Boyhood* is a mixture of fact and fiction: the truth is in Tolstoy's feelings of growing up. The Narrator is ten years old, but Tolstoy himself was eight when he first went to Moscow, where the family moved to get a better education for the boys. The journey to Moscow, like the child Aksakov's journeys, was a prolonged and extraordinary experience. With the five children went the father, the grandmother, two aunts and an adopted child of one of them, Tolstoy's father's little ward, and thirty servants. The boys could not have felt more the centre of the universe if they had been royal children. At Yasnaya Polyana everyone who passed any of the Tolstoys took his hat off, and now the other travellers took no notice of them, 'had no conception of their existence'. Nikolenka, after his talk with Katenka, after his realization that there were other people in the world with their own interests, their own concerns, says, 'Without a doubt, I knew all this before; but I did not know it as I got to know it now, I had not been conscious of it, I had not felt it. A thought changes into a conviction only in one particular way, often quite unexpected and different from the way other minds take to reach the same conclusion. The talk with Katenka, which moved me deeply and compelled me to think of her future, was my way.' Prince Andrey, a middle-aged man, knew without any doubt that other people exist with their own interests, but only in that moment of great suffering did he feel this, and it became his own conviction and comforted him. How is it possible for a child's particular moment when 'a thought changes into a conviction' and he is conscious of it and feels it for the first time, to become an adult's moment, an adult's conviction?

Dickens gives the answer: he makes it amply clear in the fragment of his autobiography given to Forster that what he, aged twelve, perceived about the prisoners in the Marshalsea, where his father was imprisoned for debt – the comic, the pathetic – he perceived as clearly as he would have as a mature man.

He told Forster that 'he had never seen any cause to correct or change what in his boyhood was his own secret impression of anybody, whom he had had, as a grown up man, opportunity of testing in later years'.

The vividness, freshness, persistence of our secret impressions is not the privilege of genius alone, nor of the artist only. It is a universal experience. Darwin's modest statement sheds some light on this: 'I think memories of events commence abruptly: that is I remember those earliest things quite as clearly as others very much later in life.' The genius is in transforming a memory into an image, a poem, as Goethe said, or into the experience of a non-self.

Mr Pickwick's advice to his friends at the election in Eatanswill, to shout with the mob who shout loudest, does not originate in the cynicism of an adult, but in the free irreverential high spirits of the boy Dickens. And before long Mr Pickwick, in prison, will feel and think like the boy-poet Dickens: 'The whole place seemed restless and troubled; and the people were crowding and flitting to and fro like the shadows in an uneasy dream. "I have seen enough," said Mr Pickwick as he threw himself into a chair in his little apartment. "My head aches with these scenes, and my heart too. Henceforth I will be a prisoner in my own room".'

I find Dickens's fragment of autobiography invaluable: it contains some of the 'impressions' printed in him by reality, and it helps me to understand how he deciphered them. But knowing his real memories, I am still in awe before his 'translation'. He told us that what Mr Pickwick saw in the Fleet he, Charles, had seen in the Marshalsea, when he was twelve years old. But only a genius could have created Mr Pickwick, an adult, with the mind and heart of an exceptional boy. If you have any doubt of his intention listen to Sam Weller on Mr Pickwick: 'His heart must ha' been born five-and-twenty years after his body at least.'

Marcel says that not only Albertine but he himself was simply a series of moments. But Marcel Proust was more than that: he was *all* 'the series of moments' that his characters were. So was Tolstoy, so was Dickens.

# AKSAKOV

IN *Design and Truth in Autobiography*, a deep study, Professor Pascal comes to the conclusions: 'It is likely that autobiography is at its happiest when recreating childhood, that is, when it is based almost solely on memory.' He goes further: 'Some of the greatest [autobiographies] rely entirely on memory, and the finest parts of Rousseau's are those for which he had no documentary sources.'

One of the reasons for this becomes clear when you read an autobiography of a distinguished politician, soldier, or scientist. Preferably he should not be a man who has been your teacher, someone with whom you have worked, or under whom you have served, for in that case you will fill in his account with your own memories. Reading an autobiography of a man you do not know personally but in whose achievement you are interested, you will often find that what he tells you of his childhood holds you, but when he comes to the years of achievement you are bored. Of the early years he writes from memory and, it is new to us because it is new to him; in recreating his adult years he relies on documents: memoranda, letters, diaries. In recreating his growing years he is making a discovery (there is hardly a well-recaptured childhood without a recovery of memories which have been buried for years); on the other hand, when relying largely on documents the writer is arranging the pieces of a jigsaw puzzle.

It often happens that an autobiographer recovers later periods of his life before the earlier ones. Aksakov and De Quincey both did this. To appreciate such an autobiographer one has to read his books twice: first in the order of the story they tell, and a second time in the order in which they were written. For the benefit of those who are not prepared to do this I shall follow the example of the archaeologist who shows us not only when and how different layers of a site were dug up, but also, by a selection of finds recovered, gives some idea of the whole site.

Aksakov was born in 1791 of a noble family but not well-off, before Pushkin, Lermontov, Gogol, Turgenev, or Belinsky; a generation before Dostoyevsky and Tolstoy. Gogol and Turgenev were his friends and, in the last years of his life, Tolstoy. He learned from all of them, for they had all produced great works of art and criticism before he wrote the autobiographical books which became classics.

He began to write his books when he was nearing fifty. He had been a dramatic critic; he spent some fifteen years, with several breaks, earning a living in the civil service, and nearly as many living on his estate, where he discovered that he had neither the gift nor the liking for managing it. He married at twenty-five a well educated and able woman, and they had a large family. Two of his sons became distinguished Slavophils, and showed more zeal for politics than their father. A conservative, his judgement was not swayed by political opinions, nor his vision obscured. At one time he worked in the censorship, but lost his job: he was too independent for the oppressive régime of Nicholas the First.

He began his writing with *Family Chronicle* in 1841, the story of his parents' life before he was born. He had learned the facts from them and others, and recreated the life of his paternal grandparents from his own very vivid memories. And then he got stuck. He put the book aside: he returned to it many times, added more and more chapters, but did not finish it till fifteen years later. Why did he start so late, and take so long to write *Family Chronicle*? He wrote to his friend F. B. Chizhev: 'To replace . . . reality with invention I am unable. The result was nonsense, and it looked ridiculous even to me.' Working on the story of his sister's terrible first marriage, he told his son Ivan that he was in despair because he could not tell the truth, and 'every lie cools my imagination'. There had been objections among his relations to his telling unpleasant truths about their ancestors, and the nearer he came to his own generation the stronger the objections grew. And so the story, 'Natasha', was left unfinished.

After Aksakov had put aside *Family Chronicle* he turned to his long experience as a fisherman 'to refresh my memories and for my pleasure'. He was in need of consolation, for he had lost the sight of one eye and that of the other was failing. His *Notes on Fishing* (1847) roused great interest, and not only among fishermen. He followed it with *Notes on Shooting* (1852); to this he later added yet another book, on hunting. These books contain a lifetime's observations of a great variety of fishes and birds, their habits and natures, all unified by Aksakov's love. He describes the skill, the patience, the art of the sportsman; the waters, the forests, the seasons. These books reveal the patience of a scientist and the sensibilities of an artist. Gogol, Turgenev, Nekrasov, were enthusiastic; much later Chekhov and Gorky echoed the admiration of Aksakov's contemporaries.

Gogol had urged Aksakov to write his memories of people, saying that they would sweeten the last years of his life, be useful to his children, and help 'his countrymen to a better understanding of the Russian'. But at that time he was not yet ready. It is fascinating to follow Aksakov's excavations of his past. He is like an archaeologist working on a site under which he has a vague notion that there are the remains of several civilizations buried. The memories of fishing and shooting were the easiest to dig up: he never quite gave up his sports, so that these memories were continually renewed, and his diaries helped as well. While working on his second sportsbook he began to recapture memories of people who had impressed him in his youth. Digging down deeper, he lived in his memories of schooldays. Now he was deeply disturbed, and wrote to his son Ivan about his dilemma. He had reached the time in his boyhood when he understood the conflicts between his parents: to pass this over in silence was impossible; to publish it was also impossible. In the end he decided to publish.

While he was descending into his boyhood days, he saw paths leading to still unexplored sites above and below. In the few years that were left to him Aksakov was exploring different levels, often two simultaneously: early childhood, of which he said that it engrossed him and needed inspiration, and his literary and theatrical memories, on which he could work without much effort.

If Aksakov had any conscious purpose in his writing it was surely the one contained in his farewell to his characters in *Family Chronicle*: 'My good and bad people . . . . You are not great heroes, not imposing personalities, you trod your path on earth in silence and obscurity, and it is long, very long, since you left it: but you were human beings, and your inward and outward life had as much poetry, was as interesting and instructive to us as our life, in turn, will be to our descendants.' Tolstoy, after listening to a reading of *Family Chronicle*, made a number of suggestions, some of which Aksakov later adopted, but not the suggestion that this epilogue should be 'expressed somehow differently'. Tolstoy was much more sophisticated than Aksakov; besides he was a young man at the time. His *Childhood* had already been published, but it was years before he began *War and Peace*.

Some of Aksakov's writings are mainly of interest to a biographer or a social historian, his sports books to sports-lovers and naturalists. But *Family Chronicle* (1856), *Years of Childhood* (1858), and *A Russian Schoolboy* (1856), as well as being period pieces, are classics. He lived in the spring of Russian literature. Autobiographers were writing like novelists, and the novelists, as Dostoyevsky said in 1847, were writing confessions.

In *Family Chronicle* we learn the background of Seryozha's parents. The Aksakovs were an ancient family of landowners, who lived in a primitive patriarchal way. The paternal grandfather was a good landlord, just and truthful, a remarkable man, but almost illiterate, and capable, as Aksakov shows, of 'repulsive and ferocious actions'. J. D. Duff, the translator, gave this book the title *A Russian Gentleman*, an English euphemism. The Zubovs, the mother's family, were of a lower class on both her parents' side. Her father, having started as a small clerk ended as a high official at Ufa, a sensitive and urbane man.

Seryozha's father had a very poor education, and held a minor job in the civil service at Ufa. He did not in the least resemble his own father. He had neither his intelligence nor his shrewdness, but he was also without his ferocious temper and tyrannical ways.

Seryozha's mother was clever, good-looking, well read, and energetic. Her mother had died when she was a child, and her young stepmother took a violent dislike to her and turned her into a Cinderella. The gentle but weak father, though he loved his daughter passionately was blind to her suffering. We follow her story through her suffering in adolescence; the reconciliation with the stepmother who, dying after giving birth to a third child, begged her forgiveness, confessed her sins against her to her husband, and implored the girl to take care of her children. This she promised to do and kept her promise. The father fell ill, and the young girl became mistress of the house overnight, looked after her father's affairs, and the children of both marriages. At the time when she met the young Aksakov, she was a fully formed and mature person. She did not fall in love with him, but looked with favour on his passionate love for her. Her father thought him too insignificant: this 'little nobleman from the country' as the Zubovs' friends called him.

She was a clever, complicated person. Her son writes 'She was endowed with a kind of artistic gift to change from one state to another, and in each state to surrender unconditionally to her thoughts and desires, utterly sincere and therefore so attractive to others.'

The Aksakov grandfather would not hear of his son's marrying a woman from a lower class, not even well off, and, worst of all, much cleverer than his son. He had not met her, but had gathered enough about her to forbid the marriage.

The son began to pine, and fell ill. It was months before he recovered and when he returned to Ufa his passion flared up again. This most obedient and weak son now showed character: he informed his father quietly that he would shoot himself, and the tyrant surrendered.

When the newly-married pair came to Aksakov the old man took a great liking to his daughter-in-law and she to him. Not surprising! Nor is her dislike of her sisters-in-law and mother-in-law. Their insinuations and malicious gossip were not different from those of the servants, for, as the writer tells us, 'they were mostly pretty close to their servants in manners and education'.

*Family Chronicle* ends with Seryozha's birth, *Years of Childhood* (the title is literally *The Years of Childhood of Bagrov's Grandson*) begins with his early memories. He gives a few fragments
of memories of babyhood. Then he fell ill, an illness which
lasted for eighteen months. Of this he remembers neither the
beginning nor the end, but only the middle period, somewhere
between the ages of three and a half and four and a half, spent
in continuous travelling.

His mother had been told that travelling might do him good
and, having tried and found it true, she began to move him
about continually. The whole family travelled. The father
was always present; and with them came nurses and many
servants. They travelled in a carriage and carts, with their
bedding, food, pots and pans and, of course, the samovar.
Aksakov says: 'I remember myself often in a carriage, not always
in motion, not even always with the horses harnessed.'

Even someone who has become impenetrable to almost all
new impressions is still capable of some alertness to the changes
on a journey. It is not surprising that this very sensitive child,
waking again and again in new places, but still with his mother
close and surrounded by familiar people and things, disturbed
but not terrified, painted so many memories of moments. Here
is one example. He was feeling so unwell that it became necessary to stop. Bedding was spread out in the high grass, and he
was laid down, almost lifeless. 'I saw and understood everything that was being done near me. I heard how my father
cried, and was comforting my despairing mother, how fer-
vently she prayed, raising her hands to heaven.' Later he came
to, and felt better and stronger than usual; he begged not to be
moved, and they stayed till the evening. 'The horses were
unharnessed and put to graze, very very near me, and this
pleased me. A spring was found somewhere; ... food was
prepared and eaten, and everybody rested, even my mother
slept long. I did not sleep, but felt an unusual vigour and inner
pleasure and peace, or, more true to say, I did not understand
what I felt, but I was blissful.'

The extraordinary characteristic of Aksakov's record is
that all his memories are, like this one, fully recaptured. How
many times have I come across such a happy fragment without

the disturbing experience of the moment before. Aksakov is a paradigm.

The doctors gave up all hope for the boy's recovery, but his mother did not. Noticing that the child was a little better after being without his medicines for a few days she gave up the doctors, and started treating him according to Buchan's *Domestic Medicine*, which had recently been translated into Russian. Soon the boy began to improve. Buchan's book and his name became a precious memory: Seryozha was taught to pray for Buchan.

Aksakov says that he does not remember the end of his illness except that he became very cowardly. Discontinuity is typical not only of a child's but also of an adult's memories. His mother had always been strict with him when sure that it was for his good; she made many rules, especially when she had to leave him for a while with the grandparents: what he was to eat, when to go out, whom not to talk to. But at the same time she gave him throughout his childhood such a sense of freedom that he never hesitated to go to her with all his impressions and problems. I believe that this freedom accounts for his many references to his being a coward: he was not afraid to be afraid.

Not long after he had recovered his mother began to ail and there was fear of consumption: 'My heart grew cold with fear; and the thought that my mother's illness was due to me was a constant torture.' She was to go to Orenburg to see a doctor, and the children were to be left with the paternal grandparents in the country. Seryozha was nearing five when they started on that fabulous journey. He fully recovered many memories which were more than sixty years old. They had to cross the large river Belaya, and he remembered the sight of the river, the ferry, the boat, the ferryman and boatmen. A ferryman, wading into the stream, carried him straight to the boat, 'while my father walked beside me along the plank, smiling and encouraging me'. He was frightened, and later, in the boat, he was struck dumb, and could not answer any questions. 'All laughed and said that fear had robbed me of my tongue; but this was not quite just: I was overcome, not so much by fear as by the novelty of the surroundings, and by the noble spectacle, whose beauty I felt, though I could not explain it.'

Fair seed-time had my soul, and I grew
Fostered alike by beauty and by fear.
(WORDSWORTH: *The Prelude*)

The Aksakovs were travelling in rich country, completely
unspoilt, crossing great rivers, sleeping now in a Tartar village,
now out of doors. Seryozha had very many new impressions,
and in nearly every memory there is a note about the mother:
'my mother said she felt better', 'my mother was preparing to
pour out tea'. At the same time for everything that roused his
curiosity, every question to which he wanted an answer, he
turned to his father; and once, after his mother had gone to
sleep in the carriage, Seryozha remained to have a chat with
his father about their next halt. In the middle of the conversation they both became thoughtful for some reason, and sat for
a long time in silence. The stars were shining, the air was
fragrant from the drying grasses of the steppe, the servants were
sitting round the blazing fire, eating their meal. His father put
him quietly into the carriage. As he was falling asleep he felt a
blissful intoxication.

A conflict was soon to appear in his life. On one of their
halts his father took him fishing, and he went mad with delight.
The father was himself a keen fisherman, and so was Seryozha's
*dyadka* (a male nanny), Yevseich. This man was a domestic
serf who had been given to the young Aksakovs as a wedding
present by the grandfather. He was intelligent and self-respect-
ing, devoted to the family and especially to Seryozha.

When Seryozha came running to his mother with the first
fish he caught, she expressed displeasure. Later, when they had
resumed their journey, she explained to him that it was bad to
surrender oneself to an amusement, and that even a clever
little boy, who forgets everything for the sake of some sport,
might become stupid.

When, on the next occasion his mother very unwillingly
gave him permission to go fishing with his father, Seryozha
could not enjoy it, and soon begged to be sent back to her.
She saw at once what was going on in him: they embraced and
cried. Now she wanted to send him back, but he refused and
stayed with his mother and sister, feeling lighthearted and gay.
The number of memories in which his mother is the central

figure is overwhelming. It is his mother's anxiety, her fear, her disturbance, which disturbs him. And so Seryozha began to fight out in his own breast the conflict between the father and mother.

He early became a voracious reader. He had no playmates of his own age, and the intimacy with his mother enormously accelerated the growth of his understanding. He wrote: 'I think it is necessary to warn my well-disposed reader that Bagrov's grandson [i.e. himself] was made unusually and even painfully precocious by his passionately loving mother.'

The parents went off to Orenburg to consult a doctor, leaving the children with the grandparents. The parting with the parents, the bad season which confined the children to the house, and the new environment – Seryozha was afraid of the grandfather, and felt they were not loved in that home – all this made him very anxious. He painted many memories, as other autobiographers of childhood have done at times of anxiety And the result in all these cases was the same: a rapid growing up. When the Aksakovs took Seryozha home to Ufa, their friends remarked on the great change in him.

After the grandfather's death, Seryozha's father inherited the estate, and they moved to Aksakovo for good. The mother had never intended to live in the country, and there was nothing about Aksakovo that she liked. Her health suffered, and she blamed it on the place, which was low and damp. Passionately as her husband loved her he was not sensitive to her moods, and was frightened of all excessive emotions. He loved Aksakovo and all country pursuits. Yevseich too was a born sportsman, and as Aksakov says, 'what made him invaluable was that every sport excited him not less than me'.

By the time the family settled at Aksakovo Seryozha was seven. Tolstoy advised his official biographer, Biryukov, to divide his life into periods of seven years. Early childhood came to a watershed at about the age of seven in Tolstoy's case, in De Quincey's, Proust's, and also Aksakov's. Every one of them, sooner or later, traced their story to the source, and found that they had experienced a great love before they were seven. Aksakov and Proust for their mothers, De Quincey for his eldest sister, Tolstoy for his eldest brother.

On their travels, and later in the country, Seryozha had discovered more and more interests and passions which he shared with his father and for which his mother had nothing but contempt. One of the most remarkable chapters in Aksakov's *Years of Childhood* is 'My first spring in the country'. He was in his eighth year. Both the father and Yevseich delighted in the spring, and *passionately loved* nature (Aksakov's italics). They were not aware of it and, as he says, 'never used such words'. Lucky for Seryozha! The father and Yevseich were like a couple of children as they described to him the coming phases of the spring. He was not allowed to go out, and he ran from window to window to watch the season's advance. But when the birds came, especially 'the real birds, game . . .' the excitement of the men and the child knew no bounds. The year before, Seryozha had been present, for the first time, when his father shot down two partridges. Pursuing, with the others, one of the wounded birds, he says 'I felt some kind of avidity, a kind of new joy . . .'

With the father's help, Seryozha finally got his mother's permission to go out. When he came in 'Clasping my father's hand . . . my mother was angry'. We can see the disturbance dropping like a stone into water. 'She threatened that she would not let me go out unless I became sensible, and cleared my head at once of ducks and snipe. Good heavens, how utterly impossible!' We can watch the memory spreading like a wave. 'Suddenly there was a report, close to the house: I rushed to the window . . .' and the old falconer Philip brought in a mallard; the colours of the bird were very bright in Aksakov's memory.

There were many disturbing events in that spring. Seryozha watched the old miller, a little tipsy, fall into the pond and drown. Then came Easter. There was so much to do, to see, to care for. The father had told him that when the nightingales begin to sing it would be even gayer. In daytime their song had not made a special impression on Seryozha and he even said that the lark was as good, but at night their music got him into a state of exaltation. But was it gayer? he asks. 'In general I cannot tell: was I gay at the time? I only know that all my life the memory of that time has spilled a quiet joy over my soul.'

The only paradises we know are the lost ones, as Proust said.

It was not until the spring had far advanced that he began to calm down. His mother told him that he had been like a madman. 'You did not take any interest in anything, you forgot you had a mother!' Tears came into her eyes, and he was overcome with remorse. He believed that he was an ungrateful son. 'Unfortunately my mother sometimes either could not or would not check my tendency to run to extremes; it was a feature of her own character.' They worked themselves up to 'violent expressions of mutual repentence and passionate affection', and at that moment the father walked in. He turned pale and asked what the matter was, and it was the child who explained. 'You are still a child, but it is a sin in your mother.' And then the mother stuck up for their sensibilities 'and said much that was offensive and unfair to my kind father.' Seryozha took the mother's side: he did not understand for years how unfair he had been to his father, he says.

The mother must have been with child at the time. But Seryozha does not mention it, or tell us about the birth of his sister Annushka (though he had earlier described at some length the birth of a brother). And then, at the beginning of the schoolboy's memories, we discover Annushka's existence. We know, from *Family Chronicle*, that the father could not understand his wife's demands on him when she was pregnant, or why anyone complained when not ill. She used to say to herself, 'A man cannot give you what he has not got', but that was not followed by calm resignation. Seryozha had everything she could have wished in a husband. 'You are no longer a child; you understand everything; . . . she was deceiving herself.' This is what the old Aksakov knows, but at the time it made him conceited and spoilt him, as he tells us.

The highest price that he had to pay for the passionate love between his mother and himself was when he was compelled to condone her unfairness to his younger sister Nadia. Aksakov found, when he got down to his infant memories, that he had loved Nadia even more than his mother. He remembered being afraid that she was hungry and cold: he wanted to give her his food and put his dress on her, but was not allowed to, and cried. His instinct must have told him that his mother

did not love her. When talking to Seryozha, as to a friend, the
mother used to send Nadia out of the room, and 'forbade me
to repeat to her our frank conversations'. But when Nadia,
feeling that she was in the way, left the room, the mother said
it was a sign that Nadia did not love her. We know from the
fragment of the story 'Natasha' that the assertion was pre-
posterous. It made Seryozha sad, but still he believed everything his mother told him. 'The truth was that her [Nadia's] love
was always much warmer and deeper than my own; but this
did not appear till later.'

As his mother forced Seryozha's understanding – 'You are
no longer little, you understand everything. What do you think
of this, my friend?' – she let the genie out of the bottle. He
asked many questions and was not satisfied with the answers.
Why was he not allowed to go and see the sluices lowered?
His mother said that the peasants were rough, and used coarse
language. But his father denied this, and said there was only
plenty of gay noise and shouting. 'I couldn't *not* believe my
mother, but there was in me a desire to believe my father
more.' She disapproved even of mushroom expeditions, but he
was allowed to go with his father and the servants. He noticed
that they were unusually gay and lively, and that the maid
Matryona sang beautifully. Seryozha praised her and asked
her why she never sang in the maids' room. 'Your mother does
not like to hear our country songs.' When he came home he gave
his mother, as usual, a full account, but left out Matryona's words.

His mind opened more and more to life around him. A vague
suspicion became a conscious thought, a conviction. Some
remark of Yevseich's, and his father's embarrassment, made
Seryozha ask his mother why his father did not go fishing,
when he loved it so much, or shooting, when he had been so
keen on it? She told him she did not forbid it, but immediately afterwards expressed scorn for such childish occupations. Seryozha felt ashamed that he himself loved all sports so
much, but not for long. 'I was a sportsman at heart', he says.
As a small child he had great pity for suffering, but 'What has
happened to it?' he asks, 'the bleeding, fluttering, beautiful
little birds roused no compassion in me whatsoever.' We answer
in his own words: he was a born hunter. It is when he describes

hawking after quails with Yevseich that we learn what it felt like to be a hunter. 'I very quickly became infatuated with hunting with "the dear little hawk", as Yevseich called it . . .', Aksakov speaks of the 'avid hawk', and 'avid' is how Aksakov had described his own feeling when the partridges were shot down. His description reveals that the avid child shares the feelings of the avid hawk.

'But alas! However hard I tried to put a favourable light on the hunt in describing it to my mother and sister, both declared that it was pitiful and repulsive.'

Aksakov, the old man, is himself puzzled. He gives a particular memory of snaring a hare, and exclaims 'What a beauty that old hare was!' And proceeds to give us a minute description of it. 'I was suffocating with rapture, without myself understanding its cause.'

Yet in his memories of his mother's objections to his love of sports, there is not one based on moral grounds, which may mean only that he did not remember that kind of argument. Anyway she was more tolerant of his passion for sports than of her husband's, but always made him feel that it was time he grew out of it. He never did. But as in a marriage of love, when one of the partners begins to feel the need to free himself somewhat, and takes a step away only to come two steps back, so did Seryozha in his love for his mother. After he had been ill again her infinite love overwhelmed him. When he understood her generosity to her sister-in-law, who had never been fond of her, 'I began to worship her, was proud of her, and loved her more with every day.'

Aksakov in old age has reached the truth. He knows that he had been a favourite, a spoilt child, that his mother had been unfair to his father and sister. But his understanding does not alter his early memories of moments. An old painter, examining his past works, can tell how one influenced the next, and see the things to which he had been blind. But the paintings themselves remain memorials to particular past moments.

*Years of Childhood* ends with the parents going on a visit to Kazan, taking Seryozha with them, and *A Russian Schoolboy* begins with that visit, and the decision that he would have to go to school there.

He had been asleep while they were talking about it, and suddenly he woke, and gathered enough. That night both he and his mother wept, and she decided, against her husband's and friends' advice, to delay his going for a year, maintaining that she and the boy needed a year to get used to the idea of school.

She spent the year preparing Seryozha for school, but could not save him from the many shocks he would receive. Among the earliest was one caused by her: following the advice of some of the teachers she decided to depart secretly, and without saying goodbye. He fell ill and had to be taken to hospital; luckily one of the teachers was kind to him, and understanding. Two days later he received a note from her telling him that after travelling ninety versts from Kazan she had come back: 'to leave without a proper parting had proved too much for her. I cannot explain to myself why I did not at the first moment feel the immense happiness which I surely ought to have felt.' The old Aksakov's attempt to explain his feeling – 'I suppose I was afraid to believe it and took it for a dream' – is a rationalization. It is not uncommon for a child, or even an adult, who has suffered greatly through an act of a beloved person to resent a subsequent act which makes nonsense of the earlier suffering.

After a short time at school he began to break down. It is easy to jump to the conclusion that it was to be expected in such a spoilt child, and that the mother's uninhibited behaviour was largely responsible. Yet that was not so. So intelligent was the child, so clear had his mother made to him the purpose of his going, that he would have managed the separation from her, the cruelty of other children, being called a cry-baby. No, the main cause was the headmaster. He had been away on leave of absence, and when he saw Seryozha he took an immediate dislike to him. 'I don't like your silent, solitary child' he told the masters. He was provoked by the love Seryozha had inspired in some of the teachers, and blamed them for making too many allowances for the child and his mother. An ever-present danger to a gifted, free, and sensitive child is the envy of a man who has power over him: a buried envy, wrapped up in principles and duties. The headmaster began to persecute Seryozha.

Seryozha fell ill, but he was not utterly alone: he had Yevseich, working as a dormitory attendant at school, to watch over him. Yevseich informed the parents of Seryozha's illness. The spring floods had begun and the river Kama was dangerous, but nothing would stop Seryozha's mother from crossing it. When she saw the state her son was in she decided at once to remove him. The headmaster was against it, and the school being a government one it was as hard to get a pupil out as to get a soldier out of the army. Aksakov's mother engaged the sympathy of some of the teachers, and of the doctor; she fought with intelligence, fearlessness, and passion. She succeeded.

She kept him at home for another year, and then, after he had quite recovered, decided that he was to go back, but only as a private pupil, living outside the school with a teacher. It meant running into debt, but they reckoned to come into a rich inheritance.

Seryozha was lucky, for the headmaster had left the school, and his place was taken by a teacher who had been very kind to Seryozha before. The next few years at Kazan were very happy. The mother, with her usual insight into people, had set out to get one of the teachers, Kartashevsky, to become his tutor. For a long time he resisted the offer, but finally agreed. He was remarkably good with Seryozha, very understanding, broadminded about the boy's infatuation for him, and very firm. He made Seryozha's last two years especially happy, and this Seryozha felt he owed to his mother's pertinacity – 'I felt how far superior a mother's love is to that of anyone else in the world.'

Here the love story between mother and child breaks, and we get only occasional glimpses of her in other books. We know the parents lived to an old age, that Seryozha used to go now and then to see them at Aksakovo. A curtain descends. What were the relations between the mother and the equally intelligent and able woman Aksakov married? From the Soviet edition of his works we learn that the publicist Pogodin, after Aksakov's death, urged his wife and daughter to write a sequel to *Family Chronicle*: 'to begin with Sofiya Nikolayevna [the mother's pseudonym]: how and why feelings changed gradually and cooled.' But if we take it that falling in love with a woman who was his mother's peer produced cracks in his relationship to his mother, what happened in the years before he met his wife? We know nothing. Perhaps his correspondence, if it were published, might enlighten us a little.

Aksakov rounded off the character of Yevseich, though he was compelled to put it in a footnote in *Family Chronicle*. We see him with the old Aksakov's eyes. Frail, bent, and quite white, he is standing by his hut, his blind face turned towards the rising sun, feeling the warmth and the gentle breeze, his expression sad-joyful. His sensitive ear recognizes Aksakov's step from afar as he comes to the stream to fish. 'Ah, it's you, my little falcon! (That is what he used to call me.) High time! God grant you a good bite!'

Aksakov must have longed to go on with the story of his major characters: the objections from some of his family could not have been the sole, or even the greatest, obstacle. Again and again one finds that an autobiographer cannot write about some of his most important adult experiences, not so much out of reticence, but because something 'palsies' him, as De Quincey puts it. Take Harriet Martineau's reticence about her brother James. She had recaptured a number of memories of him. She gives us a most minutely vivid memory of his birth before she was three, which flashed upon her after many years. It was an extraordinary experience to recapture the first sight of a person who mattered so much as this brother did to her. She loved him and used to ask his advice on all important matters: why did she leave out of her *Autobiography* almost everything about her later relationship with him? Professor Pascal tells us in *Design and Truth in Autobiography* that this was due not only to a feeling of delicacy towards her brother, 'but also to the painfulness of their estrangement'. When she reached maturity she was capable of living again in many of her fears and shames of childhood, her jealousy of other members of the family, but she still could not write about James; he had hurt her too deeply. Only in a novel could she have transmuted this experience, for then it would have become impersonal. (Even after her death he continued to attack her.)

Aksakov took his writing very seriously. The idea of manu-

facturing a book, or the craft of doing it, was entirely foreign
to him, as it was to other artist-autobiographers, then and
later. In a letter to the critic M. F. De Pool, Aksakov wrote,
shortly before he died: 'People close to me have heard more
than once that I am lacking in free creativeness, that I can
only write standing on the ground of reality, following a thread
of a true event; that all my attempts of the other kind turned
out unsatisfactory and convinced me that I do not possess the
gift of pure invention.'

He had begun *Family Chronicle* with the story of his parents
before he was born, a story he had acquired from others, but
his wonderful pictures of his grandparents are based on his own
very vivid early memories. But he got stuck, and put the book
aside. At that time, in his middle life, his childhood was dead
to him, a well-known phenomenon, described by De Quincey
in *Suspiria de Profundis*. In a letter in verse to his brother Aksakov
writes:

> I have been at Aksakovo
> Nowhere did sadness leave me.

and again:

> The past has hidden itself for ever,
> Nothing can bring it back.

At the age of sixty he wrote to his friend Dmitriev that
nothing had cooled his passionate nature, that he was still now
angry, now ill, now dissatisfied with himself: his great comforts
were still his field sports where he found 'a world of calm and
freedom', and his early memories. But when he began to live in
his schoolboy memories he became deeply disturbed by the
conflict between his parents, and by his new self-knowledge.

There is much of great interest to the psychologist in *A
Russian Schoolboy*, but I must confine myself to Aksakov's digging
up of his past. 'No period of my childhood do I remember
with more perfect distinctness than my first term at school.
I could describe accurately and with every detail (though I
certainly have no intentions of doing so) the whole course of my
strange malady.' Imagine (if you can) Dickens without his
great gift of invention, writing about his boyhood towards

the end of his life: he would have made the same statement about his time at the blacking warehouse. In both cases, Aksakov's and Dickens's, the experiences lasted only a few months, but in memory they were eternities.

At school Seryozha's thoughts always travelled to the same spot, the paradise of his country home! But how? By a rush of involuntary memories. 'When I was thinking of something quite different, even when I was entirely taken up by my lessons, suddenly the sound of someone's voice, probably like some voice I had heard before, or a patch of sunlight on wall or window, such as had once before thrown light in just the same way upon objects dear and familiar, or a fly buzzing and beating against the panes, as I have often watched them do when I was a child – such sights and sounds, instantly and for one instant, though no consciousness could detect the process, recalled the forgotten past and gave a shock to my overstrung nerves.' He gives us numbers and numbers of such involuntary memories, and adds 'the oppression on my chest came on immediately and was followed by a fit'. Again and again, he says 'the past flashed into life and brightness before me; and the familiar sensations of uneasiness were soon followed by a severe attack'.

So far as I know no psychologist has taken note of Aksakov's experience of involuntary memories, and the effect they had on his health. Many a small child has suffered great anguish at the beginning of boarding school, and sometimes has been saved by getting ill, like Churchill: involuntary memories may bring him back his home without his observing them, and precipitate his illness.

But there are many examples of involuntary memories sustaining us, helping us to live, and bringing great joy, especially late in life. The taste of the madeleine, which brought Combray back to Marcel, overwhelmed him with joy, but he was an ageing man then. In the silence of old age, after the daylight has withdrawn, 'Happy is the man', Aksakov says, 'to whom childhood is a Golden Age' (or in Proust's more precise language 'a lost paradise'), and who 'is able to recall the memory of it in later years'.

Throughout life, though, some involuntary memories are

nightmares, others bring us 'the sweet loveliness of childhood', as Proust wrote in *Jean Santeuil*. Like Aksakov, he too experienced involuntary memories as a boy and, what is more, some of them are preserved in the same sensations as Aksakov's: buzzing flies, or the light on a wooden table.

The past beckons to Seryozha at a time when, half unconsciously, he wishes that the ground would open and swallow up the present. He is like the child in Goethe's *Erlkönig*, carried by his father through night and wind, who sees the Erlkönig and listens to his enticements to go with him, to play lovely games where the bright flowers grow. The father neither sees nor hears anything, and at the end of the journey the child is dead. But not if he has a mother like Aksakov's.

In this very fully recovered boyhood there are, as his Soviet biographer Mashinsky points out, a number of factual errors. For instance, Aksakov writes that he returned to school the following autumn; not at all: he stayed at home for another six months. His conscience must have blamed him for staying away longer than was necessary, for being spoilt. But he was lucky when he returned: his last few years at school were very happy. Fragments of spring at Aksakovo came back to him sporadically: he was in the middle of a French lesson with his beloved tutor when suddenly the musical cry of a redshank reached him: he rushed to the window in great excitement, but the tutor was not amused and told him sharply to get on with work. No fainting fits now followed the return of the past to the happy boy.

In *A Russian Schoolboy* the memories of school are of individual events, and very fully recaptured, but the memories of Aksakovo in the same book are very different: they are again and again only a summary of experiences: 'Childhood was a magic world', or 'My mother loved me passionately'. Such memories are brought back, as Proust says, 'with will and intelligence': they contain information, but not the living past; that you will find in his later book, *Years of Childhood*.

With knowledge of this book, one is amazed to read in a letter to his son Ivan that when he was writing about his schooldays he was disturbed when he recovered his memories of the conflict between his parents. We know that conflict, in all its manifestations, we know how deeply it affected him from the age of five and culminating at seven, so that by the end of his early childhood, it seems, there could have been nothing more to discover. It becomes clear to us that, though he had undoubtedly had fragments of memories of those early years, most of his childhood was still buried when he was living in his memories of his schooldays, at the age of sixty-three. So was De Quincey's childhood at sixty, Stendhal's at fifty, Harriet Martineau's at the same age. And it was not only the conflict between the parents that was buried: Aksakov's fear of crossing the great river Kama is described in *A Russian Schoolboy* as if he had no earlier memories of such fears.

Of that spring, after he had left school at fifteen, and had arrived at Aksakovo, he says: 'I did not know it before, and only then saw and felt it for the first time.' But what about the spring at Aksakovo when he was seven? He has recaptured it so fully in *Years of Childhood*, transfused to us his feelings of so many memories of moments, that if the book consisted of that one chapter alone we should still know the child and its world. We can tell how it came about that he had no memories of spring between the ages of eight and fifteen. When, at eight, he visited Kazan with his parents, and it was decided that he would have to go to school there, 'shades of the prison-house' began to close upon him. When, after his first term and his breakdown, his mother brought him home in the spring, he was not only ill: he had lost, as he says, the old freedom from care and his passion for outdoor life. Even Easter brought him little happiness. During the next five years he was at school at that season, and only went home in the summer. When he left school finally at fifteen, and got home just before the snow had melted, the spring greatly affected him: it pushed out of his head all thoughts of the war with Napoleon, as well as of the comrades he had left behind. Clearly this was the first time that he became fully conscious of all the things he had loved at Aksakovo in the spring.

His father had finally come into the inheritance they had expected, and they were now well-off, but 'I can honestly say that change of fortune produced no impression at all upon me'. No reason to doubt that. What really mattered was that the home was still the same as in his early childhood. The family had grown, they could travel whenever they wanted to, and his mother was now content to live in her husband's precious Aksakovo. Seryozha had become more sure of himself, and he and Yevseich still passionately loved their sports. What mattered to Seryozha was seeing and feeling again the things he had loved as a child.

A study of a number of autobiographies has corroborated my own experience of rooting my early memories when I was about fourteen, which was the beginning of a happy period for me. I was not in the least conscious of this at the time, and indeed it was only when, in maturity, I fully recovered adolescence and youth that I realized that some of my memories of before I was seven had the same nucleus as memories of when I was fourteen. If, in youth, we are still accompanied 'by the vision splendid' it is because the vision of childhood is then reinforced.

Towards the end of recreating his schooldays Aksakov, now sixty-three years old, recovered the fifteen-year-old boy's knowledge of his parents, of Aksakovo, of habits and customs. Before the year was out in which he finished *A Russian Schoolboy*, he was already promising his granddaughter, on her sixth birthday, a little book in a year's time. The book was to be the history of a child between three and nine, and it was to be for children: for a child of twelve, he wrote to Turgenev. But *Years of Childhood* was not ready for another three years.

In the Introduction Aksakov says: 'I don't know myself whether one can completely believe everything that my memory preserved.' And he goes on to tell us that he had memories not only of early childhood, but also of infancy. 'Of course I do not remember them in connection with one another, in an uninterrupted sequence.' When he was three or four he told the people round him that he remembered being weaned: they laughed, and said he must have heard about it later. Inquiries were made and it was found that some of the things he remembered nobody could have told him. That is what Charles Darwin said about his memory of being frightened by a cow when he was three: 'I clearly remember which way the cow ran, which would not probably have been told me.' On the other hand, inquiries also proved to Aksakov that other very early memories were of things he had not seen, and could have only heard about, and he concludes by saying that he will only describe memories the reality of which he cannot doubt.

The lover of memories, like the lover of music, begins to be preoccupied with them from early childhood. Aksakov remembers describing his travels during his early illness to his sister, when he was five years old and she was three. 'The greatness and beauty of God's world had made a secret impression on my child's heart, which lived on without my knowing it in my imagination.'

Mirrored in the child's experience is the life in the days of serfdom at his grandfather's place, Aksakovo, simple and primitive, and at Churasovo, a great manor house belonging to one of their relations. But the ultimate value of *Years of Childhood* is less in what the child sees, than in the child who is looking: it is this, as Professor Pascal says, which makes the book 'unsurpassed as a revelation of childhood'.

The language is simple, direct, vigorous, perfectly suited to his sincerity and truthfulness. It was clear to him that his book must be done with perfect art. He was now more excited than ever before, and wrote to Turgenev that he could not even trust his artistic judgement. He needed inspiration, and when it did not come he set the book aside, and worked on literary and theatrical memories. A conscious effort of recollection, selection, trial and error, were sufficient for those, but not for the memories of childhood. The artistic unity of *Years of Childhood* is in the whole experience being that of a particular child, and to achieve it Aksakov had to be that child again, to recapture the child's feelings.

*Family Chronicle*, which he began in 1841, did not appear till 1856, but it was still incomplete: Two parts were still to be added, the account of the newly married couple's visit to Bagrovo (Aksakovo), and of their life at Ufa. Why could he not have written them earlier? Of course he had known the facts long before, but it is one thing to have information about the past, and quite another to bring it to life. It was only when his earliest memories of Aksakovo were revived that he could write of the early years of his parents' marriage, which was added later.

*Family Chronicle* and *Years of Childhood* became Aksakov's best loved books. Gorky wrote of *Family Chronicle* and Turgenev's *Sportsman's Sketches*: 'These books calmly formed in me a stable conviction: I am not alone in the world and I shall not perish.' Most of Aksakov's contemporaries thought more highly of *Family Chronicle* than of *Years of Childhood*. Not so Tolstoy: in his diary (1857) he wrote 'There was reading at S. T. Aksakov's. *Childhood*: ravishing.' A few days later he wrote to his friend B. F. Botkin that it seemed to him better than the best parts of *Family Chronicle*, and today most people would agree with him. Some fifty years later, shortly before his death, Tolstoy told Chertkov: 'The *Years of Childhood of Bagrov's Grandson* is interesting because he himself describes his own impressions. What is bad about novels is that description comes from the writer. One should describe how this or that is reflected in the characters.' Leaving aside the novelist's problem, this is certainly true of a writer like Aksakov who does not invent: his impressions of people come best from himself, as in *Years of Childhood*, rather than from an omniscient narrator, as in *Family Chronicle*.

Aksakov was nearly blind when his early memories became visible to his inward eye. Even after he had finished *Years of Childhood* he still continued to work on other memories. To feel the urge to go on extracting the truth of one's past while death is at the door bespeaks an indifference to death itself.

# DE QUINCEY

In 1821, when De Quincey was thirty-six, there appeared in the *London Magazine* the *Confessions of an English Opium-Eater*: pure autobiography, as the writer later plainly assured readers. To this, the first instalment of his autobiography, De Quincey later added many more, which first appeared in *Tait's* and *Blackwood's Magazines* and *Hogg's Instructor*.

The chapters of De Quincey's autobiography on which I shall dwell are scattered and buried in miscellanies. In the *Collected Edition* the *Autobiography* proper consists of nineteen chapters; some writings extraneous to his story, and others, like the *Original Confessions*, are excluded. A better selection was made and edited by Edward Sackville-West (Cresset Press), but that too can be improved. If an editor were to collect De Quincey's memories of childhood and boyhood, from the *Suspiria*, the *Preliminary Confessions*, the *Revised Confessions*, and journals (like the priceless chapter 'Introduction to the World of Strife'), we would have a work of art comparable to Aksakov's *Years of Childhood* or Stendhal's *The Life of Henry Brulard*. In his preface to the 1853 English edition of his collected works he put the *Confessions*, and its sequel *Suspiria de Profundis*, in a class apart, 'far higher' than his other works. Of these the *Suspiria* was not available in this country in its original form for about a hundred years.

The fault was partly De Quincey's: in revising his work he robbed the *Suspiria* of its beginning, 'The Affliction of Childhood', for his *Autobiographic Sketches*, and so removed its foundation. He still hoped, then, to revise the *Confessions* and the *Suspiria*. He did revise the *Confessions*, but not the *Suspiria*.*

*In 1956 it appeared in its original form in Malcolm Elwin's book, *De Quincey*, together with both versions of *Confessions* and a short biography.)

By moving his earliest memories to the *Autobiographic Sketches* De Quincey achieved an autobiographic sequence, but not an autobiography. The sketches were written at different times, from different points of view, and are of different quality. He wrote chapters of autobiography over a period of thirty-five years. To appraise his work I shall confine myself, by and large, to the parts which he claimed were works of art in conception, in the order in which they were written.

In Part I, which he calls *Preliminary Confessions*, he begins by answering the question how he first became a regular opium eater. He refutes the opinion that he practised it for the sake 'of creating an artificial state of pleasurable excitement'. True, he did occasionally take opium for the sake of pleasure for nearly ten years, but he interposed long periods of abstinence, and did not become a regular opium eater until he was twenty-eight years old. That year he suffered from a most painful affliction of the stomach which had originally been caused 'by extremities of hunger, suffered in my boyish days'. For this affliction he found only one remedy – opium.

The first chapter is a short introduction to his London adventure. The starting point is his running away from the Manchester Grammar School at the age of seventeen. He already knew more Greek than his teacher, and having an income sufficient to support him at college he wanted to go there immediately. But his guardians would not hear of it, so he decided to run away.

From his subsequent writings and letters it becomes clear that he had told us very little of what had gone before he reached London; enough only to make us understand his fear that if the guardians discovered him they would make him go back. Without this his plight in London would be incomprehensible. But it was not the whole truth: that was far too complicated.

The London adventure marked the beginning of his youth. However much Greek he knew, however much his letters and conversation had impressed people, he was still a child. But not after London: his experience there served 'to convince me how easily a man who has never been in any great distress, may pass through life without knowing, in his own person at least, anything of the possible goodness of the human heart – or, as I must add with a sigh, of the possible vileness'.

The plans that he made from the very beginning were those of a child, but not unreasonable. When he had decided to run away he wrote to his friend Lady Carbery, who 'had latterly treated me with great distinction', and asked for a loan of five guineas: she sent him ten. He hoped to borrow money on his future inheritance, but what he had not foreseen was that the negotiations would drag on for months.

Utterly alone in London, his money soon exhausted, all depended on what he meant to people and people to him. The shady attorney, his agent in all his dealings with the money-lenders, who dared not sleep in his own house for fear of debtors, allowed De Quincey to sleep there. He found there a forlorn child, who had been living in the house alone for some time, hungry, cold, and frightened. From want of furniture 'the noise of the rats made a prodigious echoing on the spacious staircase and hall'. They slept on the floor, 'with a bundle of cursed law papers for a pillow', and little to cover themselves with. 'The poor child crept close to me for warmth, and for security against her ghostly enemies.' He did not know who she was, or what she did in daytime: 'She was neither pretty, nor quick in understanding, nor remarkably pleasing in manners. But, thank God! . . . plain human nature, in its humblest and most homely apparel, was enough for me; and I loved the child that was my partner in wretchedness.'

In daytime he used to walk in the streets, often with prostitutes. They gave him what protection they could. This diminutive man, with his lovely face and enchanting manners, must have roused their maternal instincts.

Ann was among them, but not of them. She had not completed her sixteenth year, and so was younger than he. A brutal ruffian had plundered her little property, and De Quincey urged her to lodge a complaint. But she delayed taking any steps, 'for she was timid and dejected'. For many weeks they walked the streets together. One night, when he was feeling particularly ill, they left Oxford Street, and turned into Soho Square. They sat down, he leaning his head against her bosom.

He fainted, and fell backwards on the steps. Uttering a cry of
terror, she rushed away and returned with a glass of port wine
and spices. He believed it saved his life.

A moment of respite came when De Quincey met in the
street a man who had received hospitality from his family, and
who now stopped and spoke to him. He told him the truth and
asked him not to betray him to his guardians. Next day he
received a ten-pound banknote. As the money-lenders were
asking for a further guarantee, he decided to go down to Eton
and talk to his friend Lord Westport, with whom he had
travelled before he went to the Manchester Grammar School.
He gave Ann some of the money, told her of his plans, and that
he would never forsake her. He was now quite cheerful, but
she, as they kissed, put her arms round his neck and wept
without speaking a word.

They had agreed exactly when and where to meet, and she
was to come to the same place for a number of nights. When
he returned from Eton, and came to their rendezvous, she was
not there. His inquiries, his search, led nowhere. He says in
the original version that losing her 'has been my heaviest
affliction', and even years later, in the revised version, after he
had recaptured his great 'affliction of childhood', he says the
same. She continued to live in his memories and dreams for the
rest of his life.

Anything might have happened to Ann. She may have been
in the power of an evil man or woman, who used De Quincey's
absence to put an end to their meetings. She had a very bad
cough, and may have died. It is possible that she cried so
bitterly when they parted because she had decided to end their
meetings. She must have learned a great deal about him: she
knew his plans, knew he had friends among the high and
mighty, that a stranger he met in the street had sent him ten
pounds on account of knowing his family. De Quincey may
have told her that his schoolmaster had said that he could
harangue an Athenian mob better than he could address an
English one. She could have had little doubt that the boy's
sojourn in her world was temporary. And so De Quincey lost
the girl who haunted his dreams to the last.

We have read nearly half the *Confessions* before we come to the story of how he first became an opium-eater. In 1804, at the age of nineteen, while in London, he had a severe attack of neuralgia, and a college acquaintance recommended opium. He took it and his pain vanished, but that was of little importance compared with 'the immensity of those positive effects which had opened before me – in the abyss of divine enjoyment thus suddenly revealed. Here was a panacea for all human woes: here was the secret of happiness . . . happiness might now be bought for a penny.' From then on, for nearly ten years, he took it in moderation, 'seldom more than once in three weeks.' It was usually on a Tuesday or Saturday night, because it was then Grassini sang, and opium enormously increased his pleasure. At other times he used to wander on a Saturday night in markets, and join the poor, who 'are far more philosophic than the rich'. He shared their interests, 'became familiar with their wishes, their difficulties, and their opinions'. He gave them his own which 'was always received indulgently. If wages were a little higher, or expected to be so, or the quartern loaf a little lower; or it was reported that onions and butter were expected to fall, I was glad: yet, if the contrary were true, I drew from opium some means of consoling myself.'

But he admits that markets and theatres 'are not the appropriate haunts of the opium-eater. . . . He naturally seeks solitude and silence as indispensable conditions of those trances, or profoundest reveries.'

We who know his whole life story recognize these profound reveries: he had experienced the first when he was seven. Now he writes: 'I, whose disease it was to meditate too much, and to observe too little, and who, upon my first entrance to college, was nearly falling into a deep melancholy, from brooding too much on the sufferings which I had witnessed in London . . .' looked for remedies. He forced himself to go among people, and studied hard.

And so we have an indication that he suffered from deep melancholy at the very beginning of his college life, that is, when he was beginning to take opium. Though he will claim throughout his writings that he first took it by accident, as a remedy for neuralgia, and that he later became a regular opium-eater because of an intolerable affection of the stomach, he slowly uncovers many other causes, of which melancholy, 'blank desolation', was an important one.

When he recovered his cheerfulness, it was not to markets and theatres that he turned, after opium, but to the reveries of solitude. He sat from sunset to sunrise, motionless, he says, on a summer night, in a room from which he could overlook the sea and the distant town of Liverpool, in a reverie on the antagonism of 'infinite activities, infinite respose'.

He takes stock of his condition in the spring of 1812. He is living in a cottage, 'in the depths of mountains': we know this is in Grasmere. He is living on a private income and studying German metaphysics. He has been taking opium for eight years, in moderation, and is in good health. In 1813 he was attacked by 'a most appalling irritation of the stomach . . . in all respects the same as that which had caused me so much suffering in youth, and accompanied by the revival of all the old dreams'.

From 1813, he tells us, he became a regular and confirmed opium eater. The year before 'I had suffered much in bodily health from distress of mind connected with a very melancholy event'. He tells us nothing at all about this event, which was the death of Kate Wordsworth.

The next landmark in his life is 1816: in that year, after taking large does of opium for three years, he reduced the dose greatly, and without any considerable effort; again he was happy, he says, again he read Kant.

To give us an idea of his happiness in 1816 he describes an evening, typical of many. 'Let there be a cottage, standing in a valley, 18 miles from any town – no spacious valley . . .' where he knew everyone, 'let the mountains be real mountains, between 3 and 4,000 feet high; and the cottage, a real cottage . . .' with flowers upon the walls through the months of spring, summer, and autumn, but the season 'winter', in his sternest shape'. In a low room, lined with thousands of books; 'a lovely young woman sitting at the table . . . her arms like Aurora's, her smiles like Hebe's: But no, dear M., not even in jest let me insinuate that thy power to illuminate my cottage rests upon a tenure so perishable as mere personal beauty . . .' The cottage is Dove Cottage and the place Grasmere.

And who is M.? We know that she was Margaret Sympson, whom he married in 1817, after she had born him a son. He had been visiting a farm called the Nab, where the Sympson family and their eldest daughter Margaret lived. We have one definite date, Christmas 1814, of a party to which De Quincey invited the family from the Nab.

We need to know a great deal more than he tells us in the *Confessions* to see through some of the mystery which surrounds that happy year 1816, when Margaret, the beautiful farmer's daughter, was carrying his child.

These premarital relations, in a man known to have been a prude in sexual matters, shy with women, and after his marriage faithful to his wife for life, made Edward Sackville-West suggest (in his biography of De Quincey *A Flame in Sunlight*): 'The explanation, I cannot help thinking, is that the seduction was more Margaret's doing than De Quincey's.' While we cannot tell what part was played by this young, healthy, and natural girl, in love, we need never be surprised at anything De Quincey did. A Tory, a churchman, insular, and in all matters passionate, this conventional man, fastidious and extremely polite, again and again cut his moorings: ran away from school, became an opium-eater, ran away from Oxford, and married a simple country girl.

There was little money, and no kindness from the Wordsworth clan. The women – Mrs Wordsworth, her sister Sara Hutchinson, and Dorothy Wordsworth – disapproved of his relationship with Margaret and were positively unkind. But the estrangement between De Quincey and the Wordsworths had begun before Margaret appeared on the scene.

He had loved Wordsworth's poetry since he was a boy, and they corresponded. He had longed to meet him, and finally, when he was twenty-two, the meeting took place. For some years he shared the domestic griefs and joys of the Wordsworths, over and above his profound sympathy with the poet's work. In 1809, when the Wordsworths moved to a new house, De Quincey took over their Dove Cottage, in Grasmere. Chance misunderstanding between them began in 1813, but what hurt De Quincey most was Wordsworth's failure to counter the 'female prejudices', their unkindness to Margaret at the hour 'in which an act of friendship so natural, and costing so little (in both senses so priceless), could have been availing'. He wrote this in *Recollections of the Lake Poets,* in his fifties; he still could not bring himself to speak plainly about his great disappointment, but makes us read between the lines that there were deeper grounds for Wordsworth's failing him than disapproval of his misalliance and his opium-eating. He felt Wordsworth no longer needed him as he had done earlier. In 1816, Henry Crabb Robinson, visiting the Lakes, recorded in his diary the childish way in which De Quincey and Wordsworth dodged meeting one another. So when De Quincey says in the *Confessions* that the happiest evenings in that year were the longest ones, it is because it was easier on such evenings to shut out the hostile world, the Wordsworth ladies and their scathing remarks about Margaret, and his disappointment in the man Wordsworth.

To relish a winter night 'it must be divided by a thick wall of dark nights from all return of light and sunshine'. But to shut out the world is not sufficient for happiness – not sufficient to enable an addict to disintoxicate himself. The happiness was brought by Margaret; but why does he narrow the period to 'the latter weeks of October to Christmas Eve' of 1816? They had been lovers for some time. This season of happiness was not the first fine careless rapture: Margaret was in the last months of pregnancy.

I think there is a clue to the specific happiness of that winter in the revised *Confessions,* written towards the end of his life. The happiest season, instead of stretching from 'the latter weeks of October to Christmas Eve', is now shifted: 'Start, therefore, at the first week of November; thence to the end of January, Christmas Eve being the meridian line, . . . when happiness is in season.' Why that change in dates, when he rarely altered a sentence of the original version? That happiest period is more bright to him in old age than it had been in his thirties: he moved the date nearer to the birth of his first child, on 15 November, and continued it until the end of January, up to the time when he once again began to take opium in excess.

There is some evidence that the end of January marked the

end of a happy year, 'a year of brilliant water (to speak after
the manner of jewellers) set as it were, and insulated, in the
gloom and cloudy melancholy of opium.' The evidence comes
from a letter by Dorothy Wordsworth written to a Mrs Clark-
son on 15 February 1817, in which she reports that he 'takes
largely to opium'; she talks with contempt about Miss Sympson,
'who to all other judgements appeared to be a stupid heavy
girl, and was reckoned a dunce at Grasmere School', and
predicts De Quincey's ruin. Could a woman like Dorothy
Wordsworth, intuitive, spontaneous, original, write this merely
for snobbish reasons? We know how much she liked him from
the moment she met him, and how he returned her affection,
but was not attracted to her as a woman. He talks of an
'ungraceful and even an unsexual character of her appearance when out-of-doors' (*Recollections of the Lake Poets*).
Besides, she was fourteen years older than he, and at the time
she wrote that letter, forty-six. She was wrong that Margaret
was a dunce, wrong that the fireside would soon be dull, and
that she would be his ruin. De Quincey loved Margaret, body
and soul, passionately – we get glimpses of this in the *Confessions*
– and twenty years later the memory of the happiness she had
brought him was not dimmed. The all important part she
played in his life will emerge later, but in that year, 1817, when
he again took opium to excess, there began one of the grimmest
periods of their lives.

   For more than three and a half years he suffered again the
'pains of opium'. Living, as he says, 'in a dormant state', unable
to answer a letter or pay a bill; lacking even the power to
attempt, let alone execute anything, it was his memories,
visions, and dreams, which were his greatest ordeal. 'The
minutest incidents of childhood, or forgotten scenes of later
years, were often revived.' Placed before him 'clothed in all
their evanescent circumstances and accompanying feelings,
I *recognized* them instantaneously'. It was enough for him to
think of 'things capable of being visually represented' for them
to shape themselves into phantoms and transfer themselves to
his dreams. Space was 'amplified to an extent of unutterable
infinity'; but even more disturbing was 'the vast expansion of
time', and equally, if not more, 'the oppression of inexpiable

guilt'. 'A deep-seated anxiety and gloomy melancholy' brooded
over everything.

Involuntary memories, visions, dreams, and a hypersensitive
conscience, all had been there before he ever took opium.
Indeed we shall see that they were already apparent in the
child. I am not concerned with De Quincey's theory of opium,
but with his memories. Under opium he experienced a great
increase of dreams, visions, involuntary memories, and the
oppression of guilt.

Dreams, as Freud says, help us to sleep. It has been established that we have two kinds of sleep, a dreamless sleep and a
sleep in which we dream, and that both are necessary to us.
We know that some drugs suppress the dreaming sleep and
induce a long rebound on withdrawal. One thing we can be
certain of is that opium upset the balance of the two kinds of
sleep in De Quincey, and drove him to cry out in despair,
'I will sleep no more'.

Our conscience fights for our identity, but De Quincey's
conscience under opium was monstrous: 'for the weight of
twenty Atlantics was upon me, or the oppression of inexpiable
guilt.'

Sporadic involuntary memories help us to live but, as we
know from Aksakov's experience when he was trying to escape
from reality as a child, large numbers of them lead to breakdown.

There is one thing opium did for De Quincey: it multiplied
his hours of reverie and inactivity. Marcel, in *A la Recherche
du Temps perdu*, says that involuntary memories never came back
to him except when he was inactive ('qu'en dehors de l'action').
But the price De Quincey paid was exorbitant. There was no
need for opium to achieve the reverie so necessary to an artist:
Aksakov spent endless hours fishing, Tolstoy riding, Wordsworth walking; and De Quincey himself knew very well the
great benefit of walking. What a pathetic miserable lot are
those unfortunate people who try to buy an hour of reverie,
of visions, of the 'vast expansion of time' – normal attributes
of our nature which, forcibly acquired for a moment by a drug,
turn to ashes.

In spite of a great increase in the number of his involuntary memories under opium, De Quincey did not recover his most important memories of childhood and boyhood till late in life, and their excellence is matched by those of many writers who never tasted opium. The miracle is that he succeeded in saving his real memories from the fumes of the drug.

It was in 1820 when he saw 'that I must die if I continue the opium', and it was the family, dearer to him than his own life, which determined him rather 'to die in throwing it off'. Suffering from terrible dreams and a fear of insanity he wrote, in a few months, the *Confessions of an English Opium-Eater* in 1821.

We have seen that he could not be frank about his love story, nor about the Wordsworths. Least of all could he be frank about his mother. He admired her; she was an intellectual woman, but she never showed any understanding of him. As he said later in the *Suspiria*, there are 'great convulsions' about which a man 'neither ought to report, nor could report'. How did De Quincey come to write about opium-eating, a great convulsion indeed? Opium, in his time, was not a forbidden drug, it was used widely, and not only for medical reasons. De Quincey granted that 'Guilt and misery shrink, by a natural instinct, from public notice', but while he described plenty of misery, guilt he did not admit either in the original *Confessions* or at any time later.

His marriage to a simple country girl had set him free to live again in his first love, for Ann of Oxford Street. It confirmed his belief in his philosophical nature: 'A philosopher should not see with the eyes of the poor limitary creature, calling himself a man of the world, and filled with narrow and self-regarding prejudices of birth and education, but should look upon himself as a Catholic creature, and as standing in an equal relation to high and low – to educated and uneducated, to the guilty and the innocent.' To him Ann and Margaret were sisters.

But this freedom, though a necessary condition for writing his first book, would not have been sufficient for the great effort he had to make, while still a slave to opium. The happiness of 1816 was one of the great gifts which his love for Margaret had brought him: he had disintoxicated himself for the first time, and from then on knew that it was in him to do it again. He told the reader that he had struggled against opium 'with a religious zeal', and had accomplished what he had never heard any other man to have done, had 'untwisted, almost to its final links, the accursed chain which fettered me'. More than that, 'I trust that it will prove, not merely an interesting record, but in a considerable degree useful and instructive'.

In the original *Confessions* he had mentioned a melancholy event in 1812, followed by an illness. It was the death of Kate Wordsworth, in her fourth year. He was twenty-seven at the time, but it was a quarter of a century before he recreated his memories of that event, in *Recollections of the Lake Poets*. He makes the following statement: 'had I left untouched every other chapter of my experience, I should have certainly left behind some memorandum of this as having a permanent interest in the psychological history of human nature.' It is more than that: it is an indispensable chapter in De Quincey's *Autobiography*.

De Quincey was very fond of children throughout his life. From Dorothy Wordsworth we know that he took an interest in Catherine from the time she was a baby. He was in London when the news of the child's sudden death reached him. He was overwhelmed with grief. He wrote to Dorothy Wordsworth: 'Nobody can judge from her manner to me before others what love she showed to me when we were playing or talking alone. On the night when she slept with me in the winter, we lay awake all the middle of the night – and talked, oh, how tenderly together: when we fell asleep, she was lying in my arms; once or twice I awoke from the presence of her dear body: but I could not find it in my heart to disturb her. Many times on that night – when she was murmuring out tender sounds of endearment, she would lock her little arms with such passionateness round my neck, as if she had known that it was the last night we were ever to pass together. Ah, pretty, pretty love, would God that I might have seen thy face and kissed thy dear lips again . . .'*

Wordsworth left a portrait of her: *Characteristics of a Child Three Years Old*.

* Wordsworth Collection.

> Loving she is, and tractable, though wild . . .
> Even so this happy Creature of herself
> Is all-sufficient; solitude to her
> Is blithe society, who fills the air
> With gladness and involuntary songs.

But De Quincey tells us that 'she was noways a favourite' with her father.

When the news of her death reached him De Quincey hastily returned to Grasmere, and stretched himself every night, for more than two months, upon her grave. He had 'noonday visions': he saw her walking in a field, coming towards him. These visions did not originate from the fumes of opium: they were 'eidetic' visions, in which scientists are so much interested today. It was to be expected, he says, that nature 'would avenge such senseless self-surrender to passions', and so it did. He fell ill. It was a nervous malady, an indescribable torment, and he felt that 'life could not be borne'.

He left Grasmere and travelled south. After a few months the illness left him, and with it all his memories of Kate. Summing up this experience, he says 'a case more entirely realizing the old Pagan superstition of nympholepsy in the first place, and, secondly, of a Lethe or river of oblivion . . . applying an everlasting ablution to all the toils and stains of human anguish, I do not suppose the psychological history of man affords'.

Kate Wordsworth was not the first child whose life and death had 'connected themselves with the records of my own life by the ties of passions so profound, by a grief so fantastic', that he felt he must record the experience. There was another child, his sister Elisabeth, of whom he wrote in the *Suspiria*, several years after he had recaptured his love for Kate. He was sixty then, and again taking opium to excess, this time experiencing a panic that seemed worse at the time than any he had known before. He says that when he tried to disintoxicate himself he became 'profoundly aware that this was impossible'.

Thomas's childhood was spent with his three sisters, Elisabeth Mary, and Jane, 'sleeping always amongst them', a boy as gentle as a girl. Elisabeth was the eldest, then came Mary,

Thomas, and Jane. Jane was younger, yet in the *Suspiria* he makes her older than himself! It is wrong to attribute De Quincey's factual or chronological errors to opium. It is only those autobiographers who check their dates with the help of diaries and memoranda who achieve accuracy. Artists write about their impressions of dates, as they do of colours or of any other sensations. But De Quincey's juggling with his and Jane's ages is most remarkable. We know their true birth dates from the inscriptions in St Anne's churchyard, Manchester. Jane, who died in her fourth year, was the baby, and Thomas thirteen months older. A number of explanations jump to mind. He was very small, and it is possible that Jane caught up with him in height, or even overtook him, and his hurt pride made her the elder. But it is more likely that Elisabeth, the eldest girl, who had given Thomas so much love, mothered the new baby Jane, and made him jealous. Jane's early death would have further burdened him with guilt, and this he wiped out at one stroke by making himself a baby and her a big girl.

Her death made him sad, but he believed that she would come again. 'Thus was healed, then, the first wound in my infant heart. Not so the second.' Elisabeth was nine when she died, and Thomas nearing seven. From his memories she seemed to have been, like him, endowed with a superb intellect, a heart overflowing with love, and profound sensibilities. Serene and capacious as his sister's mind appeared to him later, he says, he knew that 'hadst thou been an idiot, my sister, not the less I must have loved thee, having that capacious heart overflowing, even as mine overflowed, with tenderness, and stung, even as mine was stung, by the necessity of being loved'.

When Elisabeth fell suddenly ill he grieved to hear her moan, but he believed that all would be well. When a nurse came to him in the night and assured him that his sister '*must* die', 'mere anarchy and confusion fell upon me'. 'Rightly it is said of utter, utter misery, that it "cannot be remembered" ' and he quotes Coleridge:

> I stood in unimaginable trance
> And agony, which cannot be remembered*

* Speech of Alhadra, in Coleridge's 'Remorse'.

This memory, of a moment fixed in time and space, is the first act of the tragedy. In the second, on the morning after her death, 'I formed my own scheme for seeing her once more. Not for the world would I have made this known.' He knew that one of the staircases would be deserted at midday, and that was when he stole up to her room. 'Entering, I closed the door so softly that, although it opened upon a hall which ascended through all the storeys, no echo ran along the silent walls. Then, turning round, I sought my sister's face. But the bed had been moved, and the back was now turned towards myself. Nothing met my eyes but one large window, wide open, through which the sun of midsummer at midday was showering down torrents of splendour. The weather was dry, the sky was cloudless, the blue depths seemed to express types of infinity, and it was not possible for eye to behold, or for heart to conceive, any symbols more pathetic of life and the glory of life.'

I omit, for the time being, De Quincey's digression that follows at this point, not because it is not of great significance, but because the memory itself is like a tune played on a violin, and we do not want to hear any other instrument at that moment. 'From the gorgeous sunlight I turned round to the corpse.' He had heard it said that her features had not changed: they had and they had not. 'My eye filled with the golden fullness of life, the pomps and glory of the heavens outside, and turning when it settled upon the frost which overspread my sister's face, instantly a trance fell upon me. A vault seemed to open in the zenith of the far blue sky, a shaft which ran up forever. I, in spirit, rose as if on billows that also ran up the shaft for ever; and the billows seemed to pursue the throne of God; but that also ran before us and fled away continually. The flight and the pursuit seemed to go on for ever and ever. Frost, gathering frost, some Sarsar wind of death, seemed to repel me; I slept – for how long I cannot say: slowly I recovered my self-possession, and found myself standing, as before, close to my sister's bed.'

The funeral is the third act of Thomas's tragedy. 'I was put into a carriage with some gentlemen I did not know. They were kind to me', but their conversation about things disconnected with the occasion was a torment. 'At the church, I was told to hold a white handkerchief to my eyes. Empty hypocrisy! What need had *he* of masks or mockeries, whose heart died within him at every word that was uttered . . . ?'

He says of the night of Elisabeth's death 'the night which for me gathered upon that event ran after my steps far into life; and perhaps at this day I resemble little for good or for ill that which else I should have been'.

In *A Collection of Moments* I compared De Quincey's tragic experience with Stendhal's at the same age, when he lost the person whom he loved more than any one in the world, his mother. With all the great differences between these two men, their early environments, their abilities (Stendhal shows already in his early memories the eye of the novelist, not so De Quincey), the similarities are deeper. Stendhal claims that the pattern of his love for his mother at the age of six (in 1789) his 'way of pursuing happiness was basically the same' as when he was madly in love with Albertine de Rubempré (in 1828). De Quincey's 'way of pursuing happiness' also remained basically the same as it was before he was seven, and in love with his sister Elisabeth. He says of her 'a girl was the sweetest thing which I, in my short life, had known'. In maturity he loved Kate Wordsworth as passionately; Ann was a sister to him; and so was his wife Margaret: not for nothing does he speak of her as 'my Electra'.

In a digression, which I have so far omitted, is a statement about the nature of our memories. De Quincey says that he has often been struck 'with the important truth, that far more of our deepest thoughts and feelings pass to us through perplexed combinations of concrete objects, pass to us as involutes (if I may coin that word) in compound experiences incapable of being disentangled, than reach us directly, and in their abstract shapes'. This view is shared by Goethe: 'Man knows himself only in so far as he knows the world, and becomes aware of the world only in himself, and of himself only in it. Every new object, well observed, opens a new organ in ourselves' (*Maximen und Reflexionen*).

In this digression De Quincey shows that death and summer, death and resurrection, had come to him through 'involutes' and were linked in his mind before Elisabeth died. Her death in the summer, the death of his father in the summer, not very long after, reinforced that image.

After Elisabeth's death he began to haunt solitary places and 'sought the most silent and sequestered nooks . . . into the woods, into the desert air, I gazed, as if some comfort lay hid in *them*'. He began to have noonday visions, just as he had many years later, after Kate's Wordsworth's death. 'The faculty of shaping images in the distance out of slight elements, and grouping them after the yearnings of the heart, aided by a slight defect in my eyes, grew upon me at that time.' This is what he wrote in the *Suspiria* – in the *Autobiographic Sketch* he omitted the defect in his eyes (what a pity!) and added that the faculty grew upon him 'in morbid excess'. On a Sunday morning in church he saw 'through the wide central field of the window, where the glass was *uncoloured* white fleecy clouds sailing over the azure depths of the sky'. His 'sorrow-haunted eye', and slightly defective vision grouped these elements into 'beds with white lawny curtains', and in those beds children 'were tossing in anguish, and weeping clamorously for death'. For some reason, he says, God could not suddenly release them from pain, but he suffered the beds to rise slowly through the clouds. And 'sometimes I seemed to rise and walk triumphantly upon those clouds . . . ; yes, sometimes under the transfigurations of music I felt of grief itself as of a fiery chariot for mounting victoriously above the causes of grief'.

All these memories De Quincey transferred from the *Suspiria* to the *Autobiographic Sketches*, eight years later. He is often criticized for adding, enlarging, digressing; but that is not what he did with the *Affliction of Childhood*. He cut away many of his experiences, and limited himself to a few memories of Elisabeth's death and a short description of the effects of his grief and solitude. The result is that the *Autobiographic Sketch* is an artistic improvement, but at a great loss!

The most significant omissions from the *Sketch* are of his religious thoughts and feelings. In the *Suspiria* he said that during the trance which fell upon him while he was standing by his dead sister, a dream was concealed in his sleep, 'whose meaning in after years, when slowly I deciphered, suddenly there flashed upon me new light; and even by the grief of a child, as I will show you, reader, hereafter, were confounded the falsehoods of philosophers'. He gave other promises to the reader, such as '. . . hereafter I will convince you of this truth, that for a Grecian child solitude was nothing, but for a Christian child it has become the power of God and the mystery of God'.

He also omitted his thoughts and feelings about the various passages in the funeral service, of which he was not conscious at the time but which came back to him later. He had, as we know, a remarkable verbal memory, which does not always go with a good memory of experiences. These thoughts and feelings are very interesting, but given 'in their abstract shapes' they float in time, and we cannot be certain that he is deciphering the experience of the child. What is convincing is his assertion that he had drunk in profoundly the spirit of Christianity from the many nursery readings, that he was not 'a child trained to talk religion' and that his religion was 'pure'. Unfortunately he omitted the passage 'take you no thought for the religion of a child, any more than for the lilies how they shall be arrayed . . .', as well as his belief that the two most beautiful things which God has made were 'infancy and pure religion'. His religion was 'pure' because it was direct, personal, and profound, like Aksakov's love of nature and Tolstoy's love of his brothers.

He called the *Suspiria* a sequel to the *Confessions*, yet instead of relating his long and varied experience of opium in the years between, he began with memories of early childhood. A stricter scrutiny of the past, he said, had led him to the conclusion that 'The nursery experience had been the ally and the natural coefficient of the opium'. In 1845 he not merely asserted that the child is the father of the man but recreated the memories which proved this. To the question 'Was it opium, or was it opium in combination with something else, that raised these storms?' he gave the definite answer: there were two agencies at work, the nursery affliction and opium.

What he intended to do next he makes plain: he would show how from the depths of his nursery affliction he reached, twelve and a half years later, at Oxford, a period of youthful happiness. He had said in the *Suspiria* that when he was leaving his dead sister's room there was a worm in his heart that could not die. 'For, if when standing upon the threshold of manhood, I had ceased to feel its perpetual gnawings, *that* was because a vast expansion of intellect, it was because new hopes, new necessities, and the frenzy of youthful blood, had translated me into a new creature' (omitted in the *Autobiographic Sketches*). But this new, happy creature, while still at Oxford, 'first tampered with opium'. Some ten years later De Quincey would state plainly that the taking of opium for a toothache or neuralgia 'could not have been the permanent ground of opium-eating', something that we suspect all along. He did *not* recreate his happy youth, nor show what part the revival of his memories of childhood, enormously expanded in dreams under opium, had on his persistent opium taking. He blames 'accidents of the press' for making it impossible to accomplish his purpose in that month's instalment, but I believe the reasons were more cogent: that this task was beyond him.

The *Suspiria* is full of unfulfilled promises. Imagine Dickens an artist, a poet, but unable to write novels, struggling to communicate his experiences in autobiography: how many promises *he* would have broken! De Quincey did not return to his theme in the next instalment, but wrote *The Palimpsest* instead. 'Our brain is a palimpsest', he says; 'it contains many layers of ideas, images, and feelings, each successive layer seeming to bury all that went before, but in reality not one has been extinguished.' And from his own memories of childhood he was led to this generalization: 'The romance has perished that the young man adored; the legend has gone that deluded the boy; but the deep, deep tragedies of infancy, as when the child's hands were unlocked from its mother's neck, or his lips forever from his sister's kisses, these remain lurking below all, and these lurk to the last.'

The rest of the instalments written in that year 1845 are on the theme of the power and effect of suffering. 'Either the human being must suffer as the price of a more searching vision, or his gaze must be shallow, and without intellectual revelation.' And again: 'O, deep is the ploughing of grief! But often less would not suffice for the agriculture of God. . . . Less than these fierce ploughshares would not have stirred the stubborn soil.'

Proust says that only when we are suffering, and our thoughts
are in a state of agitation and change, do they stir the depths,
as in a tempest, and reach a level where we can see that they
are subject to laws which we could not otherwise observe
because the calm of happiness leaves those depths undisturbed.
Edward Sackville-West says in his introduction to the *Recollections of the Lake poets* that De Quincey was in love with death and
suffering. I disagree, and accept De Quincey's own view of himself: his nature, he says, was joyous, and the foundation of his
happiness was 'from the first a heart overflowing with love'.
All his life was one long struggle against suffering, mysterious
illnesses, and melancholia. But now, at the age of sixty, he
realized how much he had learnt through suffering.

In *The Affliction of Childhood* he had established the link
between his grief for Elisabeth and opium. In *Levana and Our
Ladies of Sorrow* he uncovers a great deal more. Levana is a
Roman goddess who educates the child, not with the help of
spelling-books and grammars, but through grief. She uses the
powers that shake man's heart: these are Our Ladies of
Sorrow, Our Lady of Tears, Our Lady of Sighs, and Our
Lady of Darkness. They are sisters; there is no evil in the
first two, but the third is wicked: it is she who tempts and
hates.

The eldest, Our Lady of Tears, 'raves and moans, calling
for vanished faces'. She comes into the chambers 'of sleepless
men, sleepless women, sleepless children' from one end of the
world to the other. Her 'let us honour with the title "Madonna".'
Our Lady of Sighs 'is humble to abjectness. Hers is the meek-
ness that belongs to the hopeless', she visits bondsmen and
criminals. Our Lady of Darkness is 'the defier of God. She is
also the mother of lunacies, and the suggestress of suicides'.

'I wish to have these abstractions presented as impersona-
tions, that is clothed with human attributes of life, and with
functions pointing to flesh.' And so they are. Our Lady of
Tears, the Madonna, points to Elisabeth. The Madonna had
led him astray: 'From heaven I stole away his young heart to
mine. Through me did he become idolatrous. Holy was the
grave to him'. And the Madonna also stands for Margaret.
She was with him in his sleepless nights, as Margaret was; she

'stood in Rama where a voice was heard in lamentation –
Rachel weeping for her children, and refused to be comforted',
as Margaret wept for her boy William, who suddenly died at
nineteen, and refused to be comforted.

It is clear that Our Lady of Sighs stands for Ann. She
resembles the *Daughter of Lebanon*, in the revised *Confessions*,
an oriental woman, a Magdalen, whom he associated plainly
with 'Ann the Outcast'.

These sisters 'season' him, and at last hand him over to Our
Lady of Darkness. He had called opium the 'dark Idol'. The
Lady of Darkness, who stands for opium, is different from the
others: she does not move like the Madonna, 'with a tragic
grace', nor like the Lady of Sighs 'timidly and stealthily':
she moves 'with a tiger's leaps'. This wicked sister can only
approach those whose 'profound nature has been upheaved by
central convulsion'. De Quincey had already established a
connection between his intolerable suffering in childhood and
opium. But now he goes further. All the women he most loved,
Elisabeth, Margaret, and Ann, seasoned him and handed him
over to opium. All loved him and all brought him great bles-
sings. Elisabeth filled the gap left by the parents. Ann saved his
life. Margaret brought him the happiest year of his life, when
she bore him a son in 1816, the year in which he disintoxicated
himself without great effort. But every love had become entangled in a great convulsion. He lost Elisabeth at a tender age.
He lost Ann, and still searched for her years later. But what
made him suggest in his allegory that Margaret, his Electra,
handed him over to opium? We know one fact: a couple of
months after their child was born, he began to take opium in
great excess, never afterwards surpassed, and was for three and
a half years a wreck.

He was writing all this when Elisabeth, Ann and Margaret
were all dead and he was once again prostrating himself
before 'the dark idol', and this time 'towering gates' seemed to
him at last barred against his retreat. To this all his loves had
brought him.

The Madonna tells Our Lady of Darkness: 'Suffer not
woman and her tenderness to sit near him in his darkness . . .
curse him as only thou canst curse. . . . So shall he see the

things that ought not to be seen, sights that are abominable, and secrets that are unutterable. So shall he read elder truths, sad truths, grand truths, fearful truths. So shall he rise again *before* he dies. And so shall our commission be accomplished which from God we had – to plague his heart until we had unfolded the capacities of his spirit.'

'The true object of my "Opium Confessions" is not the naked physiological theme, – on the contrary, that is the ugly pole, the murderous spear, the halbert, – but those wandering musical variations upon the theme, – those parasitical thoughts, feelings, digressions, which climb up with bells and blossoms round the arid stock; . . .' But no writer should hang an unlimited number of bells and blossoms round an arid stock.

His material circumstances in 1845, at the time of writing the *Suspiria*, were very different from those of 1821 when he was writing the *Confessions*. His financial difficulties were coming to an end. His wife had been dead for some years, but his daughters, now grown up, were well educated, able, delightful women, and they took charge. In 1840 they had made a home for him at Lasswade, not far from Edinburgh. All the same we find him taking opium to excess. He had written the *Confessions* when he was in the depths of despair. Now he was writing the *Suspiria* in worse despair, and discovering that: 'Some of the phenomena developed in my dream-scenery, undoubtedly, do but repeat the experiences of childhood; and others seem likely to have been growths and fructifications from seeds at that time sown.' But just as the *Confessions* turned out a blessing, so did the *Suspiria*. In a preface to the first volume of the Collected Edition he asks the reader to judge the *Confessions* and the *Suspiria* 'in conception', since they still needed revision. Of the *Suspiria* he says 'not more than perhaps one third has yet been printed'. When they had been fully revised he would ask for judgement on their claims as works of art. The *Suspiria* remained unrevised; the *Confessions* he did revise – and almost robbed it of its claim to be a work of art.

In the revised *Confessions* De Quincey made a new and last attempt to understand how he became an opium-eater. There are in this version new, priceless memories of boyhood, there is a great deal of information about opium, and in this enormous chest, among a great miscellany of papers, we find the original *Confession*, practically unaltered. But even the revised *Confessions* is still a fragment!

Now, at seventy-one, the 'accursed chain' of opium which had fettered him for so many years was finally untwisted. He was famous, his family brought him happiness, and among his grandchildren it was still a granddaughter which was the sweetest thing. He pursued two different aims: to recapture fully his boyhood and the time before he got to London, and to try once more to understand how he became an opium-eater. With the latter I shall deal first.

'What was it that did in reality make me an opium-eater? That affliction which finally drove me into *habitual* use of opium, what was it? Pain was it? No, but misery. Casual over-casting of sunshine was it? No, but blank desolation. Gloom was it that might have departed? No, but settled and abiding darkness – "Total eclipse, without all hope of day" [*Samson Agonistes*]'. He goes on to say that this abiding darkness stem-med from his distresses in London, which had their ultimate origin in his own folly – 'one erring step', namely running away from school. Terrible remorse, a 'mighty phantom', strides after him, and dates its 'nativity from those hours that are fled by more than half a century'. This is a completely new analysis. 'Oh heavens! That it should be possible for a child not seventeen years old ... by one erring step ... to change the currents of his destiny!' This assertion remained unproven.

The most valuable addition to the original version is the expansion of the first part by new memories of boyhood. De Quincey was in his sixteenth year when he went to Manchester Grammar School, much too late! His comment, in an earlier sketch of school, that he ought to have entered such 'schoolboy servitude at the age of thirteen', sounds familiar today. He had flourished at his previous school, the Bath Grammar School, where he went at twelve, though the high praises of his Latin verses by the headmaster produced resentment among the other boys, and bullying. From his account we can tell that he was managing to hold his own, but unfortunately he met with an accident, a severe blow on the head, and was taken away. The headmaster came to his mother to apologize, and begged her to let him return, praising his ability 'in terms most flattering to myself'. This was the very worst way to set about getting Thomas back: the mother was shocked. 'It illustrates my mother's moral austerity.'

He was sent to a school called Winkfield, where he stayed for about a year. Then Lord Westport, a boy younger than Thomas, invited him to accompany him to Ireland on a visit to his father and later the boys lodged together at Eton. Those six months in his life, at fifteen, away from school, with Lord Westport at Eton, visiting London and Dublin, meeting aristocratic society and holding his own, accelerated his development. At the end of these travels he went to stay with a Lady Carbery, a friend of his mother. She was about ten years older than he and, unlike his mother, frankly admired his intellectual ability. She asked him to teach her Greek, while she tried to teach him Hebrew.

By the end of that year Thomas was no longer a boy but a youth, ready to go to Oxford. But he was still too young, and once again the question of his going to school came up. Lord Westport's tutor had expressed the hope that Thomas would come to Eton, and his mother did not object. But he would not hear of it: 'Anyone who should *attempt* to differ from the rest of the boys ... would be literally tormented to death.' He still urged that if he were to go to school, the best was the Bath Grammar School: it was better than Eton, he argued, because you did not have to be like every one else; the teaching, he reminded his mother, was good, and as for morals, were they not as good as at most places?

She did not listen, and finally the Manchester Grammar School was suggested to him. The great argument in favour was a financial one: a stay at that school for three years would give him an exhibition at Brasenose College, Oxford, of fifty pounds a year for seven years. Thomas's £150 a year was not considered sufficient. Still, his instinct was all against going to that school, but when even his friend Lady Carbery urged him to go he finally agreed.

According to his own account in the revised *Confessions*,

3

it was not a bad school. 'All punishments that appealed to the sense of bodily pain had fallen into disuse. . . . How then was discipline maintained? It was maintained through the self-discipline of the senior boys, and through the efficacy of their example, combined with their system of rules.' Of the boys at Bath and at Eton he says that though they had more polish, they 'suffered by comparison with these Manchester boys in in the qualities of visible self-restraint and self-respect'. He goes further, and expresses great admiration for these natives of Lancashire, mostly sons of artisans. He had a room to himself. 'I acknowledge with deep self-reproach, that every possible indulgence was allowed to me which the circumstances of the establishment made possible.' For a time Lady Carbery was staying in Manchester; he was allowed to visit her, and her presence made life bearable. But after she left he became more and more bored.

His main trouble was ill-health. The headmaster was a very sick man himself, and 'through pure zealotry of conscientiousness' became a curse to the boys by robbing them of their time for meals and recreation. To De Quincey walking was the breath of life and without exercise his health deteriorated quickly. Added to this was the medicine prescribed to him by an apothecary, fit, he says, for a tiger. His liver became affected, and this was accompanied by 'profound melancholy'.

His negotiations with his guardian about shortening his stay at school came to nothing.

He says that it was 'a furious instinct' which drove him to run away, and that he acted under the compulsion which makes 'the lemming traverse its mysterious path!'

Of all the new memories in this part, of the school, of an encounter with his uncle and mother, of travels in Wales, I shall confine myself, for the moment, to two: the Whispering Gallery and the night at the Shrewsbury Hotel. Both experiences occurred before he got to London. The Whispering Gallery came to him in a despondent early hour of a June day when he was waiting to run away. It came involuntarily, bringing back the moment when the whisper at one end of the gallery of the Dome of St Paul's reached him at the other end 'as a deafening menace in tempestuous uproar'. The old De Quincey could follow up his particular kind of fear, that he could never be sure that in time he 'might not feel withering doubts', and see it running as an unbroken strand through his story: as at the moment before running away from school, as when he began to take opium, when he ran away from Oxford, when he began to sleep with the farmer's daughter, Margaret. But in each case no retreat was open to him.

A couple of hours after he had set out from school on foot he reached Altrincham. A memory of seeing the Market Place, on just such a lovely morning, when he was three years old, came back to him, and he lived so completely in that past moment that he had to remind himself that fourteen years had gone since.

The boy of seventeen, refreshed by exercise and the lovely memory of childhood, breakfasted at Altrincham, and when he resumed his journey, after an hour's rest, 'all my gloom and despondency were already retiring to the rear,' – 'and as I left Altrincham, I said to myself "All places, it seems, are not Whispering Galleries".'

These involuntary memories which came to him at seventeen show clearly that if he had never tasted opium, the past would still have come back to him.

Compare De Quincey's experience with one of Proust's, as he recreated it in his novel. In *Time Regained*, the feel of a napkin, handed to Marcel by a servant at the Guermantes's party, fills him with joy as he wipes his mouth. It had the same feel as the napkin on which he had tried to dry himself in front of the open window at Balbec: it brings him back the sight of the green-blue sea. Turn back many volumes, to Marcel's original experience, and you find that that morning was preceded by a night of black unhappiness. He had come for the first time to Balbec. The great change lifted the curtain of habit and exposed Marcel to new impressions, as it always exposed Proust. The strange and lofty ceiling filled him with anxiety and alarm, the protest of an affection that survived in him for a ceiling that was familiar and low. What had brought him despair was the feeling of the death of things and of people one loved, and at the same time the acceptance of new things. This terrible night was followed by a joyful morning. He could not find in his trunk the things he needed, his effort to dry himself on the 'unyielding towel' was futile, but nevertheless, 'what a joy it was to think of the delights of luncheon and a walk along the shore, what a joy to gaze upon the sea.'

An intelligent and sensitive youth may generalize about the transience of all our love for things and people. Another youth, when taking an active step with some doubt, may conclude from previous experience that he will live to regret it. That is not what happened either to Marcel Proust or to De Quincey: a cerebral experience would not have had power to bring such despair. They were shaken to the depths of their beings.

Proust feared the death of things and people that he loved, and did his very utmost to immortalize them. De Quincey did not suffer from that fear; but he was afraid of the shifting nature of his own judgement and sympathies. Each was pursued by his own particular fear, rooted in his own nature.

The boy's memory of Altrincham was wonderfully joyful, but it was only a fragment of the whole experience. The morning at Balbec, standing before the open window and looking at the sea, was joyful, but not the night that preceded it. Both De Quincey and Proust took near-fatal doses of self-knowledge at the cost of great suffering, but these were followed by joyful consolations. Neither is for long without suffering, or without comfort.

The bones of De Quincey's and Proust's experiences in early youth are the same as in childhood: there is a great disturbance accompanied by fear and suffering, and an escape from them, to the beauty of the world, to love, to an expanding understanding.


I must skip the delightful account of De Quincey's travels, which have only one fault, common to the whole of the revised *Confessions*, that he hangs too many parasitical thoughts and digressions round the 'arid stock'. At a Shrewsbury hotel he waited for the Holyhead Mail to take him to London. It was a November day, and he had reached Shrewsbury after nightfall. Since he was waiting for the night mail, he was received not

like a pedestrian, a vagabond, but with courtesy. The four
wax-lights, which waiters carried before him, stirred his imagination, and even more so the room he was allotted: 'it was a
ball-room of noble proportions – lighted, if I chose to issue
orders, by three gorgeous chandeliers.' Moreover there was
room for two orchestras which money would have filled within
thirty minutes. All that was wanted was 'a throne – for the
completion of my apotheosis'.

The mail was not due till two o'clock in the morning and the
boy had long hours before him. Fierce winds were rising, 'and the
whole atmosphere had, by this time, become one vast laboratory
of hostile movements in all directions'. The day had been fine,
an Indian summer day, and his thoughts had been divided
between the grand Welsh mountains and London. But now, in
the night hours, London rose 'sole, dark, infinite – brooding
over the whole capacities of my heart'.

This is how Marcel Proust describes his experience on the
first night at Balbec: 'And for a neurotic nature such as mine,
one that is to say in which the intermediaries, the nerves,
perform their function badly – fail to arrest on its way to the
consciousness . . . the plaint of those most humble elements of
the personality which are about to disappear – the anxiety
and alarm which I felt as I lay outstretched beneath the strange
and too lofty ceiling, were but the protest of an affection that
survived in me for a ceiling that was familiar and low.' And
this is what De Quincey says: 'It is all but inconceivable to men
of unyielding and callous sensibilities, how profoundly others
find their reveries modified and overruled by the external
character of the immediate scene around them.' The loftiness
of the ballroom, and even more that of the adjoining smaller
rooms, affected him deeply, and his imagination filled the place
with music and 'flying feet that so often had spread gladness
through these halls on the wings of youth and hope'. In the
dead hours of night, with men asleep, the storm raving outside,
he was thrown into the 'deadliest condition of nervous emotion
under contradictory forces'. The music and dances and gladness of youth receded before the 'horror' of London. 'Thou
also, Whispering Gallery, once again in those moments of
conscious and wilful desolation, didst to my ear utter monitorial

sighs. For once again I was preparing to utter an irrevocable word, to enter upon one of those fatally tortuous paths of which the windings can never be unlinked.'

Edward Sackville-West expresses impatience with De Quincey for not having included the memories of the Whispering Gallery and the night at Shrewsbury in the original *Confessions*. But such memories cannot be called back by the power of will and intelligence. They came back to De Quincey towards the end of his life, as his first spring in the country came to Aksakov. And just as Aksakov, when he had deciphered his memories, knew the most profound truths about himself, so did De Quincey. He knew that his particular 'worm lying at the heart of life and fretting its security' was the inconstancy of our thoughts, judgements and feelings. 'Already, at fifteen, I had become deeply ashamed of judgements that I had pronounced, of idle hopes that I had encouraged, false admirations or contempts with which I had sympathized. And as to acts which I surveyed with any doubt at all, I never felt sure that after some succession of years I might not feel withering doubts about them both as to principle and as to inevitable results.' Again and again, during the weeks before De Quincey set out on his final journey to London 'the dreaded Whispering Gallery' came back to him.

One of the significant features of the old De Quincey's attempt to find the source of his misfortunes in that one error of running away from school is the power of his remorse 'towering for ever into proportions more and more colossal'. In the original *Confessions* he described the terrible sense of guilt from which he suffered under opium. But everything he experienced under opium was only an enormous amplification of his real experience. What were the 'fearful truths' that he knew, and the things he saw 'that ought not to be seen, sights that are abominable, and secrets that are unutterable'? What evil had he discovered in himself? He had led a virtuous life, apart from taking opium to excess; and whatever suffering this caused his wife and children, they continued to love him to the end.

We must look for the answer among his early memories.

He tells us that one of his infirmities when he was a child was 'morbid sensitivity to shame'. But after Elisabeth died, when he was told 'insultingly to cease "my girlish tears", that word "*girlish*" had no sting for me.' However he was not cured of this infirmity. Ten years later, imagining a person in peril, needing his aid, which he could obtain for him at the price of 'facing a vast company of critical or sneering faces' he feared he might 'shrink basely from the duty'. Not very unusual, but what is special is that to De Quincey 'to feel a doubt, was to feel condemnation; and the crime which might have been was in my eyes the crime which *had* been'.

De Quincey had first glimpsed the truth 'that I was in a world of evil and strife' when his sister Jane died. A whisper reached him that she had been treated harshly, if not brutally, by a servant, two days before she died. The effect on him was terrific.

I have remarked how strange it is that De Quincey, who was four and a half when Jane died at three and a half, altered his age to two and a half, which made him younger than Jane. There was no need for him to make inquiries in order to realize that he could not have been younger than Jane: it is clear from his other memories. What is truly amazing is that, when revising *Affliction of Childhood* eight years later, he changed his age from two and a half to one and a half! It is unrealistic that at that age he should have understood the whisper that she had been treated harshly by the servant. He makes himself into an infant, who cannot be responsible for *any* wrong. Guilt has the power not only to tamper with dates but to defy reason!

But the root of his strongest feeling of guilt seemed to have been in his feelings towards his mother. The father he never knew until he came home to die of consumption at the age of forty, when Thomas was in his eighth year. His mother was more highly gifted than his father, he says, and he clearly had great respect for her and called her 'an intellectual woman'. That was in the original *Confessions*, but he omitted it in the revised version: to the old man her intellect could not have been of much importance compared with her lack of understanding and of sympathy. Though he tells us a great deal more about her in the latter version than ever before, more striking is what he could not say, although she had then been dead ten years. He tells us much about his guardians and their objections to his leaving school, but never tells us that his mother was clearly the chief guardian, and that she was obdurate against his leaving. We know that he wrote her reasonable letters, explaining why he could not say on at school: he suggested that he could work at home until he went to Oxford; she stated plainly that she did not want him at home 'because we have very few sentiments of union between us'. She told him that he must do what he was told, for 'the glorification of God', and recommended that he 'conscientiously read every day at least a chapter of the Gospels or Epistles'. He insisted, in the *Suspiria*, that he was 'not a child to talk religion': was it because his mother never stopped?

The day before Thomas ran away he had received a letter addressed '*A Monsieur de Quincey, Chester*' which had a foreign postmark, and contained a draft for forty guineas. He knew at once that it was not meant for him and that it must belong to some emigrant Frenchman, but did not find time that day to take it to the Manchester post office. He had already given up his first plan of going to the Lakes, feeling that he could not present himself to Wordsworth, whom he venerated, in his present state. He decided instead to go to North Wales, and halt on the way at Chester, not to see his mother, but to contact his sister Mary and settle on a plan for their correspondence. The distance to Chester was about forty miles, and after a day's walking and a good night's sleep he felt much refreshed. But the 'accursed letter' now worried him. He was afraid he might be arrested, afraid to go to the Chester post office. Once more this sophisticated precocious boy is as naive as a little child! Finally he asked a stranger, a countrywoman, to take it to the post office for him, which she did. At Chester he hung about his home, hoping to get a note to his sister Mary. There he ran into his uncle, Colonel Penson, known as the Bengal Uncle, home on leave from India, and could not avoid going into the house and confronting his mother.

She had known that he had run away from school a few hours after it happened, and had also heard from the Chester post office about the letter. She thought he had gone to the Lakes, and had immediately sent off his sister Mary, accompanied by a friend, in pursuit.

Her chilling manner distressed him. But he tells nothing of what she said about the letter. Only in a roundabout way, by saying that there was one person, his sister Mary, who never doubted him, who disdained the idea that her brother had done wrong, does he let us know that his mother *did* doubt him, perhaps even believed that he had committed a felony.

Thomas's sensibilities at the moment he confronted his mother 'were morbidly and extravagantly acute;' his misery, as he says, being of the kind for which there was no relief, coming, as it did, from 'the pressure on the heart from the *Incommunicable*'. 'I sank away in a hopelessness that was immeasurable from all effort at explanation. She and I were contemplating the very same act; but she from one centre, I from another.'

The Bengal Uncle saw no great harm in the boy's running away from school, and his desire to go walking in the Welsh mountains, provided he was ready to manage on a guinea a week, and 'would gladly have had a far larger allowance made for me'. But Thomas thought he could manage on that, and at this point his mother, who had listened passively to these proposals, stated her objections to a larger allowance: 'what was it but to "make proclamation to my younger brothers that rebellion bore a premium, and that mutiny was the ready road to ease and comfort". My conscience smote me at these words: I felt something like an electric shock on this sudden reference, so utterly unexpected, to my brothers.' Some eighteen months later his brother, nicknamed Pink, did run away from school, but many years later Thomas learnt from Pink that he had not been influenced by his example.

De Quincey wrote a sketch of his brother Pink. He was a very good-looking, sensitive, and thoughtful child. He was sent to 'a school governed by a brutal and savage master'. He ran away once, and was sent back; the second time he ran away to sea. He was captured by pirates and forced to live among them. Later he escaped and joined the navy. For the rest of his life he remained an exile.

3*

The eldest boy, William, was remarkably intelligent and imaginative, and he too had been found unmanageable and sent away early to boarding school. Mrs De Quincey apparently got on with her daughters, but failed with all her sons.

Those who suffer from crimes that might have been, like De Quincey and Proust, sometimes reveal a streak of cruelty, or even sadism, which is utterly unexpected and incomprehensible to people with tougher consciences, who only pay for evil actions. Aksakov, the gentlest of children, repelled his mother and sister by his cruel hawking, and himself, in old age, was astonished at his childhood joy in killing and trapping animals.

De Quincey's interest in crime, his essay 'Murder as a Fine Art', is something more than an exercise in macabre humour. The difference between Proust and De Quincey is that the French writer was far franker about his sins than was De Quincey. Proust wrote openly of matricide, sometimes disguising it very thinly. De Quincey's sins seem trivial in comparison. He wrote in the revised *Confessions* of his sense of guilt towards his mother for his behaviour in their encounter after he had run away from school; but in both versions he described how he was pursued, under opium, by Furies as ugly 'as ever haunted the couch of Orestes.' – Orestes the matricide. In a footnote he refers us to the *Orestes* of Euripides; for only in Euripides, not in Aeschylus or Sophocles, is Electra by her brother's side when he is tormented by the Eumenides. She had sent him away when he was a child, to save him from his mother, and when he obeys Apollo's command to revenge his father by killing his mother, Electra is with him. Both are aware that the wicked deed has to be done, and both feel doomed. But the Eumenides pursue only Orestes, Electra does not see them: she devotes herself to watching over her brother. De Quincey says that he participated 'in the troubles of Orestes (excepting only his agitated conscience); and that by his bed sat 'my Electra'. He had not murdered his mother, but as Aeschylus says in the *Oresteia*, it is sufficient for a man to transgress the law of reverence to a parent, a god, a guest, to be pursued by the Eumenides.

Many autobiographies of childhood and boyhood – De Quincey's, Aksakov's, or Harriet Martineau's – are works of art which can stand comparison with great works of the imagination like Tolstoy's *Childhood*, Proust's Combray in *Swann's Way*, and Dickens's childhood and youth of David Copperfield. Biographies of adult life, if they are written on a theme, and are concerned with one aspect of life, whether it is opium-eating, the impact of a great war, a revolution, a reign of terror, are sometimes works of art, but they do not deal with the whole man: they are fragments. De Quincey's *Confessions* and his *Suspiria* are such fragments, and these were the only autobiographical writings for which he claimed the status of works of art, and then only 'in conception'. But most autobiographies of adult life, though often of great interest, are not of the same order as works of the imagination.

The histories of those great writers who wrote both autobiographies and novels confirms this division: the autobiographies of their growing years are works of art, while they either never attempted to write autobiography of adult life or, if they did, they failed. Yet they succeeded marvellously in transmuting their adult experience into fiction. Tolstoy, in his twenties, had intended to write 'Four Epochs of Growth', but after he had written *Childhood*, *Boyhood*, and *Youth*, he abandoned his plan. Proust's *Jean Santeuil* is thinly disguised autobiography: while some parts are as good as anything he wrote later, and the book is invaluable to anyone who wants to understand him, it fails as a work of art, precisely because it is *not* a fragment.

De Quincey, too, tried to write fiction. *Klosterheim*, a Gothic romance, he quite rightly omitted from his Collected Edition. More significant is his attempt to translate real adult experience into fiction in his novel *The Household Wreck*. He wrote it after his wife Margaret died, and some years before the *Suspiria*.

Reading it after his autobiographical writings one at once recognizes De Quincey in the narrator, and Margaret in Agnes. It starts with a delightful picture of marriage. Agnes is very young when she marries, and the narrator, unlike De Quincey, is also young. There is, of course, no illegitimate child, and instead of a large family there is only one little boy after four years of marriage. So far De Quincey is doing what many novelists have done, creating the marriage he would have liked his to have been. But no one has ever written a work of art merely by granting himself wishes! De Quincey kills the work when, after four years, the tragedy begins: a purely accidental happening due to the malice of a puppet villain.

Look at the real story: for four years this very young and simple girl was living with a helpless wreck on the verge of lunacy, and bearing one child after another. From 1821, when he wrote the *Confessions*, he was very often away from home; their financial state was very precarious and she was bringing up children and bearing more. In 1825 he wrote a letter to Dorothy Wordsworth, begging her to visit his wife, who 'writes me the most moving and heart-rending letters—not complaining, but simply giving utterances to her grief'. She was once again with child, and according to De Quincey suffered from 'states of dejection'. In the last few years of her life an eighth child was born. She lost two children, one aged four, and her firstborn William aged nineteen. Creditors were after them the whole time: in 1836 they sought sanctuary in the debtors' prison of Holyrood, and that is where she died a year later, not yet forty-two. The tragedy in real life was intrinsic in the union of a young, simple, healthy country girl with an older, most complex man, so finely balanced that he was always on the edge of an abyss, saving himself and destroying himself by opium. The love that brought happiness to both became entangled in 'great convulsions'.

De Quincey never wrote the true story of his love and marriage. We know what George Eliot, Turgenev, Tolstoy, and Proust did: each created a new, possible, love story, with the tragedy inherent in the characters and circumstances.

Let us for a moment assume that the reason why Aksakov and De Quincey could not write about their adult life, as they had done so well about their childhood and boyhood, was that they could not be frank. C. Day Lewis stopped his autobiography, *The Buried Day*, at the point when he was thirty-six, on the eve of ten years of which he says; 'I was never long free of a sense of guilt.' His most agonizing decisions, he says, have arisen from personal relationships, and 'of them I shall say little or nothing where the others concerned are alive'. De Quincey went even further, and said that not only could one not be frank while the persons concerned were alive, but even less so 'if themselves dead and buried, are yet vicariously surviving in the persons of near and loving kinsmen'. Good enough reason, you may say, why he could not be frank about the mother of his children.

But suppose that real artists like Aksakov and De Quincey had decided that in order to be frank about their adult lives they would have their manuscripts locked up for a hundred years; would they have achieved the excellence of their writings about their growing years? De Quincey gives us a clue: he remarks that even when an autobiographer wants to be frank, and there is no apparent reason why he should not be, he is sometimes 'palsied'. Anyone who has written an autobiographical novel knows the odd things in his life, often entirely innocuous from an outsider's point of view, which yet palsy him, and which he is only free to write about when he transmutes his experience into fiction.

The adult writing about childhood is writing about himself, but it is a self so far removed that he can be impersonal. W. B. Yeats wrote of his *Reveries over Childhood and Youth*, 'while I was immature I was a different person, and I can stand apart and judge'. The adult takes his current experiences into his conscious mind; when he does forget some of them it is only in order not to burden the mind, and if some are buried they are not deeply buried. It is not the length of time between the adult writer and his childhood self which brings impersonality to his work, but the great change between the years of growth and of adulthood, between the child's experiences not fully dealt with at the time of living, and the adult's experiences accepted and taken into the conscious mind.

I am led to the conclusion that if Aksakov or De Quincey had decided to write as frankly as they could about their adult years, and to lock the books up for a century, we would still have found them disappointing.

For the most original and profound expression of the reason of the divide between growth and maturity we must go back to De Quincey. In the Introductory Notice to the *Suspiria de*

*Profundis*, he says: 'Great convulsions, from whatever cause, – from conscience, from fear, from grief, from struggles of the will, – sometimes, in passing away themselves, do not carry off the changes which they have worked. *All* the agitations of this magnitude which a man may have threaded in his life he neither ought to report, nor *could* report. But one which affected my childhood is a privileged exception.' It is 'privileged as a proper communication for a stranger's ear because, though relating to a man's proper self, it is a self so far removed from the present self as to wound no feelings of delicacy or just reserve. It is privileged, also, as a proper subject for the sympathy of the narrator. An adult sympathizes with himself in childhood because he is the same, and because (being the same) yet he is *not* the same. He acknowledges the deep, mysterious identity between himself, as adult and as infant, for the ground of sympathy; and yet, with this general agreement, and necessity of agreement, he feels the difference between his two selves as the main quickeners of his sympathy. He pities the infirmities, as they arise to light in his young forerunner, which now, perhaps, he does not share; he looks indulgently on the errors of the understanding, or limitations of view which now he has long survived, and sometimes, also, he honours in the infant the rectitude of will which, under *some* temptations, he may since have felt difficult to maintain.'

In the impersonality of a great novelist we discover the same sense of relationship with some of his characters as the autobiographer has with himself as a child. Dickens has this relationship with Mr Pickwick and Sam Weller, Tolstoy with Pierre and Andrey, George Eliot with Dorothea, Proust with Swann and Charlus, Joyce with Stephen Dedalus and Bloom: both 'the deep mysterious identity' and 'the difference which is the main quickener of his sympathy'. However deeply these characters are rooted in the writer's real memories, they are not realizable without the inventive imagination.

# TOLSTOY

## 1. *Childhood*, Tolstoy's First Book

TOLSTOY wrote two 'childhoods': the first in his early twenties, the second in his seventies. The early one, *Childhood*, is known to every lover of Tolstoy; the later account is hardly known at all, though every biographer of Tolstoy quotes some memories from it.

Biryukov, Tolstoy's friend and disciple, was asked by a French publisher to write Tolstoy's biography. The Countess gave her blessing, and Tolstoy was very willing to help: 'I will give you unequivocal answers to your questions,' he wrote in 1901. Biryukov was in exile for his religious convictions and was not allowed to come to Russia even for a short visit. There followed a very interesting correspondence between them. Tolstoy wrote: 'I am afraid I have given you vain hopes that I would write my memories. I tried to think about it and saw how terribly difficult it would be to avoid the Charybdis – self-glorification (by silence about everything bad) – and the Scylla – cynical frankness about all the abomination of one's life.'

Biryukov continued to hope and sent Tolstoy the plan of the biography. Tolstoy wrote again that he would like to help, and finally, after a few months, Biryukov received 'the precious pages of memories'; he goes on to say: 'I hurried to make use of them and replace the pale places in the beginning of the biography with these bright colours.' He sent the revised beginning to Tolstoy, who wrote: 'My general impression is that you are using my memories very well, but I avoid going into details because it might entice me into revision, which I don't want to do. I am putting it all at your disposal, only adding that when you quote my notes in your biography, please add: from rough and uncorrected notes given to me and put at my disposal.' Though a vast amount of new material has been made available since – diaries, notebooks, letters – and Biryukov's biography has been superseded, it is still invaluable because of Tolstoy's own insertions and because Biryukov was an intimate friend and a true disciple in his love of truth.

In 1906 Biryukov's first volume of Tolstoy's biography appeared in English in an anonymous translation. It is out of print. In 1908 Aylmer Maude, in his life of Tolstoy, acknowledged his debt to Biryukov and said he found him very reliable, 'a storehouse of facts invaluable to every biographer of Tolstoy'. The reader who does not know Russian, and who turns to the Centenary Edition in English, will lose the spirit in which the old Tolstoy wrote down his memories for Biryukov. Apart from the fact that they are divided between Volumes 1 and 21, with confusing cross-references, Maude's editing is unfortunate. Tolstoy wrote a few memories for other biographers at various times: Maude lumps all these with those given to Biryukov, and calls the whole a collection of 'rough unrevised notes, not intended for publication'. Tolstoy never said that they were not intended for publication. It is true that he did not revise them – deliberately did not polish them – just as Stendhal did not when he wrote his memories in *The Life of Henry Brulard*. Both feared the snares of their art. But Tolstoy knew perfectly well that Biryukov would take his notes as gospel truth, and would not omit a word. Biryukov piously puts in a footnote every time he uses one of them, as Tolstoy had asked him to do. I shall refer to them as the *Reminiscences*. Introducing them Tolstoy says that he hoped to write the true story of the whole of his life. He actually made a plan, dividing his life into four periods: 'I should like to write a perfectly truthful story of these four periods, if God grants me life and strength to do it.'

While remembering that this is a plan made by the old Tolstoy, who underwent more changes during his life than most people, I have found the plan an aid. The first period was 'that wonderful – especially when compared with the following – innocent, joyful, poetic, period of childhood up to the age of fourteen'. The second was 'the terrible twenty years' period of coarse dissoluteness, service to ambition, vanity, and chiefly lust'. The third period, eighteen years, 'from marriage until my spiritual birth, could be called from a worldly point of view moral, namely in these eighteen years I lived a correct, honest family life, not succumbing to any vices condemned by public opinion, but with all my interests limited to selfish cares for the family, to increasing one's property, acquiring literary success, and to all kinds of pleasures'. The fourth period, twenty years, 'in which I now live and hope to die and from the point of view of which I see the whole meaning of my past life, and would not like to alter anything, apart from the habits of evil acquired in the preceding periods'.

Beginning his story, Tolstoy wrote: 'In order not to repeat myself in describing childhood I re-read what I have written under this title [*Childhood*], and was sorry I had written it: not good, in a literary sense insincerely written. And it could not have been otherwise, first because my project was not to give my own story but that of friends of my childhood, and that is why there came out an inharmonious compound of events of their and my childhoods; and secondly because, at the time of writing, I was far from being independent in form of expression, as I was under the influence of the two writers who strongly affected me: Sterne [*Sentimental Journey*], and Toepfer [*Bibliothèque de mon Oncle*].'

Tolstoy's contemporaries knew that the friends he refers to were the Islenevs. Old Islenev was a friend of Tolstoy's father; their estates were not far from one another, and there was a close conjunction between the two families. There were intimate friendships between Tolstoy, his brothers and sister, and Islenev's children. Tolstoy's future wife was Islenev's granddaughter.

Islenev had abducted a married woman, a Princess Kozlovsky, and had gone through a ceremony of marriage with her on his estate. The event created a great scandal and the marriage was declared illegal. Prince Kozlovsky refused to give his wife a divorce, and Islenev's and the Princess's children remained illegitimate. They adopted the name of Islavin. What Tolstoy meant by the mix-up of two stories became quite clear once

*Four Epochs of Development* appeared, to which I shall refer as the first draft of *Childhood*. The next two drafts came much nearer to the fourth and final version.

In this first draft the Narrator is an illegitimate son; he adores his mother, but does not respect, does not love, his father. He is unhappy. In the final version the Narrator is the child of a consecrated marriage, who loves both his parents, and whose childhood has been very happy. The abandonment of an early conception of a main character happens very often in Tolstoy's later works, as we know from drafts. As he tells us a great deal about childhood in the *Reminiscences* we can attempt to understand the process. Tolstoy's first project was to describe four stages of development in the life of an illegitimate son, an Islavin. The one whom Tolstoy knew intimately was Kostya, the youngest of Islenev's three sons, who was Tolstoy's own age. He and Tolstoy were intimate friends in youth. He was elegant, a gifted musician and very attractive. There is this note in Tolstoy's diary at the time he was working on *Childhood*: 'My love for Islavin spoiled eight months of my life in Petersburg. Though not conscious of it, I did not care about anything, except that he should like me.' He was referring to his stay in Petersburg two years earlier, an active and exciting time in his life. Kostya Islavin never married, never achieved a position in the world like his two elder brothers. He was the favourite uncle of the Countess Tolstoy and her sister Tanya, the model for the 'Uncle' in *War and Peace*. Tolstoy continued throughout life to take an interest in him, tried to find him a job, helped financially. But in the *Reminiscences* he describes how his own brother Dmitry changed from an ascetic life to one of debauchery, at the time when he himself was away in the Caucasus. 'I only know that his tempter was a man outwardly very attractive, but a deeply immoral person, Islenev's youngest son. I will tell about him if I have time.' He never did. It was this young man's story that he set out to write, beginning with his childhood. At the very start of the first draft the Narrator tells us that he is unhappy. He adores his mother and can find no fault with her except 'her unfortunate passion for my father'. He cannot love his father because he does not respect him; he dislikes his vanity and selfishness. But in spite of all this he tells

us 'How could one forget and not love childhood?' He follows
this up with his memories of love for his tutor Karl Ivanich.
He had been put to bed by him, and remembering the sad
story of his life, he shed tears. 'God grant him happiness, and
give me a chance to show him how much I love him. Where
are those brave prayers, the feeling of closeness of God?' From
this and other passages childhood appears a lost paradise. Yet
in part two the Narrator says: 'How many times have I tried
to make friends—a child's heart needs feeling—or at least to
love someone at a distance, but I couldn't.'

I believe that when Tolstoy looked at the childhood of this
Narrator of the first draft he saw that it was a jumble. And if we
look at the *Reminiscences* we can see why. Kostya Islavin lost
his mother when he was a baby, just like Tolstoy, and like him
he adored her memory. Tolstoy began by inventing the mother,
and modelling the father, as Biryukov tells us, on Islenev.
But the events of the day in the country before the boys go to
Moscow, the tutor Karl Ivanich and the boy's love for him,
the deep respect for the Yurodivis (half-wits), the nurse Natalya
Savishna, all are lifted out of Tolstoy's life and lent to the
Narrator. Tolstoy makes it plain in the *Reminiscences* that Karl
Ivanich and Natalya Savishna are true portraits, that he
learned to respect the Yurodivis early in childhood. Tolstoy's
imagination did not create a happy childhood for his Narrator,
he lent him his own, and we find it hard to believe in it. How
can that child's gift for love be reconciled with his inability to
make friends, or even to love someone at a distance? Had
Tolstoy not taken writing so seriously from the very beginning
he could have contrived to hide these contradictions in the
first Narrator, and even to have made him appear a sophisticated and profound character, as many manufactured characters
do, at least for a time.

The diary note about Islavin having spoiled eight months of
his life, which is dated November 1851, if of considerable
interest. Not long before this Tolstoy had abandoned the first
version of *Childhood*, after months of work. The note, a conscious
realization of the influence Islavin had had on him, and his
rejection of him, coincides with Tolstoy's parting from his
first Narrator.

About the new Narrator we learn in the very first sentence
of the final version that he had just had his tenth birthday, a
useful bit of information to us. But much more so to Tolstoy:
it was a line separating Tolstoy's own early childhood from his
new Narrator's. By the age of ten Tolstoy had neither mother,
father, or grandmother, all living and very important characters in the Narrator's story. Furthermore all the formative
influences on Tolstoy in early childhood, his father, Tatyana
Alexandrovna who took the mother's place, his brothers
Nikolay and Dmitry, are absent from the Narrator's story.
Tolstoy's mother died before he was two and he said he had not
one memory of her, but the Narrator has a number of memories
of his mother. His name is Nikolenka. Even a superficial study
of Tolstoy's life and work reveals that he rarely chose a name
at random. Nikolay was the name of Tolstoy's eldest brother.
From the age of five, when Leo left the nursery and joined his
three elder brothers in the schoolroom, his love for Nikolenka
runs like a thread through his life, which can easily be picked
up again and again until death parted them.

*Childhood* first appeared in the *Sovremennik* in 1852, signed
'L.N.'. Turgenev greatly admired it, but did not know who the
writer was. He read it aloud to Tolstoy's sister Marie, and she
immediately exclaimed that the book was about their family,
but thought it must have been written by her brother Nikolay.
It is not very surprising that she should have recognized their
own childhood in the book. Karl Ivanich, Natalya Savishna,
the treatment of the Yurodivis, are all special to the Tolstoy
household. Mimi, the French governess, resembled the Islenevs
governess Mimi – in short it was clearly not pure autobiography,
but fact and fiction. But it never entered Marie Tolstoy's head
that Leo had written it! Tatyana Alexandrovna knew about
his writing but she must have kept it a secret, as Biryukov
suggests. Marie thought it was her brother Nikolay because the
family already thought of him as a promising writer; and not
only his family: Turgenev said that he lacked only the faults
necessary to becoming a great writer.

It is indeed the childhood of a Tolstoy, but in spite of much
autobiographical material it is as much a work of the imagination as Proust's Combray. Nikolenka, the Narrator, is neither

a portrait of Tolstoy's brother Nikolay, nor a self-portrait.

Again and again Tolstoy will start with an unusual story in the world around him: an illegitimate son; a Decembrist returning from Siberia; a jealous woman throwing herself under a train; a man in court recognizing in the accused prostitute the woman he had seduced; a man who had an affair with a peasant woman, then married an educated girl, and three months later murdered the peasant woman. In every case the story contains an echo of a profound experience of Tolstoy's own. And in every case, not only when he was young and inexperienced, but also at the height of his power or in old age, he wrote many drafts. Gradually he moved inwards and merged with another creature – a man, a woman, a horse. The result is neither portrait nor self-portrait, but a possible Tolstoy.

That is what the Narrator Nikolenka is; he is not in the least a jumble, as the first Narrator was. We are not at all surprised when he exclaims, 'Happy, happy, irrecoverable days of childhood!': his gift of loving runs through it all. Fifty years later, in the *Reminiscences*, Tolstoy expresses the same feeling about this first period of his life.

The Narrator in the first version is fourteen, in the second ten – both are still within the poetic period of childhood. But there is a significant change in the expression of their sexual stirrings. There are two love scenes in which the circumstances in the first and final version are almost identical. In the first scene one of his little playmates is trying to pick up a caterpillar, and the wind raises the fichu on her little white shoulder. In the first version the Narrator presses his lips to it and kisses it with all his might and 'for so long that if she had not pulled away I would have never stopped'. This is omitted in the final version, and also the words 'This was the first appearance of sensuality'. In the second scene, when the children are all cooped up in a dark cupboard listening to the Yurodivy Grisha's prayer, the little girl (the same one as in the first scene) takes the Narrator's hand and asks whose it is. There follows in the first version a description of the boy passionately kissing her bare arm; she did not take her hand away, but found his head in the dark and stroked his face and hair with tender thin fingers. Only then, as if she had become ashamed of caressing him, she wanted to pull away her hand, but he pressed harder, and tears streamed down his face. Then he describes what an innocent little girl she was, and ends thus: 'How can I describe my wonderful feelings, crying and kissing her little white hand. It must have been love, probably also sensuality, but not conscious sensuality. I needed only to think that I desired N. for the desire to die. Conscious sensuality is a heavy, dirty feeling, but my feeling was pure and pleasant and especially sad. All the most sublime feelings are connected with some kind of vague sadness.' All this is reduced in the final version to the statement that someone touched his hand, he recognized who it was, and: 'Quite unconsciously I took hold of her bare elbow and pressed my lips to her arm.' She drew away her arm, the movement upset a broken chair, and they all fled.

In the first version, when the Narrator has come downstairs in the morning to greet the mother, she says she had heard a noise late in the evening in the schoolroom, 'probably it was you Karl Ivanich?' 'Poor Karl Ivanich, how confused he got! As for me, in my childish innocence, I began to tell how I saw in a dream, as if Karl Ivanich had come at night with Marpha into the schoolroom; he picked up his cap, looked in on us, and then went with her into his bedroom. Karl Ivanich's face began to burn, and he was ready to confess his sin, when maman, who at first had listened with pleasure to my dream, suddenly repressed a smile and asked so naturally and charmingly "Children have you been to see Papa . . . ?"'

Tolstoy has invented the circumstances, as he has invented the mother. He may have heard that there had been some goings-on between the German tutor and one of the maids, but the scene, as he describes it, is not part of an experience of an innocent child; and already in the second version it disappears and never comes back again. What is truly remarkable was his discovery while working on *Childhood* that innocence does not mean the absence of all sexual stirrings, but unconsciousness of them. More than that: he believes that in 'the miraculous, joyful' period of childhood, the child is unconscious of a great deal. 'The relationships between children are based on exactly the same foundation as those between grownup people, with only this difference, that everything is done unconsciously and therefore more nobly.' He goes on to give this example: if a person knows how to control himself and uses this advantage to acquire influence over another person, then his behaviour is ignoble; but if it all happens unconsciously, then, no matter what the consequences are, there is nothing detrimental in it. All this is in the first version, but in the final version Tolstoy keeps this discovery to himself, and is content merely to create an innocent child, that is a child unconscious of its sexual stirrings.

He was in the Caucasus while working on *Childhood*; he was lonely and unhappy, but looking back at this period he wrote in 1858 to A. A. Tolstoy that 'Never, neither before nor after, did I reach such peaks in thought'. He searched with all his soul, he says, he suffered and longed for nothing but the truth. 'Everything that I discovered at the time, will remain forever my conviction'; and indeed, it is astonishing to find in this protean creature, forever changing his views, a permanent belief in a number of things, for instance, the importance of unconsciousness of desires, of virginity (as he told Gorky), of patriotism, of courage. 'Only unconscious activity bears fruit', he states in *War and Peace*.

What I am concerned with at the moment is his search as an artist at that time. The changes in the book *Childhood* are as rapid and as miraculous as those of the foetus in the womb. Did Tolstoy, who by then had had much experience of sex and was living a profligate life, get to the truth of his own childhood when he created an innocent child? The proof that he did, I find in the chapters in the final version on Nikolenka's love for the boy Seryozha and the girl Sonechka. What is remarkable about these loves is the child's complete freedom to feel intense emotions without fear, shame or guilt.

Nikolenka was struck by Seryozha's original beauty from their first meeting. 'I felt towards him an insuperable attraction. To see him was sufficient for my happiness . . . All my dreams in sleeping and waking were of him . . . I could not have confided that feeling to anyone, so precious was it to me.' And the first sight of Sonechka at the party, after the shawl, the cloak, the boots, were removed and she emerged from her wrappings, defies translation. The reason is simple: the nouns that Tolstoy uses are all caressing diminutives for which there are no equivalents in English. It is as if the fable of the creation had been modified, and instead of a full grown woman a little girl Eve was created for the boy Adam. She is something completely different, and something lovely. As the evening proceeds he discovers that she has humour, intelligence, initiative, will. And later, in bed, he tells his brother: 'I am in love, Volodya, decidedly in love with Sonechka. I feel sad, and want awfully to cry, Volodya.' And he continues 'I only wish for one thing, to be always with her, always to see her and nothing more.' He wished everyone to be in love with Sonechka, everyone to speak of it.

Volodya too is in love with her, but whereas Nikolenka only wants to cry, Volodya would like to ' "kiss her little fingers, eyes, lips, little nose, little feet – the whole of her." "Nonsense!" I cried out from underneath my pillows. "You don't understand anything," Volodya said contemptuously. "No, I understand; but it's you who don't understand, and talk nonsense," I said through my tears.'

Which of the two boys is talking nonsense, or is neither? Tolstoy did not say in the *Reminiscences* whether Volodya was invented or a portrait, but his contemporaries recognized the likeness to his brother Sergey. Leo and Sergey were the only Tolstoy brothers who lived to a great age, and throughout their lives they respected one another, loved and helped each other. It is only when one considers the whole content of their lives that one can at least ask the question again: who understood and who did not? We shall see, when we follow up the lives of Leo and Sergey, both in Leo's works of the imagination and his real memories in the *Reminiscences*, that in the boys' talk that evening, the disagreement between Nikolenka and Volodya, Tolstoy extracted a profound truth about himself and his brother Sergey. Tolstoy advised Biryukov to pay attention to his artistic creations, to look at them as biographical material. I will only say now that at the end of his life Tolstoy told Biryukov that his strongest love had been his childhood love for Sonechka. So Proust, only a few years before he died, said that his childhood love for Marie de Benardaky was 'one of the two great loves of my life', and that it was completely innocent, unlike Marcel's childhood love for Gilberte.

We know from biographical sources that Tolstoy had not invented his love for the boy Seryozha or the girl Sonechka. In the book *Childhood* she was called Sonechka Valakhin, and in real life Sonechka Kaloshin. In his fourth period when Tolstoy was obsessed by sexual problems, in *The Kreutzer Sonata*, *The Devil*, *Resurrection*, he made this note in his diary in 1890: 'Thought of writing a book about love, like my love for Sonechka Kaloshin – a love that would preclude the transition to sensuality, that would be the best possible protection against sensuality.'

The Narrator's love for the boy Seryozha and the girl Sonechka were absent in the first version, and what is remarkable about them is that Tolstoy was fully able to live in his real memories from the age of about nine years old; this is confirmed by the fact that in the *Reminiscences*, written fifty years later, he had hardly anything to add: he had lived in his memories so fully and transmuted them so perfectly, that he had laid them in their graves. As Proust said, 'a book is a great cemetery'.

The wonder of the book is in the great jump the artist made: the unhappiness and sensuality of his first Narrator were Tolstoy's own at the time of writing: he swept them out of the way and discovered the child he had been thirteen years earlier.

There is no jumble in the character of Nikolenka, so where does the old Tolstoy see the mix-up of the childhood of his friend Kostya Islavin and his own? At first sight the answer is easy: Biryukov states plainly that the parents in *Childhood* are not Tolstoy's parents: in the father Islenev is depicted, the mother is invented. Tolstoy went carefully over Biryukov's manuscript, made alterations and insertions, but let these statements stand.

Consider first the invented mother, and compare her with Tolstoy's own mother as we know her from the *Reminiscences*. Both are noble characters, devoted to their families, religious; they both write simply and well. But Tolstoy had not one memory of his mother: she died before he was two. He acquired memories of her in the way that Aksakov acquired memories of his parents' love story, which happened before he was born. Many of those who knew his mother well continued to live in Yasnaya Polyana: not only members of the family, but her own nurse and maids, and the German tutor. As a young man Tolstoy spent hours listening to a cousin of his mother's, Princess Volkonsky, who had often stayed in Yasnaya Polyana.

Tolstoy's mother came of an aristocratic family, was rich and well-educated. She was not goodlooking. She was quick-tempered, but self-controlled. The maids told Leo that she never said a rough word to them: 'She did not even know any.' But his most important knowledge of his mother came from his love and intimate understanding of his brother Nikolay: he believed that, more than any of the other children, Nikolay was like her. He admired in both 'their indifference to other people's opinions and their modesty', traits which he found wanting in himself. He admired their not judging others. The mother was an entrancing teller of stories, he learned, and so was his brother Nikolay, whose stories had profoundly affected him when he was five. Her letters and diary filled him with admiration for her style. 'A third feature which distinguished my mother from her circle was the truthfulness and simple tone of her letters.'

This search for his mother was not due to lack of affection either in his childhood or later. On the contrary there was abundance. Tatyana Alexandrovna, a relation of the Tolstoys who had lived at Yasnaya Polyana throughout the parents' marriage, and after the mother died took her place, loved Leo tenderly, and he returned her love fully. He gives us memories of his passionate adoration for her when he was little, and of turning to her with problems when he was older, and in fact throughout his life. He says in the *Reminiscences* that she had been, after his father and mother, the greatest influence on his life.

It is possible that Tolstoy had to come to terms with the disaster of being robbed of his mother in babyhood. He had a gigantic ego, like Dickens and Proust. The grudges and gratitudes of these men grew to monstrous size, causing them great sorrows and great joys. Tolstoy says that he was a year and a half old when his mother died, but he was nearer two. This might be thought a trivial error, but for the fact that all such errors are in the same direction: to make oneself younger. This is what De Quincey and Aksakov did, and always in traumatic memories. It is possible that Tolstoy felt guilty about her death (she died after giving birth to his sister), and even ashamed that he, who had two memories of babyhood, had not one memory of his mother. It so happened that there was not one portrait left of her. 'I cannot imagine her as a real physical being', he says in the *Reminiscences*, and goes on, 'I'm partly glad, because there is in my imagination only a spiritual image of her, and everything I know about her is sublime.' (In *War and Peace*, written forty years earlier, another Nikolenka, Prince Andrey's child, thought his father sublime, and though there were two good portraits of him in the house never imagined his father in human form.) Tolstoy created a mother for himself, a myth. He prayed to her in the second period of his life (from fourteen till he married at thirty-four), when he was overcome by temptations, prayed to her soul, asking for her help: 'and this prayer always helped me much'. He also dreamed about her. There is a note in his diary for 1860, when he was going abroad, partly to run away from an affair with a peasant woman: 'I saw myself in a dream dressed like a peasant, but mother disowned me.' At the end of his long life the mention of his mother, according to his son Sergey, still brought tears to his eyes.

If the mother in *Childhood* brings to mind Tolstoy's mother of the *Reminiscences*, Princess Marie Nikolayevna Bolkonsky in *War and Peace* reads like her biography. In *Childhood* the mother is created out of a few memories of a child, while Princess Marie is a fully realized character. Yet according to Tolstoy she too was invented! In *Some Words about War and Peace*, the reasons Tolstoy gives for saying that nearly all the characters in that book are invented stem from this statement: 'The literary activity which consists in describing real people who exist or have existed has nothing in common with the activity I was engaged in.' Thus a character is 'invented' when it is the creation of his imagination, no matter how much it resembles a person who existed.

When one compares the mothers in the first and final versions of *Childhood* one is struck by their resemblance, in spite of their very different circumstances. Tolstoy had a great intuition for affinities. The story of the first mother is that of Princess Kozlovsky. Tolstoy had no more memories of her than of his own mother, for she died in the same year. He had this experience of being deprived of a mother in babyhood in common with Kostya Islavin, the model for his first Narrator. In fact this Narrator points out, as he addresses himself to his friend in the foreword: 'You also lost your mother in your early years, so you will understand the feeling of passionate love, worship, and sad attachment to the memory of her whose existence you could not reason about, but only feel.' Both Islavin and Tolstoy had many opportunities to acquire memories of Princess Kozlovsky from those oral biographies which flourish when people live for many years in the same place, in the same way. The mother of the first Narrator does not regret deserting her husband, and says to the father, 'I am your wife before God', just as Princess Kozlovsky used to say to Islenev. The father is selfish and vain, but the mother is nobly proud and does not even notice his vanity. Her great anxiety is about the future of her illegitimate children. She gives good commonsense reasons for her fears and begs the father to do everything to get them legitimized. We know Princess Kozlovsky used to ask this of Islenev, who tried hard but failed.

When the illegal union was replaced by a consecrated marriage, and the unhappy child who did not respect or love his father by a happy child who did, there were bound to be changes in the mother and father. And so there are. We are no longer told that the father's comforts and pleasures came before the mother's. Even his objections to the Yurodivis are not nearly as violent as in the first version. The mother's feelings of respect for these half-wits, in all versions, is rooted in her Christian humility, love, and charity; but deeper than any such feelings is her love for her family. The differences in this love between the first and final versions becomes particularly clear when one compares the letters of the dying woman to the father in Moscow. Here is her letter in the first version, a reply to one from the father in which he had informed her that he had made a big haul at cards. 'Your success at cards pleases me greatly. You know that in general I don't like you gambling, but now I'm glad because you are doing it for the sake of the children . . .' She begs him to hurry to Petersburg: 'For God's sake don't delay any longer, you know how important it is . . . go tomorrow to Petersburg and make every effort. If our children were made legitimate, I would be entirely happy and calm.'

Compare this with the mother's letter in the final version. First, he has not won a lot of money, but has lost; the mother writes, 'I get as little joy from your winning as sorrow from your losses; I am only saddened by your unfortunate passion for gambling, which deprives me of a part of your tender attachment . . . I never cease praying to Him that He should preserve us – not from poverty (what does poverty matter?) but from that terrible position in which the children's interests, which I should have to defend, would clash with our own. Till now God has heard my prayer: you have not overstepped the line, beyond which we should have either to sacrifice the property, which no longer belongs to us but to our children, or . . . it is too dreadful even to think of it, yet that terrible misfortune is always threatening us. Yes, it is a heavy cross the Lord has laid on us both!' They carry the cross together, and what marriage does not carry one?

But the mother in the first version carried it alone, though she still loves the father of her children and he loves her. She does not regret her past, but she fears that her sin will be visited on her children. It is not the fear of a puritanical conscience. In a letter to the children she writes: 'There are unfortunate people whose love is not blessed by God, and because they live against the will of God He punishes them and their children.' He has laid a cross on them, 'on me and you', she says to the children, but she goes on believing in His infinite mercy. Driven mad by anxiety about her children, she does not even mind the father's gambling; clutching at a straw, she hopes that now that he has won a lot of money he will succeed in legitimizing them. It is as if Tolstoy was testing his mother in these unusual and unhappy circumstances.

If we in our turn imagine this woman in the consecrated marriage of the final version, we feel in complete accord with the change Tolstoy had made in her. Not for social or religious reasons, but because the father is *not* the same as in the first version. The second father, unlike the first, keeps his gambling within limits. More significant still, the first father's lust has disappeared in the second. In the first version, the Narrator sees a young woman standing by the dying mother's bed in a white morning gown, 'having rolled up her sleeves a little, she was rubbing maman's forehead with eau de Cologne'. She was a neighbour, whom they called *la belle Flamande* (a real person in the Islenev household: Islenev married her after Princess Kozlovsky died). Though the boy is in great sorrow, he notices every detail: 'for instance, the half smile of *la belle Flamande* to the father, which meant: "though it is a very sad time, I am pleased to see you". I noticed how father, in one and the same moment as he looked at maman's face, glanced at her beautiful arms, bare nearly to the elbows.' The setting in the final version is very similar: the young woman in her white morning gown, 'having turned up her sleeves a little'. The new Narrator, like the first, though in distress, also notices every detail, but there is not a word about *la belle Flamande's* smile to the father, not a word about his lustful look at her arms, nor about their being beautiful: the young woman is 'a remarkably handsome girl', but her arms are not bare to the elbows. In the first version the Narrator, watching the father during the funeral service, 'for no reason' remembered his father in the confectionery shop when he tried to kiss the French woman who served them. This too is omitted in the final version.

Of course, to preserve the child's unconsciousness of sexual stirrings Tolstoy was compelled to do away with all signs of lust in the father. But it went against his artistic nature to modify one character for the sake of another. No sooner had Tolstoy abandoned the first Narrator and created a happy child, a possible Tolstoy, than there was born a new father. If Princess Kozlovsky had succeeded in getting a divorce and had married Islenev, would that have changed his nature? He 'overstepped the line' in gambling again and again, and his estates and Princess Kozlovsky's went into payment of his debts, which led to bitter disagreements between them. The father in *Childhood* has become very different from Islenev. What did the old Tolstoy mean by letting Biryukov's statement stand: 'Indeed, *as far as we know* [my italics], in the father is depicted Alexander Mikhailovich Islenev . . .'? Why 'as far as we know'? Biryukov knew very well how reticent Tolstoy had always been about his creative processes, and how he disliked all talk about his models. He must have asked Tolstoy whether he might mention that the model for the father was Islenev. Tolstoy might well have answered: 'As far as you know'.

I suggest that in the final version he has mixed Islenev with himself. Islenev had three great passions: cards, women, and hunting. All these Tolstoy had in common with him. At the time of writing *Childhood*, the passion which was causing him most trouble was gambling: he was always in debt. And all the time he was longing with all his soul and strength for the home of his early childhood, the kind of family life that his father had led. He wrote in that same year, 1852, to Tatyana Alexandrovna about his dreams for the future. He would be married, and would live in Yasnaya Polyana. 'My affairs will be in order. . . . You will take my grandmother's place, but you will be better even than she was. I shall take my father's place and the children ours.' In the final version of *Childhood* he has imagined himself married to his ideal woman, his mother. He still has his passion for gambling, a cross which they carry together, but he will never overstep the line, never endanger the future of the children. As for lust, there is none of it! She has no conflicting loyalties and believes that her love for him and his children will not end with her death.

My hypothesis that in the final version the father is a mixture of Islenev and Tolstoy himself is strengthened by the change of names. In the first version the father is called Alexander, Islenev's name; the mother has no name, she is just *Maman*. In the final version the father's name is Pyotr Alexandrovich, the mother's Natalya Nikolayevna. These names are introduced early in the book, but in conversation between the grandmother and a relation, Prince Ivan Ivanich, the homely forms, Pierre and Natasha, are used. For years I had taken no notice of these names, and I am sure I could not have given them in a school examination: I knew the parents as *Maman* and *Papa*. But once you realize that Tolstoy's names are a code, you cannot overlook the names Pierre and Natasha. Tolstoy seems to have had as great a need to leave clues as Proust, and in neither case can one be quite sure whom they are meant for: themselves or us. Not only did Tolstoy use Pierre and Natasha for the next all-important marriage which he created, in *War and Peace*, but in his earliest conception of the book, a couple of years before he himself married, he began it with a happy marriage of a Pierre and a Natasha. There are other such clues in *Childhood*. The mother is Natalya Nikolayevna: her patronymic is Tolstoy's mother's. The father is Pyotr Alexandrovich, and the patronymic Alexander is Islenev's name. There is a lot more to be said about Tolstoy's names, but here I will only mention that Pyotr is the name of the first Count Tolstoy, who was ennobled by Peter the Great.

And so Tolstoy, in his first book, lived not only in his past, but future too: he will make a good marriage, between a 'Pierre' and a 'Natasha' and will not be a womanizer, nor will he overstep the line in gambling. (Fascinating that he should have been, at that time, more afraid of his passion for gambling than women.) As we know, what his imagination had created became a reality when he married.

Tolstoy had begun with the unusual story of an illegitimate son whom he knew personally, and of course he was familiar with European novels about illegitimate children. When he abandoned his first attempt and moved inwards, he still did not write about his own childhood. There are very few of Tolstoy's real memories of before he was nine in *Childhood*. He seems to have had no more access in his youth to his early memories than other mortals have. It is true that he sometimes uses an early memory, such as that of being punished by Natalya Savishna for spilling water on the tablecloth, but it is like going into a dark room to fetch something of which you know exactly where you left it. Whenever the young Tolstoy uses an early memory of an experience which we know from the *Reminiscences* affected him deeply, as in the chapter about games, we find it is a conscious memory of the kind which Proust says is brought back by will and intelligence and in which little of the past is preserved. But long before he can bring back deeply buried experiences the imagination of a writer is capable of creating a new one, like a plant shooting up from one segment of the root. By and large *Childhood* is the creation of Tolstoy's imagination: I defy anyone to tell, without other knowledge of Tolstoy, which of Nikolenka's memories are real and which invented.

He created a possible childhood for himself, and a possible marriage as well. But the viability, the timelessness of *Childhood* is not in the satisfaction of Tolstoy's needs, but in the special kind of imagination which erects a tent and fastens it firmly to the ground of experience, a tent in which he himself could take shelter. But so can others! It was already clear to Tolstoy in his youth that what he wanted – passionately desired – was to be loved by others; and what better way to deserve it than by offering them shelter?

He learnt a great deal about his art while working on *Childhood*. Long digressions on a variety of subjects, on hunting, prayer, gambling, music, personal looks, all disappear in the revision. In the first version, for instance, Tolstoy goes into a long analysis of how to judge a woman by her physical build, which, he says, is very different in a woman of aristocratic origin and a plebeian. It is a relief to find the long detailed description of the mother greatly shortened. Her smile, and the reflection on how one can judge a face by what a smile does to it, remain, and are unforgettable.

Though Tolstoy at the end of his life asserted that *Childhood* was 'not good', and said the same of *Boyhood, Youth*, and all his artistic creations, a couple of years earlier he had placed *Childhood* among the Russian masterpieces! But as his life story shows, a tendency to inconsistencies and contradiction was a cross Tolstoy carried from babyhood to the very end. Goldenweizer records Tolstoy saying 'I think that every great artist necessarily creates his own form also . . . let us take Gogol's *Dead Souls*. What is it? Neither a novel nor a story. It is something perfectly original. Then there is the *Memoirs of a Sportsman*, the best book Turgenev ever wrote; then Dostoyevsky's *House of the Dead*, and then, sinner that I am, my *Childhood*; Herzen's *Past and Thoughts*; Lermontov's *Hero of our Time* . . .'

4

With *Childhood* Tolstoy set out on the road to *War and Peace*. Dickens, starting with a piece of hackwork, achieved with *The Pickwick Papers* what Tolstoy did with *Childhood*: Pickwick is a possible Dickens. What Pickwick sees in the Fleet Prison Dickens had seen in the Marshalsea at the age of twelve! Pickwick ends by not regretting 'having devoted the greater part of two years to mixing with different varieties and shades of human character', as Dickens devoutly hoped that he would not regret his bitter experiences in the two years when he was deprived of schooling and sent to the blacking warehouse. But it is not simply a matter of the quantity and quality of the writer's experiences which became the character's. If it were, then David Copperfield would be a more possible Dickens than Mr Pickwick, Levin a more possible Tolstoy than Pierre, Marcel a more possible Proust than Charlus. But they are not. It is a far greater feat of the imagination to produce a possible self than a self portrait. Rare indeed is a character which is a mutation of its creator as viable as if nature itself had produced it. This is what Dickens and Tolstoy conceived at the age of twenty; Proust not till he was thirty-eight.

The year that *Childhood* appeared, 1852, Tolstoy began *A Novel of a Russian Landlord*; he worked for four years on it, but all that remains of it is a fragment : *A Landlord's Morning*. In the same year he began *Boyhood*, and that he completed. The next year he began *The Cossacks*, and once again he was planning a long novel. It is a thinly disguised autobiographical story and he took ten years to complete it. He began other stories: *Tikhon and Malanya*, and *The Decembrists*, all left unfinished. On the other hand, he wrote *Youth* very quickly, and so he did *Sevastopol Sketches*. In the last chapters of *Childhood*, in its final version, Tolstoy already came very close to autobiography, and in *Boyhood* and *Youth* he gets closer and closer. His original plan was to write 'Four Epochs of Growth', but he did not go on after *Youth*: he could do no more with his years of maturity than other artist-autobiographers, that is write fragments. *Family Happiness* is fiction, but he immediately took a dislike to it: no wonder, it did not need a Tolstoy to write it. He was gaining much experience, and the question was: would he ever write a great novel?

## 2. *War and Peace*

IN *Reminiscences* Tolstoy revealed quite a lot of how he created his first book, *Childhood*: how he began it, how it changed, which characters he invented, and which were 'pretty accurate portraits'. He let us into the secret of how he created Grisha, the Yurodivy. Pilgrims, many of them beggars and half-wits, used to call at Yasnaya Polyana for food and drink on their way, and were welcomed by his mother. This tradition was carried on after her death, and Leo learned, as he says, to respect them from childhood. But the chief model for Grisha was not a Yurodivy, but the slow-witted assistant gardener Akim, who 'prayed in the large summer house, between the two orangeries, and he really surprised us and deeply moved us by his prayer in which he spoke to God as to a living person, "You are my doctor, you are my dispenser".'

It was unusual for Tolstoy to be so frank about his artistic experience and indeed, when writing *War and Peace*, forty years earlier, he was irritated by people's curiosity about his models. In *Some Words about War and Peace* he wrote that except for the historical figures only Akhrasimov and Denisov were characters to whom he had given names which closely resembled those of two actual people of that time, 'involuntarily and imperceptibly', while 'all the other characters are entirely invented and have no definite prototype in tradition or reality'. But apart from the fact that prototypes of Tushin and Dolokhov have been dug out of the archives of the Napoleonic period, the most striking thing, as Biryukov, Tolstoy's disciple and biographer, pointed out in *Autobiographical Elements in L. N. Tolstoy's Works*, is the similarity between many characters in *War and Peace*, written between 1863 and 1868, and members of his family described in the *Reminiscences* in the years 1903 to 1905. Not only are their stories similar but some of the expressions he uses to describe them are identical.

Tolstoy himself told Biryukov that in writing the biography he should pay attention to his creative work, and Biryukov, with intimate personal knowledge of Tolstoy and his family and much of what Tolstoy had done and written, came to the conclusion that the amount of autobiographical material in Tolstoy's works of art was so great that if one had no facts to draw on one could write the biography by arranging his works in autobiographical order. So how was he to reconcile all this with Tolstoy's statement that, apart from the two mentioned characters, all others were purely imaginary, without any prototypes in reality? Biryukov saw a clue in the words 'involuntarily and imperceptibly', and concluded that Tolstoy's genius often worked unconsciously.

Apart from his father and paternal grandmother, of whom he had early memories (both were dead by the time he was ten), he acquired his 'memories' of his ancestors from others, and from their letters and diaries. In the foreword, which he discarded, he says that when writing about 1812 the smell and sound of that period was dear to him. He was born sixteen years later at Yasnaya Polyana, in the same house where his maternal grandfather had lived and his mother had spent all her life. As well as relations there were many others who had known his ancestors.

Other people's memories affect us like works of art; not we, but others, have made the primary selection, born out of their perplexities and suffering, their particular way of finding comfort and consolation. If such memories make a deep impression on us we make a second selection, as we do from a story or a poem that impresses us. And though, in time, this selection is illumined by our own experiences the process is different from the growth and development of our own primary selection, our own memories which 'live in the unfathomable depths of our soul', as Biryukov says of Tolstoy's early memories of children's games. It is not surprising to find that the characters which Tolstoy created out of acquired memories, such as Count Rostov and the old Prince Bolkonsky and his daughter Princess Marie, are not very different in the definitive and the earlier versions. Nor are there very great changes in characters like Natasha or Vera, Countess Rostov, Nikolay, or Berg.

Though he has often two models for such characters, and his imagination creates something new, they are still outside him. The greatest changes, as we shall see, between the drafts are in Pierre, Andrey, and Petya Rostov: all these characters are possible Tolstoys.

The drafts make it possible for us to trace the evolution of Pierre, Andrey, and Petya Rostov, changes which resulted in the novel ceasing to be autobiography. (The English reader can follow these drafts in R. F. Christian's excellent book: *Tolstoy's War and Peace*.) In the early versions Pierre was closer to an Anatole Kuragin than to the Pierre we know. The cruelty one moment – kindness the next, the early poverty, the ambition, the jealousy of Napoleon, the trait of loving quickly and passionately and then hating the person he has loved, all these characteristics of the original Pierre disappear. It was as if Tolstoy had gone down into the underworld, had wandered among the shades of his past and brought one of them back. How did that Pierre change into the Pierre of the final version, awkward, unworldly, modest, whose kindness comes from the very depths of his being? Prince Andrey, who knows him intimately, says that he has a heart of gold. He is more like Tolstoy's brother Nikolay than Leo. Turgenev said of Nikolay: 'The attitude of humility that Leo Tolstoy cultivates in theory, was actually applied by his brother Nikolay.' Nikolay profoundly affected Leo's life, from early childhood on. He knew himself to be a genius, but he knew Nikolay to be a better man than he. As we can already see in *Childhood*, Tolstoy had a gigantic ego, but others too grew to gigantic size in his memories. Nikolay took to drink and was dead before he was forty, Leo would live more than twice as long, and write great books. But Leo knew that in essence he had a great deal in common with all his brothers and his sister: the last thing he thought of himself was that he was a changeling. Leo and Nikolay merged and Pierre was born, not a self-portrait of Leo, nor a portrait of Nikolay, but a new possible Tolstoy, a viable mutation.

At first, while Pierre was coming to life in the early drafts, there was no Prince Andrey. Even after he had conceived him, Andrey continued to give him great trouble: he was bad-mannered when jealous, as Tolstoy was; he expressed views on literature which were Tolstoy's. But only when Andrey came to resemble Tolstoy's brother Sergey, the proud, eccentric yet traditional aristocrat, was the character established and became another possible Tolstoy. He tells us in the *Reminiscences*: 'With Nikolenka I wanted to be together, talk, think', but 'Seryozha I only wanted to imitate. Nikolenka I loved, with Seryozha I was enchanted, with something that was strange to me and incomprehensible.' If Prince Andrey is another possible Leo Tolstoy, why did he need him? Why did Dickens need Sam Weller? Not merely to amuse the public. Pierre could not carry the whole of *War and Peace* on his shoulders, nor could Mr Pickwick the whole of *The Pickwick Papers*. Follow the relationships of Pierre and Andrey, of Samuel Pickwick and Samuel Weller: you will find that they have something all important in common – their deep affection for one another is the root of their deep knowledge of one another.

In an early draft Pierre's father was a Frenchman, a statesman. It was necessary that Pierre should in some ways be different, from the cradle, from the Bolkonskys and Rostovs, but making him an alien was a hopeless move. What pitfalls there would have been in Tolstoy's way with a half-French Pierre! A writer sometimes introduces a foreigner not out of artistic necessity but to make his task easier: he throws dust into the reader's eyes, and screens behind the unknown. Tolstoy took a great jump when he abandoned the French father and made Pierre illegitimate. He was deeply involved with the problem of illegitimacy from childhood on. He had an illegitimate brother, Misha, a postman. While Tolstoy's father was alive all went well with Misha, but afterwards he began to go downhill. Tolstoy writes in the *Reminiscences*: 'I remember the strange feeling of perplexity which I experienced when this brother who had become destitute – a brother who looked like my father (more than any of us did) – came to us begging for help, and was grateful for the ten or fifteen roubles which we used to give him'. It is one of Tolstoy's memories of childhood of a moment when a thought turned into an experience, and became a permanent secret inscription. Tolstoy himself had an illegitimate son before he married, who later worked as a coachman at Yasnaya Polyana. Long before Tolstoy sorted out his beliefs and principles, and asserted that his own class lived on the labour of peasants (bastards in Russia usually had peasant mothers), he had created a bastard who did not end up as a coachman or a postman. The great and rich aristo- crat Count Bezukhov had many illegitimate children of whom Pierre was the favourite. He gave him name and fortune. You discover by and by that Pierre was taken as a child to the Bolkonsky's home, where he was treated as one of the family. (The old Prince Bolkonsky, if you remember, looked down on Count Rostov.) Tolstoy was not indulging his fantasy: before *War and Peace* was finished his brother Sergey married the gypsy woman with whom he had been living for fifteen years, and legitimized his children. By making Pierre a bastard Tolstoy achieved a great deal. Pierre will learn from Platon Karatayev as neither Prince Andrey nor Count Nikolay Rostov possibly could.

Why did Tolstoy have so much more trouble in creating Prince Andrey than Pierre, and why did he keep on changing Andrey's story? Pierre, as we have seen, has much in common with Tolstoy's brother Nikolay, who had been dead several years before Pierre was conceived. But Sergey was very much alive, and his love for Tolstoy's sister-in-law Tanya falls into the period when Tolstoy was working on *War and Peace*. Prince Andrey is modelled on Sergey about whom Tolstoy has many memories of childhood. 'I was enchanted by his beautiful appearance, his singing, . . . the directness of his egoism. I always was aware of myself, self-conscious, always sensed, wrongly or not, what others thought and felt about me, and this spoiled the joy of life.'

Volodya in *Childhood* is a portrait of Sergey: the directness of his egoism, and even more his outspoken sensuality, amazed and frightened the narrator. Sergey, some two years older than Leo, was wonderfully good to him: understanding, unjudging, generous, and Leo loved him. He wrote in *Reminiscences*, after Sergey's death in old age, that 'his was a human life, very beautiful, but entirely incomprehensible to me, mysterious and therefore particularly attractive'. Here we have the reason why Andrey sometimes appears shadowy and distant: Tolstoy had merged with his brother Sergey.

It was a marvellous stroke to place Prince Andrey in Tolstoy's own maternal family. There were certain things he would never have done: for instance, be as churlish as he was (in an early draft), in a moment of jealousy. It is amusing to be told by Tolstoy's son Ilya that his uncle Sergey resembled the old Prince Bolkonsky in *War and Peace*! Prince Bolkonsky and his daughter Marie hardly change through the drafts, for very good reasons: Tolstoy is writing the 'biographies' of his grandfather and mother. The limitations imposed on Andrey's character bore wonderful fruit: the relationship of father and son, of sister and brother, never make us say 'you've thought it up', as Tolstoy often threw in scorn at other writers. He could not have conceived a more suitable son for his grandfather nor brother for his mother. But there were further gains. Between Tolstoy himself and Prince Andrey there is the gap of a generation, and the intimacy which sometimes exists between an uncle and a nephew.

Tolstoy locked up many secrets in his names. He gave his characters names of Christian saints as was the custom: there was only a limited number of such names, so that it became necessary to have some different form of a name in the family circle. Some were endearing, others were names of contempt: they were called diminutives and they were sometimes longer than the original name. In the world outside the family circle and friends the diminutive names were not used, and in official papers could not be used. There was no such baptismal name as Natasha, only Natalya, nor was there a Pierre or a Petya— both are Pyotr.

Tolstoy gave some of his characters not only the Christian names of his models, but also their patronymics. So his father Nikolay Ilyich Tolstoy became Nikolay Ilyich Rostov, and his grandfather Ilya Andreyevich Tolstoy became Ilya Andreyevich Rostov; Tolstoy's mother Princess Marya Nikolayevna Volkonsky is in the novel Princess Marya Nikolayevna Bolkonsky. There is, however, one exception: his maternal grandfather Prince Nikolay Sergeivich Volkonsky is Prince Nikolay Andreyevich Bolkonsky. Why did he change this patronymic? The maternal grandfather had no sons, and Tolstoy creates a son for him and names him Andrey. With Tolstoy's great love of details, he knew that the old Prince would have called his only son either after himself, Nikolay, or after his father, Sergey; but Tolstoy had already an important character Nikolay Rostov, and he could not very well use Sergey since his brother Sergey on whom 'Andrey' was so closely modelled was still living. And having given the son the name Andrey he felt compelled to change the old Prince Bolkonsky's patronymic to Andrey. *War and Peace* is a book of 'poetry and truth'. The more attention one pays to the Christian names of Tolstoy's characters the more striking the meaning they had for him becomes. Even the name Andrey itself is not an arbitrary choice. There was a portrait of Tolstoy's ancestor, a favourite of Peter the Great, at Yasnaya Polyana: his full name was Pyotr Andreyevich Tolstoy. By giving the young Prince Bolkonsky the name Andrey, Tolstoy linked his two possible selves: Pierre and Andrey.

Not only are there great changes between successive drafts in many important characters, but also in the opening and plot of the novel. From a letter to A.I. Herzen written in 1861 we know that Tolstoy had begun a novel called *The Decembrists*. Pierre, an aristocrat who had taken part in the uprising in 1825, was exiled to Siberia; his loving wife, Natasha, followed him there. They returned to Russia with their children in 1856 – the year after the tyrant Nicholas I died. Tolstoy had created a good marriage between a Pierre and a Natasha in his book *Childhood*, but they were the children's *Papa* and *Maman*. In *The Decembrists* Pierre and Natasha have grown up children, and are still happy after long years of marriage. Tolstoy only wrote a few chapters, and then gave it up. Not till he married, in love and full of hope, did he begin to realize the new Pierre and Natasha in *War and Peace*. That was at the beginning of 1863; but in 1861 he had felt he was getting old (he was 33), his last teeth were crumbling, and the dream of a wife and family was no nearer. He knew quite a number of eligible women, and sometimes a fever seized him and he was ready to rush into a marriage, but he soon calmed down and retreated. And then it happened: he fell in love with Sonya Bers and was married by the end of 1862; and early in the following year he was already at work on a book with the title *Three Eras*: it was to

4*

come out in serial form. In 1864 he wrote a Foreword which he later omitted, in which he tries to explain how he had gone back from 1856 to 1805: 'From the present (1856) I involuntarily moved to 1825', but even then his hero, he says, was a grownup man with a family, and to understand him he moved back to his youth, in 1812. This did not satisfy him either: 'I felt ashamed to write about our triumph in the struggle against Bonapartist France without having described our failure and shames.' And so finally, he began in 1805. Tolstoy was rationalizing, as he did throughout his life. 'Involuntarily' he omitted to tell us that by starting in 1805 he could recreate his parents' youth and his grandparents' still active life in their own period. Princess Marie Bolkonsky is twenty-one years old in 1811, which was exactly the age of his mother, Princess Marya Volkonsky.

Even when he had settled on starting with the year 1805 he still tried many different beginnings. Some of these appear satisfactory to us: why did he reject, for example, the night before the review of the army by the Russian and Austrian Emperors in November 1805? What is there special about the one he finally chose, the soirée at Anna Scherer's? On the face of it he uses it to introduce many of his characters, but more important is the contrast between all the other relationships and the meeting of Pierre and Andrey.

Unlike Tolstoy, Dickens was not in a position to make many beginnings and reject them when he was writing *The Pickwick Papers*. He started it as a piece of hackwork, and it came out in instalments: he had to earn a living and make his way in the world: Tolstoy did not have to do either. Dickens began without Sam Weller just as Tolstoy began without Prince Andrey. The marvel is that Dickens should have conceived the meeting of Samuel Pickwick and Samuel Weller. Dickens was twenty-three when he began *The Pickwick Papers*, Tolstoy thirty-five when he began *War and Peace*. The contents of the two books could not be more different, so what is the point of the comparison? I want to state here that I do not believe for a moment that *War and Peace* was influenced by *The Pickwick Papers*; but there was a parallel development in the growth of these two books. I shall try and show that both Dickens and Tolstoy were writing about their 'splendid vision' of childhood which was still attending them.

Mr Pickwick's past is practically unknown to us, except that he had been in business and was well-off. But so is Pierre's: he was illegitimate, his father sent him abroad with a tutor when he was ten, and when he returned ten years later his father, before dying, gave him his name and fortune. It is clear that we are deliberately not told about the formative years of Pierre and Mr Pickwick: their creators did not want to pledge the future.

Apart from charity, the most inalienable trait in Pickwick is his innocence of love and sex. Pierre had the experience of both, but 'it was plain that l'amour which the Frenchman Ramballe was so fond of was not that lower and simple kind of love that Pierre had once experienced for his wife, nor was it the blown-up romantic love that he experienced for Natasha'. Pierre is as innocent of Tolstoy's own experience of love as Mr Pickwick is of Dickens'. Pierre had not injured anyone – Tolstoy had seduced a girl working in the house of his aunt, who drove her out; Pierre had never had such an experience as Tolstoy's of coming to a peasant woman 'like a stag', as he writes in his diary, then beginning to feel towards her like a husband, having a child with her, and then of leaving her. In the weeks when Pierre felt that he was getting nearer and nearer to the abyss, that is to a marriage with Hélène, he found that he lacked resolution, and 'an unperceived feeling of the guilt of that desire paralysed his will'. And 'Pierre was one of those who are only strong when they feel themselves quite innocent' (literally: 'entirely pure'). But Tolstoy had expressed his conviction, in an early draft for *Childhood*, that so long as the child is unconscious of his own stirrings he acts more nobly than the adult: and Pierre is *unconscious* of his guilt. When Pierre found himself burdened with his unfaithful wife, became disappointed with the Freemasons, when life was grim and without meaning, we are told he took to drink and women. Tolstoy shows us that an extra bottle of drink simply brought a little relief to Pierre, but what about the women? Are we to understand that he was going to brothels but was even less affected by women than by alcohol? It must be so, for at the same period young ladies, both married and unmarried, liked him because without flirting with anyone he was friendly to all: 'Il est charmant, il n'a pas de sexe', they said. And just as Tolstoy was driven to create a possible self without a conscious sense of guilt in sex, so Dickens was driven to create one without the humiliation he himself had experienced in love. In Pierre and Pickwick Tolstoy and Dickens started their lives all over again.

We know a great deal more about the formative years of Sam Weller and Prince Andrey than about those of Mr Pickwick and Pierre. We know something about their childhoods, and about their relations with their fathers; but in their cases too sex has not disrupted their lives. There is nothing humiliating in Sam Weller's experiences, and his story ends in marriage. Prince Andrey is married when we first meet him. His wife is a woman of his own class, a child who has had no experience of life. Princess Marie says: 'She is a complete child, such a charming gay child, I have grown to love her.' If anyone is surprised that Prince Andrey should have married a woman who was not his equal intellectually or spiritually, he only has to remember that Tolstoy, aged twenty-eight, nearly married Valerya Arsenev, a young woman who was 'trivial', as Tolstoy called her. He did not marry a trivial woman, but though his wife was very young, and growing before his eyes, nevertheless, annoyed by a quarrel about her not nursing their first child, he decided to go to war: not against a foreign intruder, but against the poor Poles who had risen against their oppressor, Russia! When Prince Andrey said 'I'm going to the war because the life I'm leading here does not suit me' he expressed Tolstoy's own feelings. Fortunately Tolstoy changed his mind, but Andrey *did* go to war. After his experience, after he has been wounded, when everything he knew seems to him insignificant, his thoughts turn to 'quiet family happiness', to his wife and un-born son. He is too late! his wife dies in childbirth, and he is filled with bitter regrets: this 'gay and charming child' might have become a real woman if she had had children and a husband who cared for and understood her.

By this conventional marriage, Andrey is spared Pierre's 'lower and simple' kind of love; later he, like Pierre, has the experience of 'a romantic love' for Natasha, but again he is

too late: he only forgives her infatuation for Anatole after he
has been mortally wounded.

Nikolay Ilyich Rostov and Marie Nikolayevna Bolkonsky are
free biographies of Tolstoy's father Nikolay Ilyich Tolstoy, and
his mother Marya Nikolayevna Volkonsky. (In an early draft
the name is not Rostov but Prostoy: the word means 'simple'
and the sound is close to that of Tolstoy; but his intuition was
right, the name Prostoy gave away too much to a reader –
Rostov is preferable.) Many of Nikolay Rostov's experiences
are Tolstoy's own: of war, of hunting, of losing a fortune in
gambling. But Nikolay is not a possible Leo Tolstoy. However
different, at times, Pierre and Andrey are from Leo, he still
could imagine merging with either of them. But not with
Nikolay. Without underlining it Tolstoy informs us that Pierre
and Andrey are both clever. A painter will sometimes portray
himself in the garb of a prince or a beggar, a saint or a rake;
he may change not only his clothes but even some of his
features, and yet he will treat some as inalienable: his eyes,
perhaps, his hands, or even his ears. Nikolay is not clever.
(The Russian adjective '*umny*' comes from the word '*um*', mind,
and it is a trait wholly desirable.) Moreover Nikolay could not
bear to see in men the expression of a spiritual life: that is why
he did not like Prince Andrey. It is left to Natasha finally to
disqualify Nikolay from being a possible Leo. She loved her
brother and knew him well: 'Nikolay has one fault: he cannot
like a thing unless everyone else likes it first,' she says.

One of the most important traits of all possible selves is the
great love they have for one another, out of which grows profound understanding. Mr Pickwick knows that Sam is an
original; Sam Weller knows that although Mr Pickwick is sure
that he has finished with adventures he is still so young in
heart that he may start again. Prince Andrey states at the very
beginning of the book that Pierre is very dear to him, and
Pierre has great respect and admiration for his friend. And at
the very end, talking of Pierre after Andrey's death, Princess
Marie, who loved and knew her brother as Natasha did
Nikolay, says to Natasha: 'I understand, that *he* (Prince
Andrey) never loved anyone as he loved him.' The love between two possible selves created by the imagination surpasses

the love of friends in real life, of lovers, of parent and child, for very good reasons: the affinity goes deeper and the love is freer. Though Nikolay sometimes acts as Leo had done, he is still not a possible Leo. He does not feel any affinity with Prince Andrey or Pierre: he takes a dislike to Prince Andrey at their first meeting, and he feels unfriendly towards Pierre and sides with Dolokhov in their quarrel.

But there is one trait which Nikolay shares with Pierre and Andrey, and the whole of the Bolkonsky and Rostov clan: innocence. While at the front Nikolay comes across a Polish family in distress, a father, daughter and her baby. He takes them into his lodgings, and when a fellow officer begins to make jokes about Nikolay's relation with the pretty Polish woman Nikolay is ready to fight him, and is only saved from a duel by his great friend Denisov. Nikolay explains: 'She is like a sister to me, and I can't describe to you how insulting it is . . . because . . . well . . . the reason . . .' Denisov is profoundly affected and though he jokes 'This is your Rostovsky nature', he is moved to tears by Nikolay's innocence.

Many lovers of *War and Peace* must have wondered why the only member of the large Bolkonsky–Rostov clan, to which Pierre belongs though he is not quite one of them, who is shown to be *not* innocent, and whose life is disrupted by sex, is Natasha. Even if Tolstoy had never told us that he mixed his sister-in-law Tanya with his wife Sonya and out came Natasha, we could still tell, from memories, letters, diaries, that Tolstoy used both of them as models. Again and again we find experiences of Natasha's for which now Tanya, now Sonya, have posed. You will find many examples in Troyat's excellent biography of Tolstoy, and might conclude that Natasha before her marriage to Pierre is a portrait of Tolstoy's sister-in-law, Tanya Bers, and in the early years of marriage of his wife Sonya. Moreover where Natasha is concerned Tolstoy was not as reticent about his model as he usually was. Tanya used to stay for weeks at Yasnaya Polyana, and Tolstoy informed her that she was not living there for nothing, that he was observing her. When he received the painter Bashilov's drawings of the characters in *War and Peace* he asked him, 'Could not she [Natasha] be made to look more like Tanya

Bers in the kissing scene?' Tanya's love stories, which began with her flirtation with her cousin Kuzminsky and ended in her marrying him, fell almost entirely into the period of the writing of *War and Peace*; but in creating Natasha's love stories he could not have diverged more completely than he did from Tanya's.

Though Tolstoy had known his mother-in-law since childhood (she was an Islavin, the illegitimate daughter of Islenyev, the family he combined with his own in *Childhood*), and only a couple of years older than himself, her children belonged to a social group not well known to him. Their father was a doctor of German origin and his daughters were more practical than daughters of the aristocracy, and were being trained for professions. Tolstoy's son, Sergey, goes so far as to give as one of the reasons for his father's choice his intention 'to marry out of his own noble class'.

Tolstoy became very fond of his young sister-in-law Tanya: like Dickens when he married, he adopted his wife's whole family. He loved Tanya's dancing and singing, her vitality and intuitions, and she returned his affection. He did not hesitate to ask her searching questions about herself, and she confided in him, relying on their mutual affection and trust. She wrote her memories in her book *Tolstoy as I Knew Him* many years after *War and Peace* appeared and, knowing the book so well, she very likely embroidered them. But we need only a few of the facts she gives and can check them against other people's diaries and letters. Her affection for her cousin Kuzminsky did not stand in the way of her becoming infatuated with Anatole Shostack, a second cousin whom she met when her father took her to St Petersburg. Soon after Tanya went to stay with the Tolstoys and Anatole followed her. Unlike the Anatole of *War and Peace* he was not married, nor had any intention to abduct her. Neither he nor Tanya Bers were well-off, and both were too prudent to marry without money. However this did not stop them flirting, and Tolstoy and the Countess asked him to leave Yasnaya Polyana. Tanya Bers says that she was upset because the Tolstoys had humiliated Anatole, and that he must have thought them provincials. The important point is that it was only *after* this infatuation that she fell in love with Tolstoy's brother Sergey. He was twenty years older than she, and had a family. All that Tanya knew at the beginning was that Sergey had a boy who used to come to Yasnaya Polyana; and when she asked who his mother was she was told only that he was illegitimate. 'The word illegitimate meant to me "not belonging to anybody".' All the ensuing conflict, all the vacillation, was in Sergey: he was in love with Tanya but could not turn his back on his past, especially because his mistress, Masha, was so undemanding, and he felt he could not abandon his children. No wonder that Tanya's parents, when they learnt some of the facts, had little faith that the marriage would ever come about, and this is faithfully reflected in the Rostov's lack of belief that the marriage between Prince Andrey and their Natasha would take place. To make a long story short, Tanya attempted suicide (nothing whatever to do with Anatole). After she recovered there were other eligible suitors, but in the end her affections turned to Alexander Kuzminsky, and Tolstoy wrote 'She's going back to her first love'. Kuzminsky was rich and altogether a most eligible man, and besides, Tanya Bers showed from the early days of their marriage that she was not going to be ruled by her husband as her sister Sonya was by Tolstoy.


The heroines in Russian literature are a match for the heroes, just as the goddesses are for the gods in Greek mythology. Where Natasha differs from Pushkin's Tatyana, Turgenev's Liza, Tolstoy's own Anna, is that she is a type while everyone of the others is unique. She was as much a Russian type as Goethe's Gretchen was a German. There was no puritanism in the bringing up of Russian children, no principle that the young need a hard schooling before facing life: on the contrary the delight of the young in growing was smiled on by the older generation. There were demands by parents and teachers, rules of manners and behaviour. In short, the attitude to children in nineteenth-century Russia was closer to our attitude today than to that of the Victorians. Since there was no established middle class, no bourgeois morality or manners, consciously and unconsciously people modelled themselves on the gentry. Natasha's spontaneity, her delight in life, her dancing, her flirting, were not at all confined to the gentry: it was not uncommon among the daughters of professional people, officials, and even shopkeepers. Idleness before marriage, and a sense of freedom both before and after, were inalienable in this type, and only when a Natasha became a revolutionary, or merely a conscious member of the intelligentsia, did she cease to be a Natasha.

(I was amazed, when I first became a student in Berlin, at the lack of style at students' parties and dances compared to those in my school in a Russian provincial town. Many of my school-mates 'danced' into life although they were, like my German fellow students, children of professional and business people. From these dancing girls to Diaghilev's Ballet was only a step.)

One of Natasha's important traits is her *chutkost*, a blend of sensibility and quick perception: in this she closely resembles both her models. Natasha did not deign to be clever, as Pierre told Princess Marie. Nor did Tolstoy's wife: they had not been married a month when Tolstoy noted 'she senses everything', and a few days later, in a letter to his relation and great friend Alexandra Tolstoy, he wrote 'she refuses to understand (besides she does not need to understand)'. This trait in Natasha is *not* aristocratic condescension. It was quite clear to Tolstoy that a man reaches the truth 'after wrestling with a long, laborious and painful series of doubts and suffering' while a woman gets there by intuition. And this was true of his sister-in-law Tanya, of his wife, Sonya, and also of his Natasha.

I do not want to detract from Natasha's charm, her vitality, her excellence as a wife, but she is a type, a character in a best-seller, unwittingly achieved occasionally even by a great artist. She falls in love with Anatole in the midst of her great love for Prince Andrey. From the beginning she is bewildered by Anatole, a man 'who could rouse in her a feeling incompre-hensible and terrible'. And after a mere three days she con-fesses to Sonya that she feels she has been in love with him a hundred years, and that it seems to her that she has never loved anyone else before. 'I felt that he is my master and I his slave.' Swept off her feet by a purely sexual passion she feels, after a couple of encounters with Anatole, that there is no barrier between them, that he has only to whistle and she will follow him.

What was driving Tolstoy to burden just one member of the large Bolkonsky–Rostov clan with a bare sexual passion, and, what is more, at the time of her great love? Was it his ambivalence towards women: love and hate – a characteristic he gave to Pierre in an early draft – or was it, after all, dictated by the demands of the plot? I had never been quite satisfied. Tolstoy took his writing of fiction as seriously as an autobiographer his true story. But once I had fully realized Tolstoy's great faith in marriage at the time he was creating *War and Peace* I was near the answer. Natasha's passion for Anatole is purely sexual, hence her blindness. Her wonderful intuitive knowledge of people is this time in complete abeyance: she thinks that both Anatole and Hélène are good; her old self seems quite dead. Her readiness to elope with Anatole shocks everyone round her: Sonya, Marie Dmitrievna, everyone who loves her; and even Pierre in the first moment says 'They are all the same'. He is thinking that Natasha is no better than Hélène, – so he is not the only one to have tied himself to 'a disgusting woman': it has happened even to Andrey whom he admires and looks up to. He sees Andrey deeply wounded, bitter and proud: he could never forgive a fallen woman. But the very next time Pierre sees Natasha he feels differently. Pierre uses his intellect in search of the truth, but deep down he is guided not by reason but feelings: he sees that Natasha is very unhappy, and says to her that if he were the handsomest, cleverest, and best man in the world, and were free, he would that very minute beg on his knees for her hand and love. He says this because he realizes that she is still the same Natasha as before. This is the parting of the ways of the two friends, Pierre and Andrey. Is this due in the main to Pierre's love for Natasha being deeper than Andrey's?

Before the battle of Borodino, Andrey is bitter about life, pessimistic, and dwells on his three great sorrows: Natasha's betrayal of their love, his father's death, and the French invasion which now covers half Russia. The pessimism is in himself. His father's befriending of Mlle Bourienne has made Andrey openly critical of him, and his sister Marie very unhappy; but the old man puts his aberration aside in time, and shows his great love for Marie. Natasha's sexual passion passes like an illness, and leaves no trace in her character. The French, ruined and humiliated, will leave Russia, and she will triumph. Only after Andrey has been mortally wounded at Borodino, after he has seen his enemy Anatole in agony when his leg is cut off, does his hatred depart and memories of childhood come back to him. He also remembers Natasha as he saw her first, at the ball, and love and tenderness for her reawakens in him. Too late.

Some thirty years ago Sir Edward Marsh asked me whether I did not think that Natasha's passion for Anatole was out of character. I reminded him of the circumstances: the rebuff Natasha had suffered from the old Bolkonsky and Princess Marie, what a bad letter writer she was and the consequent lack of communication with Andrey during his year of absence, and lastly the fact that her mother was away from home at the time of her infatuation. Marsh was not convinced, and in time I began to doubt my own reasons. John Bayley, in *Tolstoy and the Novel*, says: 'We know there is not the slightest chance of this seduction coming off.' So what made Tolstoy invent Natasha's infatuation? What did he achieve? If not only a man but a girl, a Natasha, could be momentarily blinded by a sexual passion, even while in love with such a wonderful man as Andrey, and survive it and be her old self again, how much more easily could Tolstoy become once again the child he loved, the child he was till the age of fourteen, before his terrible years of profligacy. Pierre had realized in no time that the sexual passion had not corrupted Natasha. No wonder that Tolstoy's earlier title for the book was *All's Well That Ends Well*.

Though Natasha is the only member of the large Bolkonsky-Rostov clan to be overwhelmed by a sexual passion, none of the others are white angels. Every member, including Pierre, has some human weakness. A few examples will suffice: Prince Bolkonsky causes great suffering to his daughter, Count Rostov squanders a fortune, Sonya schemes to marry Nikolay, and even Princess Marie is capable of selfish thoughts and, worse still, of envy. Before she had met Natasha she was already ill disposed towards her 'because of her involuntary envy of her beauty, youth, and happiness, and because of jealousy of her brother's love'. But allowing for such human frailties they are all sincere, affectionate people, free of corruption and of depravity. Vera is an unsympathetic person, but her faults are venial; and only when she marries Colonel Berg does she become an outsider: she and her husband seem then to belong to a 'Veneering circle' rather than to the Bolkonsky–Rostov families.

A few people, friends of the clan, are like them: for instance, Marie Dmitrievna and Denisov; but there are others, of their own class and social group but strangers to them, who are evil, and bring them nothing but suffering, like the 'depraved' Kuragins. The father Prince Vassily is a wily unscrupulous statesman, a turncoat, a man ready to steal a will. Everything bad that Tolstoy could say about a woman he says about Princess Hélène. Though born and bred in the highest society she uses coarse and vulgar language; she is stupid; she has been in love with her brother and he with her; she connives at the attempt to seduce Natasha; she marries Pierre only for his wealth, with no intention of giving him a child; and, as if all this is not enough, she becomes a Roman Catholic in the hope that will enable her to enter another marriage; in the end she tries to cause an abortion and dies of an overdose of the drug. Society admires her: not only Anna Pavlovna Scherer, the maid-of-honour to the Dowager Empress, but a sophisticated man like Bilibin, and even Kutuzov; but not once does Tolstoy reveal anything admirable in her, apart from her beautiful body.

There is an equally sharp division among the soldiers who serve in the war: there are members of the clan and their friends, and there are outsiders. Among the 'friends' are Denisov who loves all the Rostovs, the brave Tushin to whom Prince Andrey does a good turn, Kutuzov who, when he learns that the old Prince Bolkonsky is dead, tells Andrey 'I am a father to you'. But there are others: famous generals, who bear foreign names such as Pfuel, Barclay de Tolly, Bennigsen, Wolzogen, Paulucci: we do not see their courage, their humanity, as we do that of Tushin, Denisov, Bagration, Nikolay Rostov,

Prince Andrey. It is with Andrey's eyes that we see Barclay de Tolly who receives him 'drily and coldly', speaking with a German accent; it is from Andrey that we learn that Pfuel is an absurdly self-confident man, as only Germans can be, who believed in military science. Andrey pities him. The Marquis Paulucci, 'an excited Italian', goes on talking to the Emperor, 'oblivious of decorum', according to Prince Andrey. When Bennigsen insists, after the battle of Borodino, that Moscow must be defended, Kutuzov sees clearly what his aim is: in case of failure he will put the blame on him, if there is a success he will claim it for himself. Bennigsen displays his patriotism so passionately that Kutuzov cannot help frowning. And like Prince Andrey we trust Kutuzov mainly 'because he is Russian'. Kutuzov knows in his bones that in spite of all the losses in the battle of Borodino it has been won, and when Wolzogen comes from Barclay de Tolly and tells him that the battle is lost, Kutuzov gets really angry. ' "How ... how dare you! ..." ' he shouted, choking and making threatening gestures with his trembling arms. "How dare you, sir, to say it to me. You know nothing ..." All were silent and the only sound audible was the heavy breathing of the panting general, "They are repulsed everywhere, for which I thank God and our brave army. The enemy is beaten and tomorrow we shall drive him from the sacred soil of Russia," said Kutuzov crossing himself, and suddenly he sobbed as his eyes filled with tears.'

At least as convincing to us as the judgement of Kutuzov the Commander-in-Chief is that of Pierre, who was in the midst of the battle of Borodino, in his white hat. The soldiers recognize a gentleman (a *barin*), in him and treat him in a friendly manner: all men are brothers in the hour of grave danger. Pierre had experienced fear: ' "Oh, how terrible fear is and how shamefully I surrendered to it! But they ... they remained firm, calm, to the end," thought Pierre.'

The Kutuzov of the final version is not the same as the one in the early drafts, which was based on authentic sources; but Tolstoy felt himself as free to invent a Kutuzov as a Pierre or a Natasha or a Sonya.

In *Some Words about War and Peace*, Tolstoy wrote 'What is *War and Peace*? It is not a novel, even less is it a poem, and still less a historical chronicle. *War and Peace* is what the author wished and was able to express in the form in which it is expressed.' Dickens could have claimed the same for *The Pickwick Papers*, and indeed the skeleton of *The Pickwick Papers* shows a marked resemblance to that of *War and Peace*. Just as Tolstoy created a clan so did Dickens the Pickwick Club: just as the members of the Bolkonsky–Rostov clan have human faults but none of the vices which would shatter a child's world, so the members of the club suffer from venial short-comings, but not vices. At the root of Tolstoy's knowledge of the clan and their friends, just as of Dickens's knowledge of the club and friends, is the knowledge of a child of his family and friends, and out of the security of childhood each watches the world outside as through a window. But Dickens was only twenty-five when he finished *The Pickwick Papers*, Tolstoy forty when he finished *War and Peace*, and he made good use of his wider experience as man and artist. He hid successfully the dividing line between the members of the clan and out-siders.

Tolstoy's great experience as a writer before he began *War and Peace* gave him freedom to create a vast variety of characters. What is so interesting about Anatole Kuragin are the many characteristics Tolstoy gives us about him all at once: some-thing he seldom does. 'Anatole was always content with his position, with himself and others'; 'he was not a gambler, at any rate he did not care about winning. He was not vain. He did not mind what people thought of him. Still less could he be accused of ambition . . . He was not mean, and did not refuse anyone who asked him a favour. He was incapable of con-sidering what the gratification of his tastes entailed for others, he honestly considered himself irreproachable, sincerely despised rogues and bad people, and with tranquil conscience carried his head high.' An inventory. Let us put down what we know about Tolstoy, from the impact he made on others and, above all, from his own memories: he was a gambler, he was vain, never indifferent to what other people thought of him, ambitious, sometimes miserly. He was never pleased with himself for long and reproached himself often. In short Anatole is in everything the reverse of Tolstoy. Did he create him to a formula, by placing him at the opposite pole from himself? No, not quite. One unbroken strand in Tolstoy is the contradiction in his nature. He was at times generous as he was mean at others; he ceased to gamble; the very ambitious man put his ambitions outside himself; even his awareness of what the gratification of his tastes and desires entailed to others ceased at times to torment him. He must have had fun in creating Anatole to a formula, but then, since nothing human was alien to him, *he breathed life into him*.

The years between the end of happy childhood and the beginning of the happy period when both Tolstoy and Dickens wrote masterpieces contained shattering experiences. With the most personal and traumatic of these neither Dickens nor Tolstoy dealt till decades later. What they both did at the time was to use isolated experiences from the traumatic period, a dark room on which they had closed the door, but from which they now and then fetched a memory of a manageable experience. So Dickens brought out his experience of the Marshalsea, of elections, of courts, and of perfidious lawyers; Tolstoy of war, hunting, gambling away a fortune.

I believe that the model for Dolokhov comes from that period, which Tolstoy later called 'terrible'. V. B. Shklovsky writes in his biography of Tolstoy: 'In his youth, Tolstoy did many things, imitating Kostya [Islavin]. Unlike his two elder brothers, Kostya had neither a position in the world nor any property, and was, as Troyat says 'a rake'. But there was another side to him: he was very musical, and was loved by his nieces, the Countess Tolstoy and her sister Tanya. In *War and Peace* the poor 'Uncle', at whose house Nikolay and Natasha stop while out hunting and Natasha delights everyone when she joins in a country dance, is also modelled on Kostya Islavin. That is one aspect of him. The other, I believe, is Dolokhov, 'a deeply immoral person', but fascinating. Nikolay Rostov and his brother Petya both fall under Dolokhov's spell, just as Leo Tolstoy and his brother Dmitry fell under Islavin's. John Bayley argues cogently that Dolokhov can be regarded as a character with whom Tolstoy failed, and asks: 'If nothing Dolokhov says rings quite right, is this because he is "insincere", or because his nature is genuinely incomprehensible to Tolstoy?' I am inclined to the second suggestion, especially because Tolstoy had failed, too, with the Narrator of the first draft of *Childhood*, who was modelled on the young Kostya, and because his promise, in old age, to 'write about him later if there is time' was never fulfilled. Just as we know that a scientist, who at times produces a viable and indeed a great hypothesis, fails to do so on another occasion, so even a Tolstoy occasionally produced a flawed character.

There are more of Tolstoy's early memories in *War and Peace* than in his book *Childhood*. He carried over objects, names, customs, traditions, and breathed the very air of his childhood. Prince Andrey's child Nikolenka is born on the leather sofa on which Tolstoy and all his own children were born. His mother's nurse Praskovya Isaievna appears in *Childhood* under the name Natalya Savishna, and this was, he said in old age, a pretty accurate portrait; in *War and Peace* she reappears as Princess Marie's nanny, Praskovya Savishna. There was a somewhat unusual habit in the Tolstoy household of adults and children kissing each other's hands on greeting: Prince Andrey and Princess Marie keep this custom.

Tolstoy as a child was very unhappy about his looks. He wanted to be like his brother Sergey, and Sergey was goodlooking. One day he cut off his eyebrows, but they soon grew again. 'I had the strangest idea of beauty . . . so that every reference to my appearance offended me painfully', he wrote in *Childhood*. The mother says 'No one will love you for your face, so you must try and be a clever and good boy'; he goes on: 'These words not only convinced me that I was no beauty, but that I should certainly be a good and clever boy. In spite of that there were moments when I was overcome by despair . . . and all I then had and everything I might have in future I would have given for a handsome face.'

In *War and Peace* he never mentions Hélène or Anatole without reminding us how goodlooking they were. Hélène has beautiful shoulders, she has the smile of 'a completely beautiful woman'; he even goes as far as to allow her some virtue when talking of her beauty: it seemed as if her great beauty even embarrassed her sometimes. And her brother Anatole is more than 'handsome'; it would be nearer to the original *krasavets* to translate it 'an Adonis'. By contrast Pierre is stout, awkward, and shortsighted; Princess Marie is ugly, her only redeeming feature her eyes. (People used to say this of Tolstoy.) In Natasha he points out physical imperfections too. Dominated by a memory of childhood he links plain looks, in the characters he loves best, Marie and Pierre, with goodness, while the two depraved people, the brother and sister Kuragin, he endows with outstanding beauty.

The linking of plain looks with goodness, like De Quincey's linking of July splendour with the darkness of the grave, is of course not a universal statement. Many poets have linked beauty with goodness, and death with autumn. But Tolstoy and De Quincey both transfuse into us the intensity and truth of their childhood experience, and this too is poetry.

Andrey, Pierre, Petya Rostov, Tolstoy's possible selves, gave him the greatest troubles. In the early drafts, when Petya joined the army in the field, he experienced 'a painful feeling of disillusionment and dissatisfaction with himself'. Such a feeling, Tolstoy informs us, 'is always the stronger the better the young man is at fighting'. We also learn that 'Petya was endowed with great ambition'. Once again Tolstoy is writing about himself. Only in the final version does Petya cease to be a self-portrait and become a possible young Leo. As usual he has a secondary model, his young brother-in-law Petya Bers. 'When Petya joined the army at sixteen, he was in a state of blissful excitement of being grown up and in a perpetual hurry not to miss any chance to do something really heroic.' He is a very kind-hearted and affectionate boy. There is a delightful scene, entirely unsentimental, about his feelings and behaviour towards the French boy who had been taken prisoner. He admires greatly the daredevil Dolokhov. When he hears him argue with Denisov that it is no use taking French prisoners, that it is better to shoot them, Petya feels uncomfortable and restless, but he thinks 'If this is what grown-up well-known men think, it must be that it is necessary, it must be that it is good.' In the *Reminiscences* Tolstoy gives us three memories of just such an experience in childhood. A dog ran under the horses' feet and its leg was broken: when Leo heard the tutor say that the dog would be hung, he felt it was bad, but did not trust his feelings. He had a similar experience when, coming home from a walk with the other children, he saw the steward leading away the assistant coachman to be flogged, a married man no longer young. This was the first time he had heard of such a punishment being given at their home: his father had been a gentle master, but was by then dead. When he told Tatyana Alexandrovna what he had seen, she asked, ' "And how is it that you did not stop him?" Her words grieved me even more . . .'. It happened a third time when he heard Temyashev, his father's friend, tell how he had pressed one of his serfs into the army when he found that he had eaten meat during Lent. In each case he felt that something bad was being done, 'but being firm decisions of older and respected people, I dared not trust my own feelings.'.

Petya, who longed for heroic exploits, was determined to accompany Dolokhov, who was going to the French camp to spy. Denisov, who was devoted to all the Rostovs, did not want him to go, but the boy refused to listen. And so he set out with Dolokhov, both dressed as Frenchmen, on their adventure. Dolokhov's behaviour among the French, especially when they began to grow suspicious, filled Petya with great admiration. When they finally got back to safety, and Dolokhov said good-bye to Petya and gave him a message for Denisov, Petya seized hold of him. ' "No" he cried out, "you are such a hero! Ah, how good! how splendid! How I love you!" "All right, all right," – said Dolokhov. But Petya did not let go of him, and Dolokhov saw through the darkness that Petya was bending towards him. He wanted that they should kiss. Dolo-khov kissed him, gave a laugh, and turning his horse disappeared in the darkness.'

Tolstoy had experienced passionate love for old and young, men, women, children, and animals. He had early memories of passionate love for Tatyana Alexandrovna. 'I had outbursts of rapture, tender love for her. I remember how once, on the sofa in the drawing-room, when I was about five, I lay behind her; and she caressingly touched me with her hand. I caught her hand and began to kiss it and to cry from tender love for her.' In *Childhood* Tolstoy recreates his passionate love for the boy Seryozha. 'I could not have confided that feeling to

anyone, so much did I treasure it.' This passionate love recurs
again and again. Here is what he wrote in his diary in 1851.
He describes travelling with his friend Dyakov, at night, in a
sledge: 'I wanted to kiss him and weep. There was voluptuous-
ness in this feeling, but why it occurred here it is impossible
to say, for my imagination did not paint lascivious pictures.
On the contrary I had great aversion to them.' And Petya's
enthusiasm in fighting is equally Tolstoy's. In the last terrible
moment Petya rushes into the thick of the battle with the wild
enthusiasm and fearlessness of Tolstoy when hunting, both as a
boy and as an adult.

To repeat De Quincey's statement in the Introductory
Notice to the *Suspiria de Profundis*: 'He acknowledges the deep,
mysterious identity between himself, as adult and as infant,
for the ground of his sympathy; and yet, with this general
agreement, and necessity of agreement, he feels the difference
between his two selves as the main quickeners of his sympathy.'

For a parallel with Petya Rostov consider Dickens's Jo, the
boy crossing-sweeper in *Bleak House*. Jo has no surname. He
does not know his father or mother, he does not know what his
name is short for. He is a tramp, always on the run for no fault
of his own. He goes, one day, to Blackfriars Bridge, 'where he
finds a baking stony corner, wherein to settle to his repast'.
Dickens used to walk this way every day, when he was twelve
years old, from the blacking warehouse where he worked to the
Marshalsea where his father was imprisoned for debt. Jo looks
up and sees the Great Cross on the summit of St Paul's Cathedral, glittering above a red and violet tinted cloud of smoke.
So did Dickens look up from the top of Bayham Street, 'at the
cupola of St Paul's looking through the smoke.' (This comes
from Dickens's fragment of autobiography.) He felt at eleven
as much an outcast as Jo. Jo sits there, he sees 'the sun going
down, the river running fast, the crowd flowing by in two streams
– everything moving on to some purpose and to one end – until
he is stirred up, and told to "move on" too'. This is Dickens
deciphering what he had felt in cipher, to use De Quincey's
felicitous expression. 'From the boy's face one *might suppose*
[my italics] that sacred emblem to be, in his eyes, the crowning
confusion of the great, confused city; so golden, so high up, so

far out of his reach.' Why is Dickens an onlooker here? Why so
tentative? Because he does not remember what the sight of
St Paul's did to him in his miserable hour, and living in Jo
his primary concern is the truth. Dickens is not the only writer
who revered his childhood memories.

It is marvellous how Dickens throws overboard all that he
himself had learned at that age. Jo did not know one prayer,
what his name was short for – 'Never knowd nothink sir' –
but his memory for the minute details of his disturbing experience of taking Lady Dedlock to the grave of her lover is
as good as Dickens's own. More than Esther, the flesh and
blood child of the unhappy union, Jo is their child.

He remembers Lady Dedlock perfectly, but there is no love
for her in his memory, any more than there was in Dickens for
his mother. We know that Lady Dedlock was indirectly the
cause of Jo's great misfortune – of his always having to 'move
on'. But there is great love in Jo for the lover, and gratitude for
his unforgettable kindness; and we see with Dickens that 'there
is something like a distant light' in Jo's oft-repeated words:
'He was very kind to me, he was'. And this is Dickens's profound belief that even if he had been Jo, the last of men, he
still would have seen 'something like a distant light'.

Jo dies young, so does Petya Rostov. In the early drafts of
*War and Peace* Petya was not going to die. Nor was Prince
Andrey. A Dickens, a Tolstoy, who like a god decides who is
to live and who to die, is not, surely, dictated to by his plot.
These possible selves, created with such love, had died in their
creators: they were not viable.

An autobiographer's all important images are to be found in
his memories – not surprising this; but it is also true of the
images of great inventors. Proust, in *By Way of Sainte-Beuve*,
writing about his reading of Tolstoy, talks of the 'inexhaustible
fund of creation' in *War and Peace* and *Anna Karenina*; but he
goes on to point out that Tolstoy repeats some themes, disguised and reshaped. 'The stars and the sky Levin rivets his
gaze on, are pretty much the same as the comet that Pierre
saw, as Prince Andrey's wide blue sky.' Had Proust known the

fragment *A Landlord's Morning* he would not have failed to see the origin of the sky image.

Tolstoy was nineteen when the brothers and sister divided their inheritance in great amity and Leo became master of Yasnaya Polyana. He left the university, without finishing his course, decided to run his estate, and invited his relation Tatyana Alexandrovna, who had brought him up, to come back. Nekhlyudov, the hero in *A Landlord's Morning*, decides to leave university at the age of nineteen, just as Tolstoy did, and informs his aunt, who 'according to his ideas was his best friend', of his plans to improve the lot of his peasants. After a year of managing his estate, no longer green in either the practical or theoretical knowledge of husbandry, he sets out one morning to visit his peasants. On that morning the young Nekhlyudov returns home terribly disappointed and discouraged: neither the successful peasant nor the ne'er-do-wells showed the slightest sign of trusting him or wanting to collaborate with him. Walking towards his house, along the shady avenues of his overgrown garden, plucking a leaf absentmindedly, he thinks: are all my dreams about an aim in life, and duties, nonsense? He lives in his imagination, with extraordinary vividness and clarity, in the happy memory of a morning the year before, when he was dreaming of things to come. He had risen early 'and, painfully disturbed by some hidden longings of youth, eluding expression, he went out aimlessly into the garden. . . .' Wandering in the forest on that May morning, he had pursued his feeling, searching to find an expression of it. One moment his imagination had put before him a voluptuous image of a woman, and it seemed that this was his hidden desire, but another, more exalted feeling had told him 'That's not it'. His inexperienced enthusiastic mind had lifted him higher and higher into a sphere of abstract thought: it seemed to him that he was discovering 'the laws of existence', and he dwelt with delight on these thoughts. But once again his feeling had told him 'That's not it', and again he searched, and again was excited. Finally, exhausted, 'he lay on his back, under a tree, and began to look at the transparent morning clouds, passing over him in the deep, infinite sky. And suddenly, without any reason, tears came into his eyes, and God knows by what way, a clear thought came to him, filling all his soul, which he grasped with delight – the thought that love and goodness are truth and happiness, and the only truth and only possible happiness in the world.' This time his exalted feeling did not say 'That's not it'. To be happy one must be good, he had decided, so why search for a sphere of activity – he had his peasants? And apart from this 'who was to hinder him from being happy in love for a woman, and finding happiness in family life?' He imagined himself 'loving his wife as no one has ever loved anyone, of their living in the country, with their children and the old aunt, and both having one aim, to do good'.

These were his dreams a year ago, and now he is disappointed and unhappy. By the steps of his house he finds a number of peasants waiting for him, and he returns from his dreams to reality. He listens to their petitions, complaints, gives advice to some, promises to others to attend to their affairs, and with 'a mixed feeling of fatigue, shame of impotence, and regret, he entered the room'. A little later he sits at the piano and begins to play; the notes are not even quite correct and show no musical talent, but they bring him 'a sad delight'. 'The chief delight came from a greatly increased activity of the imagination, disconnected and intermittent, but with astonishing clarity showing him all kinds of mixed-up and meaningless images and pictures out of the past and the future.' In the end he is fascinated by the vision of a troika drawn by well-fed horses, driven by the strong and handsome Ilyushka, the carter son of the rich peasant he has seen that day. It is Ilyushka's free life, his sound carefree sleep, his dreams of seeing the world – Kiev, Odessa, Tsargrad, that make Nekhlyudov whisper to himself 'Lovely', and the thought also comes to him: why is he not Ilyushka? And that is what Tolstoy did next: he set out to see the world.

As Proust recognized, Tolstoy's image of the sky recurs again and again. Pierre has been a prisoner of the French for a month; he has known great privations, was shattered by the inhumanity of man, but Platon Karateyev has restored his faith. He rises early one morning, comes out of the shed at dawn, sees the crosses of the monastery and the country around him, and the rim of the sun solemnly appearing from behind a cloud: 'Pierre felt a new, never before experienced feeling of joy and vigour of life'. This feeling had been strengthened in him by the high opinion his fellow-prisoners had formed of him. 'And Pierre felt that their opinion placed responsibilities on him.' The morning sky, the joy of life, and the duties towards men, are all linked together in Pierre's experience, as they had been in Tolstoy's own.

Levin, after spending a short summer night with the peasants in the meadows, wakes at dawn and 'glancing up at the stars realized that the night was over.' He will live like a peasant, 'convinced that he would find satisfaction, peace, and dignity ... "this night has decided my fate". . . . "How beautiful" he thought, looking up at a strange mother-of-pearl coloured shell formed of fleecy clouds in the centre of the sky just over his head.' Soon afterwards he sees a carriage on the road, and inside it is Kitty. He looks up at the sky hoping to see the shell he had admired before, but it is a new sky again, 'which has turned blue and grown brighter', and now he realizes that he loves Kitty and that he cannot turn to the life of simplicity and toil.

Prince Andrey discovers the lofty sky after he is wounded at Austerlitz, and is lying on his back: he opens his eyes hoping to see the end of the struggle between the Frenchmen and the gunners, but he sees nothing. 'Above him there was nothing but the sky – the lofty sky, not clear, yet still immeasurably lofty, with grey clouds crawling over it. . . . "How is it I did not see this lofty sky before? And how happy I am to have found it at last! Yes! everything is empty, everything is a lie except that infinite sky. Nothing, there is nothing apart from it. But even it isn't there, there is nothing there but silence and tranquillity. And thank God".' This moment of peace becomes an eternity, preserved in the sensation of the lofty sky.

Tolstoy turns to the many others taking part in this great battle: their hopes, fears, disappointments. Meanwhile Andrey is bleeding profusely, groans, and towards evening loses consciousness. Suddenly he feels himself alive, and suffering from a lacerating pain in his head: his first thought is 'Where is it, that lofty sky that I did not know till now, but saw today?

And this suffering I did not know either. Yes, I did not know anything at all till now. But where am I?'

He begins to listen, and hears the sound of approaching horses, and voices speaking French. He opens his eyes. 'Above him was again the same lofty sky with swimming clouds which had risen higher, and through them was visible blue infinity.' Judging by the sound of hoofs and voices Andrey realizes that the riders have stopped near him. It is Napoleon, accompanied by two aides-des-camp. 'That's a fine death!' said Napoleon, gazing at Bolkonsky. 'Not only did the words not interest him [Andrey], but he took no notice of them and at once forgot them. His head was burning, he felt himself bleeding to death, and he saw above him the remote, lofty, and eternal sky. He knew it was Napoleon – his hero, but at that moment Napoleon seemed to him such a small insignificant creature compared with what was passing now between himself and that lofty infinite sky with the clouds running over it.' He is glad that people have stopped near him, he wants someone to help him and bring him back to life, 'which seemed to him so beautiful because he understood it differently now'. He gathers all his strength in order to move, and utters a sound; Napoleon hears him, and gives the order that he should be taken to the dressing-station. Andrey again loses consciousness. Later still, when Napoleon sees him again and remembers him, and asks, 'And how do you feel, *mon brave*?' Andrey is silent, 'so insignificant at that moment seemed to him all the interests that engrossed Napoleon . . . compared to the lofty, just and kindly sky which he had seen and understood, that he could not answer him'.

By now Tolstoy has driven the sky image to death. We have followed the signposts willingly, expecting Andrey to discover the meaning of life. We accept from Tolstoy that Andrey, seriously wounded, does feel 'It would be good if everything were as clear and simple as it seems to Princess Marie . . . How happy and calm I should be if I could now say "Lord, have mercy on me!"' With hindsight, with what we know will happen to Andrey when he is mortally wounded at Borodino, we accept that at Austerlitz he only got as far as to know that 'There is nothing, nothing certain, except for the insignificance of everything that is understandable to me, and the greatness of something incomprehensible, but the most important!' And yet we are made uneasy by the recurring sky image. We know from our own experience that in a traumatic moment our eyes turn to something in the world outside and find comfort. So when Andrey was wounded, and luckily falls on his back, and the lofty sky makes him feel 'nothing but quiet and peace. And thank God' we feel with him and know that we shall never forget the link between the lofty sky and terrible fear and suffering. But when the sky speaks to him again and again, when in a different moment its infinity makes him realize that Napoleon is insignificant, we feel that this realization is insignificant. The image is now a ghost of what it was in the first moment of his falling wounded; and what is most painful is our conviction that Tolstoy is contriving it, making it up. He was pitilessly scornful of writers who 'thought up' things, and, true enough, he very rarely did it himself.

In Tolstoy's real memory the sky was accidental – he might have wandered on that May morning to the stream, and the meaning and purpose of life might have been preserved in the sight and sound of flowing waters. In Pierre's experience, in Levin's, Tolstoy recreated the whole memory: a memory of a moment when he got hold of the meaning of life, preserved in the sensation of the lofty sky. But in Andrey's experience Tolstoy splits his memory: at Austerlitz 'the lofty, just, and kindly sky' makes him feel that life is beautiful and he is certain of the unimportance of everything he understood, and the importance of something incomprehensible. Seven years later, at Borodino, the incomprehensible becomes comprehensible. The doctor who is attending Andrey knows that there is little hope. After his terrible pain and suffering he experiences a bliss such as he has not known for a long time. 'All the best and happiest moments of his life – especially his earliest childhood, when he used to be undressed and put to bed, and when his nurse, leaning over him, sang him to sleep and, burying his head in the pillow, he felt happy in the mere consciousness of life, presented themselves to his imagination, not even as the past but as reality.'

Such comfort brought by memories in a traumatic moment, when the past becomes the present, are to be found in the

5

writings of autobiographers, novelists, poets. Psychoanalysts have described this phenomenon, and physiologists will one day account for the comfort, and the greatly increased activity of the mind, in such moments. Andrey recognizes in the weeping man whose leg has been removed, Anatole Kuragin, 'And suddenly a new unexpected memory out of his childhood world, pure and loving, presented itself to him.' And immediately he remembers Natasha as he saw her for the first time at the ball, and pity and love for Anatole fills his happy heart. 'Compassion, love of our brothers, for those who love us and for those who hate us, love for our enemies; yes that love which God preached on earth and which Princess Marie taught me and I did not understand – that is what made me sorry to part with life, that is what remained for me had I lived. But now it is too late. I know it!'

The happy early memories of being put to bed, which came back to Prince Andrey as he lay wounded at Borodino, are Tolstoy's own, recorded in his youth, in middle life, and again in old age. Does Tolstoy convince a sceptical reader that the sceptic Andrey became certain, in the end, 'that love which God preached on earth and which Princess Marie taught me' made life meaningful? To me, a sceptic, the answer is in the character of Princess Marie, whose profound religious feelings are an inalienable part of her, and of her influence on her brother Andrey in childhood.

I will not deny that my conviction is strengthened by my knowledge of the influence of Tolstoy's mother: without one memory of her he felt her posthumous influence on their home and its inmates, he searched for her, he prayed to her, he dreamt of her, and she became a myth to him.

A plain girl, motherless, Princess Marie has spent her life in the country, in the home of her autocratic father. He laid down rules for the house, the peasants, himself and his daughter: she was almost a prisoner but, himself a sceptic, he respected her freedom of conscience. She is very human: she is envious of Natasha; much as she respects and loves her father, she looks forward to the time when she will be free and perhaps even have a husband and children, and this realization comes to her when he is dying. When she does marry, fulfilled as a wife and mother she feels a submissive tender love for her husband. But from early girlhood she has had a life of her own: her care of pilgrims, her fellow-feeling with them, are rooted in profound religious experiences; she is not a lady bountiful, she is not sentimental, she has stowed away a pilgrim's outfit and hopes to go on a pilgrimage herself. Her father remains a sceptic to the end, but his last words, 'Put on your white dress, I love it', speak of his great love for her: it is a fear of words which makes him say 'I love it', not 'I love you'; he has not deceived himself or her about her plainness, but it matters little in the hour of death, when he thinks of her in her white dress. She had failed to infect her father with her faith, but not her brother: when mortally wounded he remembers what she taught him when he was a child. Just as she accepted her limitation where her father was concerned, so she does with her husband: she will not try to change his reactionary views, but she will improve his temper, and he will feel ashamed that in a passion he beat his serfs. And she will influence her own children, as we see in the Epilogue to *War and Peace*, at least as much if not more than she had her brother Andrey.

It is often said that it is not legitimate to call on our knowledge of a writer's experience to shed light on his work. I do not know what is 'legitimate' but I know what helps understanding. Tolstoy, whose most striking feature is his continual ending and beginning anew, and looking at his past from a different height, still says, in *Father Sergius* written very late in his life, that his childhood faith was never destroyed. John Bayley writes that 'almost everything in *War and Peace* springs out of the childhood world and returns to it for judgement'. That pleased me greatly.

Pierre, like Andrey, was a seeker, and he blundered and erred more than Andrey; but he was a less rational, less proud, more intuitive person, and like a child he heard the tones of truth. For him it is never too late. He had searched for an aim in life, and 'had equipped himself with a mental telescope to look into remote space', but found nothing except 'pettiness, worldliness, and senselessness.' But after his suffering as a prisoner of the

French – and without suffering, he says, one would not achieve self-knowledge– after his meeting with Platon Karatayev, he was like a man who 'after training his eyes to see into the distance, finds what he has sought at his very feet'. To the question 'What for? a simple answer was now always ready in his soul: "Because there is a God, that God without whose will not one hair falls from a man's head".'

When Pierre, after his long search, begins to bring out in everyone what is best in them, we feel that this is the truth, and it helps us to know that this too begins in Tolstoy's own experience. He writes in the *Reminiscences* 'The people round me in childhood, from father to coachman, seemed to me entirely good people. Probably my pure loving feeling, like a bright ray, revealed to me in the people their best qualities (they are always there), and the fact that all people seemed to me entirely good was a great deal nearer the truth than when I saw all their faults.'

A Russian critic remarked that when we read *War and Peace* we wonder where Gogol's Russia came from, but Tolstoy was indifferent to such criticism. His parents' and grandparents' home and those of their close friends had been tolerant and civilized.

Here is one of his childhood memories, given to Biryukov. It is evening, the father is sitting beside the grandmother, helping her with her game of patience. 'Father was polite and kind to everyone, but to grandmother he was always somehow specially kind and submissive.' In the middle of the game of patience, while an aunt was reading aloud, the father interrupts the reading and, pointing to the mirror, whispers something. They all look in the mirror and see the butler Tikhon walking on tiptoe towards the study to help himself to tobacco from the father's pouch. 'The aunt laughs. The grandmother does not understand for a long time, and when she does she too smiles joyfully. I am in raptures about father's goodness, and saying goodnight I kiss his white sinewy hand with special tenderness.' The father died when Leo was nine.

But *War and Peace* is not an autobiography. He had not been married long before his ideal of a happy family at Yasnaya Polyana was becoming a reality, and at once he began to write the book which in the end became *War and Peace*. He spanned the second period of his life – what he called 'those twenty terrible years' – by building a bridge between childhood and marriage. We find that for the Bolkonsky–Rostov clan, and for Pierre, he is using experiences of his childhood or his married life. His wife, her two sisters, her mother, all are models for characters in the clan. Countess Rostov, when she learns of the death of her son Petya, talks to him as if he were still alive. So does the grandmother in *Childhood* talk to her dead daughter. He had painful real memories of his grandmother going nearly out of her mind when the news came that his father had died. But Countess Rostov's intimacy with Natasha is a translation of his mother-in-law's closeness to her daughters Sonya and Tanya. To be able to walk safely across the bridge between childhood and marriage, he made Natasha, whom he modelled on his sister-in-law and his wife, into a member of the Rostov family, a sister of Nikolay; in other words he imagined her as a Tolstoy and, unlike her models, a countess. We have his own reasons for making Prince Andrey into a son of the old Prince Bolkonsky and a brother of Princess Marie. In a letter in May 1865 to L. I. Volkonsky, Tolstoy attempted to answer her question: who was Andrey Bolkonsky. He asserted, not for the only time, that he was not a writer of memoirs. 'I would be ashamed to go to print if all my labour consisted in portraying, finding out, remembering.' He tells Princess Volkonsky he needed a brilliant young man to be killed at the battle of Austerlitz. But later he became interested in him, and spared his life and only had him seriously wounded. And 'since it is awkward to describe a person not connected to anyone else in the novel, I decided to make the brilliant young man into the son of the old Prince Bolkonsky.' And he ends: 'So there, dear Princess, you have an entirely truthful, and because of this not clear, explanation of who Bolkonsky is.'

Very well. Now let us compare Prince Andrey with Leo's brother Sergey. As Sergey grew older he more and more resembled Prince Bolkonsky, Andrey's father. His estate, unlike Leo's, was orderly, and the peasants, though afraid of him, respected him. He loved his three daughters, and they were still old maids in their forties, as Princess Marie would have remained if her father had not died. There was between Sergey and Leo a deep undemonstrative affection, but Sergey not only did not share Leo's opinions, he detested the Tolstoyans. He was dying of a painful cancer and his family were afraid to ask him to take communion: he had long since given up practising religion. They entreated Leo to approach Sergey, and Leo, the excommunicate, did so, and Sergey consented to see a priest. Whether he did this for the sake of the family, or because early memories of his mother came back to him as they did to Prince Andrey at Borodino, we cannot tell. So, some forty years after Tolstoy had conceived Andrey, Sergey, the sceptic, died reconciled with the Church in his last hours – for whatever it was worth – while Leo refused to the last to see a priest. What is the most striking is Tolstoy's great insight into the affinity between people: of his grandfather Volkonsky's four grandsons, only Sergey was like him, only he lived the life of Prince Bolkonsky of the novel, the eighteenth-century independent landed aristocrat, cultured and agnostic. Guided by his great intuition Tolstoy imagined the relationship between the father Bolkonsky and his son Andrey, with what a sure touch, what excellence! Tolstoy's assertion that he had to attach Andrey to a family is true; everyone in *War and Peace* is attached to some family. As for the creative process, he not only did not want others to know anything about it, he was not quite conscious of it himself. But a great work of art, more than a hundred years old, can bear the weight of our wider knowledge of how it was born.

Far below, under the bridge, were the years of Tolstoy's life between childhood and marriage. 'Those dreadful twenty years, the period of coarse dissoluteness, of service to ambition and vanity, and, above all, of lust', he called them in his seventies. In his early fifties, in the autobiographic fragment *Notes of a Madman,* he summed up that period somewhat differently: 'These twenty years of my healthy life passed in such a way that I hardly remember a thing, and now remember only with effort and revulsion.' The summaries do not quite tally, of course, and what we know of Tolstoy during that period is something quite different again: vain, snobbish, a gambler and a womanizer, he was also, throughout, struggling with himself, and becoming an artist: he was searching hard for the meaning of life, teaching peasant children and dreaming of a family life like his father's. What is more, the two years in the Caucasus in his early twenties were 'a painful but good period in my life', he wrote to Alexandra Tolstoy six years later, when he looked deeper into life than ever before or after, and discovered 'that there is immortality, there is love and that one must live for others in order to be forever happy.

While he was writing *War and Peace*, dominated by his 'poetic, innocent childhood' which made the book joyful, he did not want to remember those twenty years. But he could not do without them altogether. It was not that bringing back his memories of his tempter Islavin and creating a Dolokhov was a hard task. What he chiefly needed from that twenty years was his maturing. This need to cease to be a child and become an adult is much plainer in *The Pickwick Papers*, a less complex book than *War and Peace*. Pickwick's experience in the Fleet prison is indispensable: step by step we follow him, as he enters prison a boy and comes out a man. We know from Dickens's fragment of autobiography that what Mr Pickwick saw in the Fleet he, Dickens, had seen in the Marshalsea prison; but we also know that of all Dickens's traumatic experiences the least painful and most manageable was his prison experience. What Tolstoy lifted out of that twenty years' period was his gambling away a fortune (not once but many times), the death of his beloved brother Nikolay, and, more important than anything, his experiences of fighting in the Caucasus and in the Crimean war. Prince Andrey and Pierre matured in the wars: if there had been no Napoleonic war, Tolstoy would have had to invent one. He might have had to resort to a literary trick, like Dickens when he put Pickwick into prison.

A most surprising thing is the absence of Platon Karatayev in the early versions of *War and Peace*. In a cancelled Preface to *1805* (the original title of the first volume) Tolstoy says: 'The lives of officials, merchants, theological students, and peasants, do not interest me and are only half comprehensible to me; the lives of the aristocrats of that time, thanks to the documents of that time, and for other reasons, are comprehensible, interesting, and dear to me.' Tolstoy does himself less than justice: we know from his earliest writings that the peasants were no less comprehensible, interesting, and dear to him. Moreover his statement about aristocrats is very curious. John Bayley is wrong when he asserts that 'Russia belonged to Tolstoy because Russia belonged, literally, to his class'.

The peculiar thing about Russia was that it did not belong to any class, it belonged to the autocrat: no class had any rights of which it could not be deprived by the autocrat raising an eyebrow; and this was as true of Nicholas II right up to 1917, as it was of Nicholas I a century earlier. An aristocrat could not be sure of or claim an inviolable right, any more than a member of the privileged class in the Soviet Union, the Communist Party, can today. On the mere suspicion of some unimportant official Tolstoy's home was literally ransacked, policemen camped in the house, demanded food, searched letters and diaries. And that was not in the time of the tyrant Nicholas I but of the liberal Tsar Alexander II. Tolstoy writes in the *Reminiscences* that his father refused to serve the conquerer of Napoleon, towards the end of Alexander I's reign; moreover, he goes on to say, his father and their friends, out of self-respect, had no dealings whatsoever with any officials. Not to serve the autocrat, except in time of war, was a badge of honour. And yet a most remarkable and little understood feature of Russian life was the feeling running through the whole people, from aristocrat to peasant, that Russia belonged to them. Patriotism was based on the certainty of the greatness of Russia, the land and the people, and on a faith that the future was bright. This pride of every good Russian was unselfconscious, and I remember the scornful remarks of Russian émigrés, my fellow students in Berlin in the early twenties, about the Germans' vociferous love of their country. 'How beautiful life will be in three or four hundred years . . . all the earth will become a flourishing garden', wrote Chekhov, a great humanist. This does not mean that Chekhov, or any of the men of hope, were free of fear and doubt, or ever ceased to probe their faith or search for ways. Chekhov was not a revolutionary; it was Tolstoy who imagined himself taking part in the Decembrists' revolt against Nicholas I and, as Pierre, exiled to Siberia. *The Decembrists* remained a fragment, and the remarkable thing was that after he had written *War and Peace* and *Anna Karenina* he again returned to the theme of the Decembrists, studied the period and collected material. But once again he abandoned it. And in the end Tolstoy rejected the revolution of 1905.

Chekhov, the son of a serf, felt that Russia belonged to him no less than Tolstoy did. Even a minority, not only oppresssed but shamelessly used as a scapegoat, the Jews, abounded in Russian patriots. Babel, Pasternak, Mandelstam, Ilya Ehrenburg, all had great faith in the future of Russia. I have confined myself to writers because they had the means of bringing about a change. If you had asked an intelligent teenager, before 1917, what about the good scientists, doctors, teachers, Zemstvo workers, he would have promptly retorted 'Nothing more than a drop in the ocean'. Only the writers and revolutionaries inspired faith in all thinking men. There had never been in Russia a class, solid, powerful, capable of defending its rights, as in Western Europe the feudal aristocracy, the bourgeousie, the proletarians, only an intelligentsia fighting with the pen and the gun. It was the intelligentsia who replaced the autocrats and became an autocracy itself. No wonder that the rulers of Russia are so afraid of writers: Solzhenitsyn belongs to the old Russian tradition of men who refused to serve the autocrat, except in time of war, and who had faith in the bright future of Russia to be brought about by the power of the pen.

Tolstoy's snobbishness, if one can call it so, at the time when he began *War and Peace*, was not shared by his brothers. Nikolay, the eldest brother, was a member of the intelligentsia, his best friends were writers: he used to make fun of Leo's desire to be *comme il faut*. All three brothers were eccentrics: there is a good portrait of Dmitry in *Anna Karenina* – he ended preaching communism and living with a woman whom he took from a brothel. Sergey carried on the life of a landed aristocrat: he would not serve the state any more than Leo, and was as proud as he, but unlike Leo, he would never have said that only aristocrats were dear to him.

5*

Snobbishness is almost invariably rooted in comparisons with people only just above and just below you, and Tolstoy certainly suffered from it. He had a painful memory of childhood, of an insult to himself and his brothers at a Christmas party. The Tolstoy children had recently been orphaned and were in straitened circumstances. At that party they were given cheap rubbishy little presents, while the children of a family of their own relations, but important in the eyes of society, had very grand expensive presents. Leo never forgot that moment, and some sixty years later, in *Resurrection*, he translated his experience into one of a working boy, at a Christmas party given by the owner of the factory: he received worthless presents while the owner's children are given fabulous gifts. This event entirely altered the boy's life. He ends as a revolutionary and is among the convicts on their way to Siberia. An unrealistic story in nineteenth-century England but possible in Russia.

After Tolstoy's failure to improve the lot of his peasants, he returned to a wild life in Moscow, and once again registered his intention to 'seek out the society of people more highly placed than I'. In the Caucasus, when he decided to enter the army and needed patronage, he hoped to get it from 'the mighty Prince Baryatinsky': his striving for social advancement makes one more tolerant of that other great writer, Proust, who worked so hard to get into French high society. Even at the age of twenty-six, after Tolstoy had found himself as a writer, after *Childhood* had been well received, and his mind was teeming with new ideas, he still felt an outsider. He made a remarkable sketch of himself in his diary. It is long, and I will quote a few sentences only. 'What am I? One of the four sons of a retired lieutenant-colonel . . . without any great fortune or any solid position in society. I am ugly, awkward, untidy and socially uncouth. I am irritable and tiresome to others, immodest, intolerant and shy as a child. In other words, a boor . . . I love the path of virtue . . . and when I depart from it I am unhappy and am glad to return to it. Yet there is one thing I love more than virtue: fame. I am so ambitious. . . .'

For some two hundred years the Tolstoys' position in society resembled that of many county families in England in that they produced no men of distinction or power in the state or in any other field; but, in spite of ups and downs of fortune, continued to live the life of a traditional landed gentry, sure of themselves and quietly proud. When there appears in such a family a member of exceptional ability and ambition, he claims, for quite good reasons, that his family belongs to the highest in the land. The great difference between Leo and his brothers was that they did not care to press this.

In *War and Peace* Tolstoy, like Goethe, is following a tendency 'from which I have not been able to deviate my whole life long, to transform everything that gladdened and tormented me, or that preoccupied me in some other way, into an image, a poem, and thus to come to terms with myself, both correcting my ideas of external things and inwardly quieting myself about them' (*Dichtung und Wahrheit*). Pierre is the son of a powerful, rich aristocrat, Count Bezukhov; Prince Andrey the son of an equally proud, rich aristocrat, the eccentric and cultured old Prince Bolkonsky. Andrey even declined the favour of the Emperor: he had received a message that the Emperor wished to see him personally, and question him about Turkey. It was at Drissa. Andrey and another Russian, Chernychev, were in the porch, and watched the Emperor arrive and dismount. Marquis Paulucci began talking to the Emperor, who listened with a dissatisfied air. The Emperor, recognizing Bolkonsky, turned graciously to him and said, 'Glad to see you: go through there where they have assembled and wait for me'. My translation is literal, in an attempt to preserve the tone: it is of a senior public school boy saying something to a boy somewhat his junior.

We are not told anything about the Emperor's talk with Andrey on the subject of Turkey, and are merely informed that next day at the parade the Emperor asked Andrey where he would like to serve. 'And Prince Andrey lost for ever his standing at court by not having asked to remain with the Sovereign, but for permission to serve in the army.' In other words he had slighted the Sovereign, as Andrey, a very clever man, must have known beforehand. Tolstoy here is as cunning as Shakespeare: he leaves to our judgment whether Andrey's action is due to his conviction, expressed a little earlier: 'And only in the ranks one can serve with certainty that one is useful', or that his refusal is a move in the silent battle between autocrat and aristocrat. Leaving it to us to disentangle motives the writer comes close to real life. The odd thing about Andrey's losing his standing in court 'for ever' is that there were no more occasions for his appearing at court: he was mortally wounded at Borodino and died soon after. The passage may have been left over from an earlier version in which Andrey was not to die, but to follow the Emperor to Paris. (There are quite a number of other errors in *War and Peace*.)

What is more surprising than Tolstoy's snobbishness is his assertion in the discarded preface to 1805 that the peasants were neither comprehensible nor dear to him. He had known and understood them since childhood; he had had love affairs with peasant women, he had taught peasant children, and had painted wonderful portraits of them. One need only turn to *Childhood* and read about Natalya Savishna, a character that still pleased him in his seventies because 'it is a pretty accurate portrait', to realize the affinity between her and Platon Karatayev. Both have self-respect, commonsense, shrewdness, love of truth, and goodwill. Natalya Savishna was a serf, almost a prisoner; but so was Platon Karatayev, for a soldier in those days was conscripted for almost a lifetime. Their goodwill is not that of slaves. Platon has no grudge against Pierre, the rich, privileged, free, gifted, famous man, as if the existence of such fortunate men made his own life more meaningful. This humble illiterate Platon saved Pierre from despair; no wonder: he loved the truth, he loved mankind, he sang like a bird and talked like a poet.

There is the same 'glory and freshness of a dream' about Platon Karatayev as there is about Nikolay Rostov and his marriage to Princess Marie, about the death of Prince Andrey. This Tolstoy knew very well: before *War and Peace* was completed he wrote: 'The poet skims off the best of life and puts it into his work. That is why his work is beautiful and his life bad.' Once again Tolstoy is doing himself less than justice. By incorporating his dreams, his vision, Tolstoy extracted profound truth, and as always he was the primary beneficiary: after writing *War and Peace* he was a different man and a different artist.

In the Epilogue we have two happy marriages. Nikolay's impression that Pierre is under the thumb of Natasha shows once again that Nikolay is not a clever man: if anything he is more under the thumb of his wife, if for no other reason than that she is spiritually superior to him. Pierre is superior to Natasha: just as Natasha looks up to Princess Marie, so she does to Pierre. The dialogue between Pierre and Natasha, free of the rules of logic, incomprehensible to an outsider, is a flow of feeling and understanding between them. The ability of Natasha to run her home, her family, and her husband is willingly delegated to her by Pierre, who has more important things to do. The famous remark that 'Only what was really good in him [Pierre] was reflected in his wife, all that was not quite good was rejected' fits the conclusion of *War and Peace*. Tolstoy will never say anything like this in later books.

Pierre did not regret his experience in the war; Mr Pickwick says that he will never regret the two years devoted to mixing with different varieties and shades of human character. Both Pierre and Pickwick have suffered, both have matured, and now their aim in life is to work for the happiness of others. 'The happiness of young people,' he [Pickwick] said, a little moved, 'has ever been the chief pleasure of my life!' Pierre tells Natasha of his success in Saint Petersburg: 'It seemed to him, at that moment, that he was called to give a new direction to the whole of society and the whole world.'

Both Dickens and Tolstoy, at the time of writing these conclusions, have realized their own dreams: they have achieved happy family lives, and fame – to both not an empty worldly reward but the stuff of the love of men.

In the preface to the first version of *1805*, which I have quoted earlier, Tolstoy wrote: 'However much I tried at first to think up a novel-like plot and denouement, I was convinced that it was not within my means, and I decided, in describing these people, to bow to my own practices and my own powers.' He knew that, guided by a mere plot, he could not work out all the possible characters and their relationships, no more than could Kutuzov take into account all the possible turnings of the Great War, all that could happen in a battle. And just as Kutuzov believed that the fate of a battle is decided 'by that intangible force called the spirit of the army', and that he himself was the best man in Russia, at that time, to watch that force, and guide it as far as was in his power, so Tolstoy believed himself to be the guide of the spirit of his book.

## 3. *Anna Karenina*

In the spring of 1869 Tolstoy at last completed *War and Peace*. In August he set out to buy a new estate: he had read a notice of the sale in a newspaper; it was some five hundred miles away from his home and he took with him his favourite servant Sergey Arbuzov. They travelled by train the first part of the way, and then hired a coach. As the day declined Tolstoy was assailed by all kinds of fear and, coming to the town of Arzamas, he decided to break the journey and stop there for the night.

Despair overwhelmed him. He wrote to his wife next day that it was 'a terror such as I have never experienced before'. More than a decade elapsed before he described the night at Arzamas, in *Notes of a Madman*. 'Why this anguish, what am I afraid of?' he asked himself. ' "Of me", the voice of death answered inaudibly, "I am here".' He tried to shake off the horror, he lit a candle: 'The red flame of the candle, its size, a little shorter than the candlestick, – were all saying the same thing. There is nothing in life; there is death, but there should be no death. The anguish was like the one before one is going to vomit.' He reasoned, he got up and went to look at his sleeping servant, tried again to sleep: 'the horror was the same, red, white, square.'

Tolstoy had known fear at times in hunting and fighting. In one of the raids in the Caucasus, when men were dropping dead round him, he experienced great fear, and some fifty years later said that it 'was the greatest I have ever known'. This became Pierre's experience on the day of the battle of Borodino. Tolstoy was never afraid to be afraid. But such fear when facing death had little in common with his fear at Arzamas, the fear that the existence of death makes life meaningless. He remembered to pray. 'It was a long time, some twenty years, that I had not prayed, and had not believed in

anything, although for the sake of decorum I took the sacraments every year.' Prayer did not help him. In the morning he
resumed the journey, and fresh air and movement made him
feel better. 'But I felt that something had now deposited itself
in my soul and poisoned all my past life.'

That the horror was not passing, temporary, due simply to
exhaustion following his great labour, we know: years after
Arzamas he recreated his despair both in fiction and autobiography, in Levin's despair in the midst of happy family life
in *A Confession*, an intellectual record, and later, in *Notes
of a Madman*. What he tried to be and what he was in the next
forty years of life lead straight out of the Arzamas horror.
But Tolstoy's search for the meaning of life did not begin at
Arzamas. He searched for it at nineteen, as we know from
*The Landlord's Morning;* he searched for it in the Caucasus a
couple of years later, as we know from a long letter of 1858.

Each time he believed he had succeeded. His realization of
the purpose of life at nineteen was followed by a dissolute life:
gambling, womanizing, idleness. Again, after he had reached
certainty in the Caucasus, his old passions got the better of
him, but this time he added to all his other passions a new one,
writing, a passion which outlasted all others.

One asks: how could Tolstoy, who wrote *War and Peace* with
the seriousness of an autobiographer, and created a joyful
world, a world which, in spite of errors, disappointment,
slaughter in war, was without fear (Pierre says in the end
'nothing is really terrifying in life'), how could he experience
such despair so soon after he had finished the book?

Tolstoy had lived with unbelief in Christian doctrine for
over a quarter of a century. He says (in the letter to Alexandra
Tolstoy of 1858): 'As a child I believed passionately, senti-
mentally, and without thinking, up to the age of fourteen.'
Then, he says, he found religion unsatisfactory, felt it was his
duty to destroy it. Now, at the height of his fulfilment, the horror
of death came to him at Arzamas, and he was threatened with
despair. We know from the experience of our own time that
in hours of despair, of realization that what was happening in
Stalin's Russia, in Hitler's Germany, was destroying the roots
of our life, we still carried on work, had children, made friends,

did not give up hopes and joys. Tolstoy at Yasnaya Polyana felt secure; general political solutions to problems did not interest him much, and when a stupid governmental action, directed at him personally, offended him, he at once threatened to emigrate to England. His vitality, his great appetites, passions, gifts, pushed down doubt and fear and, happy in the early years of marriage, he felt free to embody the splendid vision of his childhood.

After the night at Arzamas, the Narrator in *Notes of a Madman* does not buy a new estate, as he had set out to do; at home he finds no comfort in family life or in his duties as a justice of the peace; he still gets a little joy out of hunting, and comfort from reading the New Testament and the *Lives of the Saints*, but not for long. Tolstoy, after Arzamas, bought more estates, had more and more children, and wrote more books. The Narrator moves directly and quickly to a climax: not so Tolstoy, who took over a decade. *Notes of a Madman* ends with the Narrator's discovery that all men are brothers, sons of the Father, and his rejection of the sacraments. This is where Tolstoy had got to thirteen years later at the time he wrote the fragment: he believed in God and immortality, and in Jesus: not a God but a perfect man, whose example it is joyful to follow.

Tolstoy's mind was a vast forest of memories, many of the direct impact of experience on him, but also a considerable number about his ancestors and their contemporaries which he had acquired from others. There were trees of every kind and size in his forest, straight and twisted, as well as stumps, bushes, and undergrowth; there were flowers in his forest of memories, fragrant scents of which he could not always tell the source. At no time was he aware of the whole of his vast domain, but got to know first this and then that part, selling it off in lots, as the great Russian landlords sold parts of their endless forests.

Tolstoy said of *War and Peace* that it was what the author wished to express, but that he did not know, when he began, what that was. *War and Peace* was not a novel, according to him;

*Anna Karenina* was, but even then, to judge by the many changes of opening and plot, and of individual characters, he did not know what he wished to express when he started. The changes in the drafts of all Tolstoy's books are not of the kind that every work of art demands: cutting, coordinating, polishing, achieving greater clarity and more felicitous expression. His changes seem to originate in successive waves of inspiration, a new one often obliterating the preceding, as if each came from a greater depth and with mounting power.

The sources of these waves are not only in past and present experiences, but in the future as well. In *Anna Karenina* Tolstoy was prophetic. I shall attempt to show that there was nothing supernatural in this, that poets and novelists live in their future as well as in their past; and further, that this is not an uncommon experience.

Francis Galton writes in his *Memories of My Life*: 'By much dwelling upon my memories they became refurbished and so vivid as to appear as sharp and definite as things of today. The consequence has been an occasional obliteration of the sense of Time, and its replacement by the idea of a permanent panorama, painted throughout with equal vividness, in which the point to which attention is temporarily directed becomes for that time the Present. The panorama seems to extend unseen behind a veil which hides the Future, but is slowly rolling aside and disclosing it. That part of the panorama which is veiled is supposed to exist as vividly coloured as the rest, though latent. In short, this experience has given me an occasional feeling that there are no realities corresponding to Past, Present, and Future, but that the entire Cosmos is one perpetual Now. Philosophers have often held this creed intellectually, but I suspect few have felt the possible truth of it so vividly as it has occasionally appeared to my imagination through dwelling on these "memories".'

It is strange that Galton, in 1908, seems unaware of this experience in De Quincey. In *Recollections of the Lake Poets* De Quincey wrote that if the 'recall of the real be affecting, much more so to me is the aerial and shadowy anticipation of the future'. While still a stranger to the valleys of Westmorland, he says, 'I viewed myself as a phantom-self – a second identity projected from our own consciousness, and already living amongst them', and again, 'during the noviciate of my life, most truly I might say "In Today already walked Tomorrow".' (Galton may never have seen this passage, which appeared in *Tait's Magazine*, for De Quincey omitted it when revising *Recollections of the Lake Poets*, for the *Collected Edition* of his work in 1853.)

I could give several examples of people's experiences of a future moment becoming a *now*, some of which I have read, others heard from friends, and some of my own. But they would be of little value without circumstantial evidence, and to give this would mean a long digression. I believe such experiences are far more common than people realize.

The future moment becoming a *now* has much in common with a past moment becoming a *now*: it is surprising, disturbing, emotional. I have described De Quincey's sudden realization that what was begun to an accompaniment of 'sullen whispers' might end in 'volleying thunders'. It was not just a thought, an intellectual conclusion, but a deeply emotional experience, when in a particular moment a thought became, as Tolstoy says, a conviction. It happened to De Quincey when a past moment became a present one; the same happened when reality evaporated and a future moment took its place. Not only the child but the adult also deals only partially with a fright, a shock; he preserves something of it in his conscious mind, while some he pushes under the threshold of consciousness and it remains subliminal. From the totality of our experience, conscious and unconscious, there comes a fear of something which is latent: we cannot deal with it – we do not want to. But now and then, usually in a happy state of mind, a future moment becomes a *now*. The censor may be nodding in a happy moment, so that a disturbing experience comes through, or perhaps it is very cunning and lets through a painful conviction when we are capable of dealing with it. Such experiences resemble moments of inspiration, explosions in the mind, in that they are lost if there is no conscious record of them either in our memory or written down, fixed in external circumstances. Of course the unconscious mind has no absolute knowledge of the future, but since it can draw on the totality of our experience the probability that reality will come close to its forecast is considerable. Proust says of the poet 'his life will resemble his work, and in future the poet will scarcely need to write, for he will be able to find in what he has already written the anticipatory outline of what will then be happening'. (*Time Regained*. A. Mayor's translation, p. 274.) The poet is privileged, for he can transmute the heart of a moment untrammelled by evanescent circumstances. Not so the novelist. Tolstoy in Anna Karenina created a whole world of people, their experiences fixed in their time and circumstances, by living in his recent past in Levin's story, and in his future in Anna's: a wonderful example of Galton's 'permanent panorama'.

In an early draft the heroine is called Tatyana. Tolstoy says she does not come from the best society, has bad manners—a habit of taking a pearl of her necklace between her lips, talks too loudly; 'a revolting woman', who ruins both her husband and her lover. In the final version all that is changed: she comes from a very old family, she is well educated and she is lovely. Chekhov, in a letter describing a long dreary train journey says he was reading *Anna Karenina* through the night and was comforted by 'dear' Anna. How did it come about that Tolstoy started with a woman he called 'a devil', and in the end would not hear anything bad said of her, as he wrote to Alexandra Tolstoy, for he had 'adopted her'?

But before I come to this marvellous creation, of whom (to quote John Bayley) Tolstoy would have been fully justified to say 'Anna c'est moi', it is necessary to contrast the world of *War and Peace* with the world of *Anna Karenina*.

*Anna Karenina* was written in the late seventies and the story is placed in that period. Between this and the Napoleonic Wars lay a mere fifty years. But in Tolstoy's mind there is an immeasurable gulf between the books, as great as between *The Pickwick Papers* and *Little Dorrit,* the gulf between the child and the man.

In *War and Peace* all the important characters have parents living till they reach maturity: both the Rostovs' parents are alive, Andrey and Pierre each have one, a powerful father. Boris and Dolokhov have devoted mothers, and the latter is an excellent son. In *Anna Karenina* all the important characters, except Dolly and Kitty, have been orphaned in childhood. Karenin did not remember his father, and his mother died when he was ten; the Oblonskys, Stiva and Anna, were orphaned as children; Vronsky had not known any family life: his father he hardly remembered, his mother had many love affairs, and he neither respected nor loved her. Levin hardly remembered his mother, and as a student he was greatly attracted to the Shcherbatskys' home, because he had been deprived of just such an aristocratic educated home by the death of his father and mother when he was a child. Tolstoy himself was a complete orphan by the age of ten.

Almost all the marriages in *War and Peace* are happy. Of the people who were, or had been, close to Tolstoy, his brother Sergey had had a mistress for some fifteen years and then married her. His sister Marie, who was orphaned at the age of eight, was brought up by an aunt and married at seventeen, just like Anna; she had been deeply unhappy, and at the age of twenty-seven parted from her husband. His brother Dmitry had taken a prostitute out of a brothel, who lived with him till he died. His sister-in-law Lisa Bers, and his brother-in-law Alexander, were both divorced.

The marriages of the main characters in *Anna Karenina* are not happy: Oblonsky is constantly unfaithful to his wife, Karenin's marriage ends in disaster, and the only exception is Levin's.

In *War and Peace* none of the main characters serve the state, except in war. In *Anna Karenina*, Oblonsky, Karenin, Vronsky, all serve in peacetime, and again the only exception is Levin.

Kitty's father, Shcherbatsky, is a prince; so is Stiva Oblonsky, who traces his family back to Rurik, a thousand years, like an Englishman who claims his family came over with William the Conqueror. Of Karenin we only know that when he was left an orphan, and poor, he was helped by an uncle, an important bureaucrat. Vronsky is a count, rich and well educated. But this is what Levin says about him to Oblonsky: 'You consider Vronsky an aristocrat, but I don't. A man whose father crawled up from nothing at all by intrigue, and whose mother – God knows whom she was not mixed up with. No, excuse me, but I consider myself aristocratic, and people like me, who can point back in the past to three or four honourable generations of their family, of the highest degree of breeding (as for talent and intellect, of course, that's another matter), and have never curried favour with anyone, never depended on anyone for anything, like my father and my grandfather.' Kitty's father confirms his opinion, and adds much more. 'But if he [Vronsky] were a prince of the blood, my daughter need not run after anyone' and 'Levin is a thousand times the better man. As for this little Petersburg swell, they are turned out by machinery, all on one pattern, and all precious rubbish.' The Prince, like Levin, is talking in a passion, but Tolstoy will later show more dispassionately that neither Karenin nor Vronsky are real aristocrats like Levin, Oblonsky, and Shcherbatsky.

At the races Anna 'saw her husband now responding con-descendingly to an ingratiating bow, now exchanging friendly nonchalant greetings with his equals, now assiduously trying to catch the eye of some great one of this world'. Vronsky was asked to look after a foreign prince and show him the sights of Saint Petersburg: 'he was a gentleman—that was true, and Vronsky could not deny it. He was equable and not cringing with superiors, free and simple in his behaviour with equals, and contemptuously good-natured with inferiors.' Vronsky was like that himself, and considered it a great merit; but to the prince he was an inferior, and the prince's contemptuously good-natured attitude to himself revolted him. That code was all right for a Vronsky or a foreign princeling, but not for a Russian aristocrat. Oblonsky, a womanizer and spendthrift, a man ready to compromise with the rising bourgeoisie, did not treat people according to their social status. His liberalism was 'not one he had learned from the newspapers, but which was in his blood, in virtue of which he treated all men equally and exactly the same, whatever their fortune or calling might be'. As for Levin, he had seriously thought of marrying a peasant and becoming one himself. So had Tolstoy.

All the main characters in *Anna Karenina*, except Kitty, belong to the middle age group: Anna has a child of eight; Karenin is twenty years older than she, Vronsky a little younger; Oblonsky is thirty-four, and Levin about the same age.

*War and Peace* is about adult people too, yet most of their experiences are translations of Tolstoy's memories of childhood. In *Anna Karenina* all the adult characters are created out of Tolstoy's adult memories. Neither Levin nor his brother Nikolay remember their childhood, they merely refer to it. It is this Nikolay, who proves that Tolstoy had now shut the door on his memories of childhood. He is modelled on Tolstoy's brother Dmitry. Tolstoy stated in *Reminiscences* that he had no childhood memories of this brother Dmitry, and he is the only brother not recreated in *War and Peace*. In his childhood and youth Tolstoy neither loved nor admired Dmitry as he did the two other brothers, Nikolay and Sergey. He died long before *War and Peace* was written, but by the time Tolstoy was writing *Anna Karenina* he had begun to understand him.

Before we meet Nikolay in *Anna Karenina* we learn that he has dissipated most of his inheritance, and keeps the strangest and lowest company. We can tell from Tolstoy's *Reminiscences* that Nikolay is a true portrait of his brother Dmitry. Levin remembers how as a student his brother lived like a monk, shunning all pleasures and especially women; and how he later burst out, made friends with very bad people and gave himself over to a life of dissipation. Levin remembers many dreadful things about him, but to him they did not seem as frightful as they might have to people who did not know the whole of his brother's story, 'did not know his heart'. Levin speaks for Tolstoy when he says 'I know his soul and I know we are alike'. Tolstoy went to see his brother Dmitry when he was dying, but he had not the patience or love to stay with him, as he stayed till the end with his beloved brother Nikolay. The profound affect of Nikolay's death he recreated in *War and Peace* in the death of Prince Andrey, and now in *Anna Karenina* he once again writes of the death of a brother whom he has given the name Nikolay. Levin is already married when he is summoned to his dying brother; Kitty insists on going with him. She turns out a wonderful help.

The difference between the two deaths, Andrey's and Nikolay's, reveals the different spirit of the two books. Both men are doomed: the doctor knows that Prince Andrey's wound is fatal, and so is Nikolay's consumption. Both get great comfort from women: Andrey says to Natasha 'Nobody gives me such great comfort as you, such light. I want to cry for joy.' Nikolay 'smiled, kissed Kitty's hand, thanked her with tears in his eyes', saying that he was feeling well. Both men are struggling against death. Andrey, after he has dreamed that he has already died, says 'Yes, it was death. I died – I woke up. Yes, death is an awakening.' Nikolay has lived through a hopeful hour, and he too goes to sleep peacefully, but when *he* wakes he knows at once that he has been deluding himself: 'And suddenly all hopes disappeared, in the people round him and in himself.' All his self-deceit is gone – death is not an awakening to him. 'It was for her sake [Kitty's] that I went through that farce,' he says.

In *Anna Karenina* the glory and freshness of a dream has departed from death as well as from life.

The name Levin is derived from Tolstoy's Christian name Lev; many of his experiences are Tolstoy's own, and not more than some ten years old. Kitty has much in common with Natasha. Proust recognized that Tolstoy is using the same image for both. Both are spontaneous, sincere; neither deigns to be clever. Both are modelled on Tolstoy's wife and her sister, but unlike them Kitty and Natasha both come from aristocratic homes. Prince Shcherbatsky's presence is not as ubiquitous as Count Rostov's, but we are left without a doubt of Levin's love for him. When Levin, after his marriage, is dissatisfied with himself, with the work he does for others, Kitty asks him if he thinks her father is a poor creature 'as he does nothing for the public good'. 'He – no! But one must have the simplicity, the transparent clarity, the goodness, of your father, and have I got it?'

The story begins with Kitty in love with Vronsky, and her rejection of Levin's offer of marriage. The circumstances are plausible: Count Vronsky is a most eligible man, and Kitty falls in love before Levin has revealed his intentions. No one would ever call Kitty depraved, as everyone did Natasha when she became infatuated with Anatole Kuragin. There are no extenuating circumstances for Natasha's love for Anatole. Later, after Kitty and Levin have declared their love for one another and are wonderfully happy, Kitty asks Levin if he can forget her infatuation. 'May be it is for the best. You will have plenty to forgive,' he replied, intending to give her the diaries of his depraved youth. And so once again, as in *War and Peace*, Tolstoy seemed to find it necessary, as a prelude to a happy marriage to a man who had had a depraved youth, to make the woman not a complete innocent but one who had had an infatuation for a man very different from the man she marries, and who has some regrets and feeling of shame.

Levin's and Kitty's love story is full of light and happiness. When Levin knows that Kitty loves him, he wanders about seeing everything like a poet in an hour of inspiration. When he arrives at her home to ask for her hand, 'The first person he saw was Mademoiselle Linon. . . . Directly she had gone out, swift, swift light steps sounded on the parquet, and his bliss, his life, himself – what was best in himself [just what Pierre said of Natasha], what he had so long sought and longed for – was quickly-quickly nearing him. "Can it be true?" he said at last in a smothered voice, "I cannot believe that thou lovest me".' She smiled at the 'thou' and the timid look he gave her.

' "Yes!" – she said significantly and slowly.'

I will skip the honeymoon months, that depressing and degrading time that neither Levin nor Kitty could bear to remember.

All ends well: Kitty turns out a wonderful homemaker, a companion, and a help with his dying brother; and his happiest time is when she is expecting a child. He now experiences that 'delight, new for him and joyful, entirely pure and free of sensuality, in being near to the beloved woman'. By the end of the book, Levin and Kitty have one child and the marriage is not more than two years old. By the time Tolstoy began *Anna Karenina* he had six children and the marriage was ten years old. Tolstoy continues to translate his own story, the beginnings of which were already visible before he started on that book. But first let us briefly recapitulate Anna's story.

Anna was an orphan, and was married off by an aunt when she was in her teens to Karenin, who was some twenty years older. Karenin wavered, but the aunt frightened him by letting him know that he had already compromised Anna, and that if he did not marry her the consequences might be bad for his

career. That was not anything out of the ordinary at the time.
Anna married like other women of that period whose youth
was not very happy, and who did not wait till love came.

Anna was a good wife to Karenin before she met Vronsky.
Nothing that happened to her husband used to pass unnoticed
by her, and, on the other hand, she used to communicate to
him at once all her joys, gaiety, and sorrows. Her love was
centred on her boy. Summoned by her brother Stiva Oblonsky,
whose wife had become terribly unhappy when she discovered
her husband's unfaithfulness, Anna walks into their home of
turmoil and misery, and shows great sympathy, understanding,
and tact; the help she gives is not that of a conventional woman
with definite principles, but of a spontaneous, sincere, and at
the same time practical and realistic person. Kitty's impression
of Anna, before she had any cause of jealousy, throws a valuable
light on Anna: she was not, Kitty thinks, like a worldly lady,
or like the mother of a child of eight but, to judge by the supple-
ness of her movements and the freshness of expression and
liveliness of her face, like a young woman of twenty, if it had
not been for the serious and, at times, sad expression of her
eyes. 'Kitty felt that Anna was perfectly simple and did not
conceal anything, but that she had in her another, somehow
higher, world of interest inaccessible to her, complex and
poetic.'

Anna and Vronsky fall in love at first sight. He is an experienced man, while she has never been in love before or since
her marriage, and her innocence, clear conscience, and sense
of security, all generate in her anxieties, fears, and a readiness
to struggle against her passion. When she returns to Petersburg
her husband meets her at the station. ' "Oh, my God,! Why
have his ears become like this?", she thought, looking at his
cold and presentable figure and particularly at the cartilages
of his ears which struck her, supporting the brim of his round
hat. . . . Some unpleasant feeling was pinching her heart when
she met his fixed and weary gaze, as if she had expected to see
him look different.' She was particularly struck by the feeling
of discontent with herself which she experienced when she met
him. 'The feeling was that old familiar one, resembling a state
of dissimulation, which she had experienced in relations with

her husband; but formerly she had not noticed it, now she was clearly and painfully conscious of it.'

She had for years suppressed both her physical dislike of her husband and the feeling of pretence in her relation to him, but now they had broken into her conscious mind, and would from now on assert themselves.

As in Pierre and Andrey Tolstoy had merged with his brothers Nikolay and Sergey, so in Anna he merges with his sister Marie. There was a deep lifelong affection between Marie and Leo.

Marie, like Anna, was married at seventeen, to a Tolstoy cousin: it was a bad marriage, and ten years later she left him for good, taking her children. Most revealing is Leo's opinion of his brother-in-law years before the marriage broke up, 'an honest, sober fellow, but devoid of that delicate sense of honour I deem essential in all to whom I give my friendship'. Honour means different things in different languages. By the time Tolstoy began *Anna Karenina*, in 1873, Marie's life story was before him, but far more important than the bones of it was her character. After she had been married for ten unhappy years, Turgenev was very attracted to her, and found her childish face frank and her manner unaffected. Tolstoy was pleased with the relationship that was blossoming between them, and disappointed later that Turgenev did not marry her. (I believe that Marie must have been the inspiration of the character Liza in Turgenev's *The Nest of Nobles*, among the best beloved characters in Russian fiction. Liza ended in a nunnery, and so did Marie; and when Tolstoy ran away from home he went straight to her.) From all we know about Marie, after ten years of neglect and insults in her marriage she remained frank and unspoilt. And so was Anna when she and Vronsky fell in love.

What sort of a man was Vronsky? He had had a coarse youth: he lived the life of a rich Petersburg officer, and had love affairs outside of society. When he came to Moscow he was attracted to Kitty, and experienced delight in coming close to a society girl, charming and innocent, who loved him. But he had no thought of marriage! The idea that Kitty might be unhappy if he did not marry her, would have surprised him: 'He could not believe that something which gave such great

and good pleasure to him, and especially to her, could be
wrong. Even less could he have believed that he ought to marry
her.'

Though Levin had had a depraved youth, it is quite un-
thinkable that he should have had Vronsky's views about a girl
like Kitty; nor would Oblonsky, the womanizer. Only a man
from the westernized St Petersburg, not from the Russian
Moscow, according to Tolstoy, could have been so insensitive
to the feelings of a young woman like Kitty.

But Tolstoy, the man of contradictions, and not 'a man of
St Petersburg', had behaved towards Valeria Arsenyev in a
way very similar to Vronsky: after courting her for some time
he broke with her, rousing indignation even among people
who loved him greatly: his aunt, his sister, his friends. In his
endless battle with himself the creation of simple single-minded
characters was a help. 'In his [Vronsky's] Petersburg universe
people were divided into two totally different types': one was
vulgar and stupid and believed that a husband should sleep
only with his wife, a maiden should be pure, a married woman
chaste; the other made it a rule to be elegant, free with money,
and abandoned themselves to every passion without scruple.
Vronsky feels at home with this second type. He abandons
himself to his passion for Anna: talking about her to his cousin
Princess Betsy, an immoral woman, he tells her 'I begin to lose
hope', meaning to lose hope that she would ever be his. He
goes on to say 'I'm afraid I'm becoming ridiculous'. He knows
that this is not true: he might be ridiculous if he were the un-
successful lover of a girl, 'but the position of a man pursuing
a married woman . . . has something fine and grand about it,
and could never be ridiculous; so it was with a proud glad smile'
that he looked at his cousin.

It seems we have another Anatole Kuragin, but Tolstoy
proves us wrong. Anatole never changes – the Kuragins, according to Pierre, were 'a depraved breed' – but if Vronsky begins
as one of them, his love for Anna changes him.

Of the first time that Vronsky and Anna live together,
Tolstoy tells us that 'that which for nearly a year had been
for Vronsky the sole and exclusive desire of his life' had been
fulfilled. For Anna it is 'an impossible, terrible, but all the more

entrancing dream of happiness'. She had been married for some ten years, had suppressed her physical dislike of Karenin, and remained innocent. Now she was sobbing: 'She felt herself so criminal and guilty that it only remained for her to humble herself and beg forgiveness.' When she says 'I have nothing but you left. Remember that,' he assures her that he can never forget: 'For one moment of that bliss . . .' She interrupts him: ' "What bliss?" she said with horror and loathing, and horror involuntarily communicated itself to him.' She begs him not to say another word.

If you think that now, a hundred years later, this dates, read on. 'She felt that she could not at that moment express in words her feelings of shame, joy, horror at this stepping into a new life, and did not want to talk about it, to vulgarize that feeling by using inaccurate words.' Why do words matter so much to her? 'Later on, the next day and the next, she still could not find words to describe all the complexity of those feelings, and could not even find thoughts with which to reflect on all that was in her soul.'

Anna becomes Tolstoy, an artist. He knew intimately people endowed with wonderful imagination, profound sensibilities and a feeling for words, who yet never wrote works of art. Such was his brother Nikolay, such was his mother, from what he knew of her. Anna's experience is plummeting into the depths of her soul, as had happened to Tolstoy many times, and like him she is filled with apprehension.

And yet the most crucial hour in her life was not the occasion of her living with Vronsky for the first time. It came on the morning after the races. The day of the races, in which Vronsky was taking part, turned out a great ordeal to Anna. She had told Vronsky, before the race, that she was expecting a child. Later, when her husband arrived, she had a talk with him in a light-hearted tone, which she never afterwards remembered without shame. She was now consciously dissimulating: Tolstoy never ceases to remind us that a conscious wrong is always worse than an unconscious. The races were so full of hazards, so many riders and men were hurt, that it was enough to unnerve anyone, but Anna hardly seemed to understand what was happening, and her eyes were fixed on Vronsky.

When he fell she lost her self control, 'she began fluttering like a caught bird', and later, after she had realized that Vronsky was alive, she hid her face behind her fan and wept. In front of society and the court! Taking her home Karenin told her that she had behaved improperly. If only he had made a scene, accused her of loving Vronsky! But there was lack of all communication between them, and he, not having an idea of what was going on in her, that she was thinking only of Vronsky, was deluded by a hope that perhaps all was well, and that he had wronged her. ' "If so, I beg your pardon." . . . "No, you were not mistaken" she said slowly, looking desperately into his cold face . . . . "I love him, I am his mistress." '

Even on the eve of the 1917 Revolution the Russian word *lyubovnitsa* – mistress – was more repulsive than 'prostitute' (there was brazenness in the former, and compassion in the latter: most likely the influence of literature). When Anna called herself *lyubovnitsa* it was as terrible to her as it would have been to Desdemona to call herself a whore when she eloped with Othello.

Vronsky was to come that night to her, and after Karenin had left for Petersburg, and Anna had a note from the Princess Betsy to say that Vronsky was all right, Anna thinks 'So he will be coming', and tells herself that it was a good thing that she told her husband everything. 'She said to herself that she was glad, that everything would now become definite, and at any rate there would be no more lying and deception.' That night, she does not tell Vronsky anything of what has happened, though it was necessary to tell him in order that the position should become definite. Next morning, the words she had used to her husband seem to her terrible: she cannot understand how she had decided to utter such strange coarse words; and when she asks herself why did she not tell it all to Vronsky, she understands that she was ashamed to do so. Her situation now seems to her hopeless, especially as she doubts Vronsky's love. When her boy comes in she feels he is her last hope. She will take him and go away with him. She tries to write to her husband: 'After what has happened I cannot remain in your house. I am leaving, and taking my son with me. I don't know the law . . . But be magnanimous, and leave him with me!'

This letter did not please her, nor could she write to Vronsky. This is a frightened, ashamed, torn woman, but her fate and the fate of the two men is decided not by her, but by Karenin's letter, and by Vronsky's behaviour at their next meeting.

In his letter Karenin writes that after careful thought his decision is that their life must go on as before. After she has finished reading it she feels cold, and that a terrible misfortune, the like of which she did not expect, has come down on top of her. To Anna, her husband's desire to keep up the appearance of a marriage after all that had happened is terrible. 'In the morning she had regretted what she had said to her husband, and only wished that the words had not been spoken. And here his letter came, and regarded the words as unspoken – what she had wished for. But now this letter seemed to her more terrible than anything she could have imagined.'

It is an unkind and ungenerous letter. Karenin is a hypocrite when he writes, 'I do not consider I have a right to sever ties with which a higher power has joined us.' We know what he was thinking before he wrote it: how he could not bear the thought of Vronsky having her and of Anna being happy with him, and we hate his threats – 'you can imagine yourself what is awaiting you and your son' if she does not comply. We agree with her: 'Yes he is a mean, disgusting person.' We know that she feels that she could have faced it if Karenin had killed her, killed Vronsky, that if she did return to Karenin nothing but lies and deception would come of it. But we do not know everything. We know from Karenin himself that Anna had in the past been very sensitive to his needs, and had tried to share her joys and sorrows with him. But now what she had suppressed for so long came out: 'They do not know how for eight years he has been smothering my life. They do not know how at every step he used to insult me, and remain self-satisfied. Have I not tried with all my strength, to find a justification of my life? Have I not tried to love him, love the boy when it was no longer possible to love my husband? But there came a time when I understood that I couldn't deceive myself any longer, that I am alive, that I am not guilty, that God has made me like that, that I need to love and to live.'

'After reading her husband's letter she was in despair; she

knew in the depth of her heart that all would remain as it was.'
Yet when she asks Vronsky to meet her: 'She hoped that that
meeting would change their situation and save her. If when he
heard what had happened, he firmly, passionately, without a
moment's hesitation, said to her "Leave everything and run
away with me" she would abandon her son and go with him.'

There has been a great change. The day before, when
Vronsky had suggested they should run away, she had not
been able to face what it would do to her son and 'like a woman,
could only try to comfort herself with lying assurances that everything would remain as it always had been.' But by the next day
she had lived through an eternity: her fears for Vronsky in the
race, the shame of her words to Karenin, his coldheartedness;
and now the moment had come when the only salvation was
to leave everything and run away with Vronsky.

When she tells him that she has told her husband that she
cannot continue to be his wife, Vronsky, thinking that now a
duel is inevitable, straightens his back, and his face takes on a
proud and severe expression. A duel has never entered her head,
and she explains his expression differently. We have seen plenty
of misunderstandings between Levin and Kitty, but they are
only temporary, they do not and cannot destroy their love and
life. Anna hands Vronsky Karenin's letter: again he is imagining himself at the duel, how he would shoot into the air and
would stand bravely facing the bullet of the injured husband;
but something else comes into his head too, something he and
his friend Serpukhovsky had talked of, and he himself had
thought about, that morning: it was better not to tie oneself.
He knows he cannot tell her that. 'In his look there was no
firmness' and it was the end of her last hope.

When he fails to sense the change in her, to sense her great
need, she is ruined, and in the end both are. We all blunder,
we again and again take the wrong turning, but there are some
blunders that are fatal. Vronsky had made terrible mistakes on
other occasions. Remember the race the day before.

Frou-Frou was a wonderful mare, a thoroughbred. When
Vronsky got ahead in the race 'his excitement, his delight, and
his tenderness for Frou-Frou grew keener and keener'. There
remained only one obstacle to cross: for a moment both he and

the mare hesitated, but she knew what he wanted, and cleared it. 'Oh my lovely!' he thought of Frou-Frou. Now there was one last ditch; the mare was tiring: using the last reserve of strength she flew over the ditch like a bird. Then, to his horror, he realized that he had made a 'fearful, an unpardonable mistake as he came down into the saddle. His clumsy movement had caused her to break her back.' The way he treats her now is quite horrible: she falls, struggles to get up, but fails, and 'with a face hideous with passion, his lower jaw trembling, and his cheeks white, Vronsky kicked her in the stomach . . .' A moment later he realizes that it was his fault, 'shameful, unpardonable! And the poor darling ruined mare! Ah! what have I done!'

Tolstoy spent an incredible number of hours riding in his life: even when he was over eighty, and had had a grave illness, no sooner was he on his feet again than he went out riding. He knew that the best rider could make a wrong movement, a fatal one, but never, never, could he, or for that matter either Levin or Oblonsky, have behaved like Vronsky, either to a horse or to a woman.

Vronsky had committed other mistakes: Tolstoy would have said of him, as he had of his brother-in-law, that 'he was devoid of that delicate sense of honour I deem essential to all to whom I give my friendship'. Wishing to show his independence, Vronsky had refused a post that was offered to him, hoping that such a refusal would heighten his price and advance his career. 'But it turned out that he had been too bold, and he was passed over.' That mistake Tolstoy called 'coarse'. Neither Levin nor Oblonsky could ever have committed it, though they had all kinds of faults; for example, when out shooting each was envious of the other whose bag was fuller. When Levin discovered for the first time that Kitty had not married Vronsky and was very ill, he felt pleased, glad because he could still have hope, but also because she who had made him suffer was now suffering. He was ashamed of it, but like Tolstoy he was concerned with the truth.

Consider Vronsky's and Karenin's ambition. 'Ambition was the old dream of his [Vronsky's] childhood and youth, a dream which he did not acknowledge even to himself but which was so strong that now [when he fell in love with Anna] this passion was battling with his love.' Karenin was also a very ambitious man, and was already set on the road to success when he married Anna; by the time we first meet him, a man in his late forties, he is a distinguished government servant. But it is not ambition which makes Karenin and Vronsky so different from Levin and Oblonsky. Both Karenin and Vronsky have a set of rules 'defining without any doubt what to do and what not to do'. Such rules were reliable until something happened out of the ordinary. Karenin feels lost from the time Anna falls in love with Vronsky: he cannot talk to her; Vronsky feels lost when his affair with Anna does not take on the light character that such affairs usually did, but becomes, as his mother terms it with horror, 'a Werther one': Vronsky could no longer find the leading thread.

If only Vronsky had told Anna at that moment that they were going to run away together, as Islenyev had told Princess Kozlovsky at a similar moment. As I have shown, the very first draft of *Childhood* tells their story. Like Anna, Princess Kozlovsky came of an old family; she was married and had a little boy. She ran away with Islenyev, and she used to say that he was her husband before God. She was a good influence on Islenyev: she hated violence, and was the only person who could restrain his severity with his serfs. All their efforts to get a divorce from Prince Kozlovsky failed, and their children remained illegitimate. He was a terrible gambler and squandered a fortune, but she never regretted running away with him. When after fifteen years she died, he was desperate. There was an oil painting of her, and for hours he sat before it. But unlike Vronsky he did not seek death; he married again, and lived to see the granddaughter of Princess Kozlovsky married to Leo Tolstoy. As always, Tolstoy's digression from his models, as from this illegal but still blessed union to the tragic fate of Anna, and not less of Vronsky, lets us into his great secrets.

Anna's grave illness after the birth of her child, puerperal fever – and her belief that she is dying (a belief shared by the doctors) – is an episode created by supreme inspiration, in conception and exploration. Before Anna's confinement Karenin had been to see a lawyer about a divorce. A most painful experience for Karenin, as is everything out of the ordinary. After that he has to go to some remote provinces, to do with his work, and he stops at Moscow on the way. He runs into his brother-in-law Oblonsky, who is surprised that Karenin has not told them about his visit and begs him to come to a dinner the next day. Next day Oblonsky visits him and Karenin informs him that he cannot come to dinner, that he is starting a divorce action. Before Karenin has finished his sentence, Oblonsky is behaving 'not at all as he had expected'. Oblonsky never does. He groaned and sank into an arm-chair. Karenin is put out by Oblonsky's reaction, his compassion and suffering. ' "Please, do come. And above all, talk it over with her [his wife Dolly], she's a wonderful woman. For God's sake, on my knees, I implore you!" ' Karenin does go to the dinner, and there are interesting people and interesting conversations, but the chief moment comes when he is about to leave, and Dolly talks to him. Dolly is not as clever or perceptive as Anna, but in her talk to Karenin she reveals what a genuine person she is: loving Anna, unable to believe in her adultery, deeply compassionate, so that her feeling for Karenin makes him respond like a human being, which he very rarely does: for once he loses his self-possession. Next day he gets a telegram from Anna: 'I'm dying; I beg, I implore you to come. I shall die easier with your forgiveness.' He returns to St Petersburg.

Tolstoy says that *Anna Karenina* was the first novel he wrote, and indeed Anna is the greatest creation of his imagination. He does not spell out what is contained in Anna's fear of words, and in her entreaty to Vronsky not to talk after they had lived together. Coleridge says that ordinary dramatists 'combine their ideas by association, or by logical affinity'; the man of genius 'transports himself into the very being of each personage'. Tolstoy does not even hint that Karenin's talk with Dolly, the unexpected deep contact with another human being – we know he had had few in his life – is unconsciously acting on him when he sees his wife near dying. Anna is delirious, but what she says is far from mad. What one says in delirium, as sometimes when one has had too much to drink, is thrown up by a kind of explosion, and among the debris there are nuggets of truth.

She says, 'I'm not afraid of him [Karenin], I am afraid of death . . . Now I understand, and understand everything, I see everything. . . .' What does she understand, and how is it that she looks with enthusiastic tenderness at Karenin, the like of which he has never seen in her? All vanities, ambitions, and above all, passion, have retreated into the far distance and shrunk to nothing, and all that she sees is man's goodness. To Anna this truth comes when death approaches. 'Now I am the real one, I am the whole of me.' And this real Anna only wants to be forgiven by Karenin, and for Karenin to forgive Vronsky.

The truth of Anna's experience is seen in the effect it has on Karenin and Vronsky. Though Karenin had all his life wanted to follow the Christian religion, he had never thought that it demanded forgiveness and love of enemies, but now, under the influence of Anna's state of mind, 'a joyful feeling of love and forgiveness of one's enemies filled his soul'. And 'she embraced his head which was going bald, moved towards him, and with defiant pride lifted her eyes'.

The effect on Vronsky is even greater and more lasting than on Karenin. He is once again thrown off the track, and all the habits and rules that he has lived by now seem false and inapplicable. The important thing is not his attempt at suicide, but his new feelings for Anna. His passion has been cooling. In the months before the baby was born, Anna, living in Karenin's house and continuing to see Vronsky, in a false situation and without hope for the future, had changed morally and physically for the worse. She became very jealous of Vronsky. 'He looked at her, as a man looks at a flower which was plucked by him and now has faded, in which he hardly recognizes the beauty which made him pluck it and ruin it.' But now something new is born in him. 'He has seen the whole of her in her illness, learnt to know her soul, and it seemed to him that he never till then had loved her.'

The reader must have asked himself why did Tolstoy give the same Christian name, Alexey, to Karenin and Vronsky, the husband and the lover. After she lived with Vronsky, Anna had a recurring nightmare in which 'both were lavishing caresses on her. Alexey Alexandrovich was weeping, kissing her hands, and saying "How happy we are now!" and Alexey Vronsky was there too, and he too was her husband.' If Anna thought of her husband in the formal way 'Alexey Alexandrovich' the only reason for it would be that he was so much older than she; but why is the lover 'Alexey' to her? To Sonya Tolstoy, her husband was not Lev, but Levotchka; to Tolstoy, his sister was not Marie but Mashenka. Vronsky was Alyosha to his friend Yashvin, and also to his mother. If Anna did not like to use the same endearing form as the mother, she could have made up a new one. If the reader has any doubt of the meaning of Karenin and Vronsky's having the same name, let him think of this: 'Anna was talking rapidly in a ringing voice with exceptionally correct and expressive intonations "For Alexey – I am speaking of Alexey Alexandrovich – what a strange and awful thing that both are Alexey, isn't it?" '

Anna's tragedy is that the two Alexeys, husband and lover, are very much alike, but the difference to her is that she had never been physically in love with her husband Alexey Alexandrovich, and fell passionately in love with Alexey Vronsky.

When Anna does not die, but begins to recover, it very soon appears that she has not been changed by her experience. She cannot bear Karenin physically, she cannot bear his damp hand with the large swollen veins. 'She kept on looking at him with the painful feeling of physical revulsion, for which she reproached herself, but could not overcome.' Her brother comes to see her. No one could be more pleasure-loving and worldly than Stiva Oblonsky, and he too, has many rules. He does not think it wrong for him, still so young and vital, while his wife has become old, to have affairs; he thinks it is wrong for a man to have an affair with a governness while she is still living in the house, but all right after she has left. He is a man of his time and society, with definite ideas of right and wrong. But his feelings are spontaneous and govern his actions.

Oblonsky arrives, and in the doorway he meets Betsy, a woman who manages to have affairs and keep her position in society. He stops her, flirts, insists on kissing her hand, and does the same when they part, 'kissing it above the glove, at the point where the pulse beats, and, murmuring to her unseemly nonsense'. Although in a mood of bubbling gaiety, no sooner does he enter Anna's room than he immediately and naturally changes to that compassionate, poetically emotional tone which suits her mood. He is, as Tolstoy says, 'a very imaginative and sensitive man'. He finds Anna in tears, in a very gloomy mood. She tells her brother, 'I hate Karenin for his virtues. I can't live with him. Do understand, the sight of him has a physical effect on me, I get beside myself.' Oblonsky smiled. No one else, Tolstoy says, having to do with such despair, would have allowed himself to smile, but in his smile there was so much sweetness and almost feminine tenderness that it did not wound, but softened and soothed. And just as a child secure in the love of a parent dares to be afraid, so does Anna dare with her brother. ' "No, Stiva," she said, "I'm lost, lost. Worse than lost . . . It has not ended yet: it will end terribly".' This despair had risen from the depths in her before: when she first lived with Vronsky, and also when he did not ask her to run away with him. But her brother encourages in her the desire to survive, and uses commonsense arguments: she made a mistake in marrying Karenin, but it was not fatal; divorce would solve all her difficulties. The look which lights up her face tells him how much she longs for this. ' "How happy I should be if I could arrange things" he said, and now smiled more boldly. "Don't speak, don't say a word. If only God granted me to speak as I feel. I'll go to him." '

Oblonsky goes to talk to Karenin, and to his own surprise he feels embarrassed. 'That timidity was so unexpected and strange that Oblonsky did not believe it was his conscience telling him that what he was about to do was wrong.' Karenin hands Oblonsky the letter he has written to Anna asking her what would give her real happiness: 'I submit myself entirely to your wishes and sense of justice.' Tears are choking Oblonsky, but he finally expresses his opinion that the only solution is divorce. Karenin has earlier discussed divorce with a lawyer, and dreads it. But he agrees, and with his bitterness is mixed 'a sense of joy and emotion at the greatness of his own humility'.

Meanwhile Vronsky has recovered from the wound of his attempted suicide, and has decided to take a post at Tashkent, but wants to see Anna once more. But the moment he sees her his passion seizes him, and communicates itself to her: they are again in its power as they were at their first meeting. Anna tells Vronsky that Karenin will agree to anything, 'but I cannot accept his generosity . . . Nothing matters to me now. Only I don't know what he will decide about Seryozha.' Vronsky cannot understand how at the moment of their re-union she can 'think about her son and divorce. As if all that were not immaterial'. They go off to Italy 'not only without getting a divorce but having resolutely refused it'.

Much as Karenin and Vronsky have in common (their treatment of people according to their social status, their great ambitions, their living by rules), Vronsky is not as lonely a person as Karenin. Yashvin is a good friend to him, so is his sister-in-law. Karenin has been hardly changed by his years of marriage to Anna, but Vronsky has already changed. He has given up his ambitions, he loves Anna more deeply now than when he was pursuing her and his one dream was to possess her. In Italy, with her recovered health, with Vronsky and his child, she feels 'unpardonably happy. The more she got to know Vronsky, the more she loved him. She loved him for himself and for his love to her. Her complete ownership of him was a continual joy to her.' He is not perfectly happy, and suffers from boredom. As he had had a taste for painting as a child, he now takes it up. Here Anna and Vronsky meet the Russian painter Mikhailov. Vronsky begins to paint Anna's portrait, and commissions Mikhailov to paint another. From the fifth sitting Mikhailov's portrait impresses everyone. 'It was strange how Mikhailov could have discovered just her characteristic beauty. "One needs to know and love her as I have loved her to discover the very sweetest expression of her soul," Vronsky thought, though it was only from this portrait that he had himself learned this sweetest expression of her soul. But the expression was so true that he, and others too, fancied they had long known it.'

The two portraits 'ought to have shown Vronsky the dif-ference between himself and Mikhailov; but he did not see it'. Since Vronsky 'drew his inspiration, not directly from life, but indirectly from life embodied in art, his inspiration came very quickly, and he easily succeeded in painting something very similar to the sort of painting he was trying to imitate'. Did she not realize that Vronsky was not an artist at all? It is true that people of her class felt themselves superior to artists and to men of genius. But we must not take it that Anna's experience in Italy, her encounter with a great artist which showed that Vronsky was an imitator, has no effect on her. She is first and foremost a woman, and closes her eyes to many things, as she had done when married to Karenin. Bored with Italy, Vronsky and Anna return to Russia; her main object is to see her son. One of her real sorrows is that she cannot share with Vronsky this longing: throughout the boy seems of little significance to him, and he behaves as if he expects her to forget him. She finds that Karenin has become ensnared by Lidya Ivanovna, a malicious person, whose husband had left her after only two months of marriage, and had detested her ever after. She is a follower of a new interpretation of Christianity, fashionable in Petersburg, and sets out to convert Karenin to it: 'It is not you who have performed that great act of forgiveness which fills me and everybody else with rapture, but He that dwells within your heart,' she tells him. And meanwhile she undertakes to look after Seryozha together with Karenin, and Anna has to ask her permission to see the boy. She decides to refuse her, to hurt Anna to the depths of her soul, and she gets Karenin to agree. In her letter to Anna she writes: 'I beg you to take your husband's refusal in the spirit of Christian love. I pray the Almighty to be merciful to you.'

The same man who had written the heartless letter to Anna after she had told him that she was Vronsky's mistress, also wrote the self-sacrificing letter to her that Oblonsky read; the man who sincerely forgave her and experienced such joy in doing it, cruelly refuses to let her see her boy. How did he come to adopt the bogus teaching of such a horrible person as Lidya Ivanovna? Tolstoy says that 'Karenin was quite devoid of that deep imaginative faculty of the soul by which ideas aroused by the imagination become so vivid that they must be brought into conformity with other ideas and with reality.' Lidya Ivanovna had told him that his wife was very guilty towards him and that he had behaved like a saint, but at home, alone, memories of his life with Anna come back to him and torment him. He is tormented by remorse that when he had first heard that

Vronsky was her lover, he had demanded of her only external propriety; tormented that he had not challenged Vronsky; but no less tormented by his forgiveness and his care for another man's child. All his past with Anna fills him with shame and regret, even 'the awkward words in which, after much hesitation, he had proposed to her.' His memories make us understand why Anna said to her brother 'I hate him for his generosity'. To Karenin neither the memories of his meanness nor his generosity, his cruelty nor his kindness, are of use. He is no fool: he has already vaguely felt the frivolity and falseness of Lidya Ivanovna's Christian teaching, of the view that 'he was not living for the present temporal life but for eternal life'; but he needs 'that tranquil elevation, thanks to which he could forget the things he did not wish to remember'. And he does not wish to remember anything.

Anna has to bear alone all the cruelty of the prohibition to see Seryozha. The surprise visit she does pay to the child, the joy of seeing him and the suffering of parting, is followed by a nagging doubt of Vronsky's love. One Anna is living an everyday life, making the best of it, while the other is 'flying headlong over some precipice' as she had told her brother. Now and then the second Anna breaks out, as when she chooses to go to the theatre. Even without warnings, she is much too intelligent not to know that there are cruel, vulgar people in society who will not lose an opportunity to hurt her. Some critics have told us that Anna is ruined by the intolerance and cruelty of society: nothing could have been further from Tolstoy's thoughts. He had the behaviour of Princess Kozlovsky before him: she never went into society after she ran away with Islenyev, and was content with friends among her neighbours. More than that, Tolstoy was pleased that his mother had been well content to live in the country: he could not imagine his family life based on a city – it must be in the country, and he expected this of his wife.

Anna and Vronsky go to his country estate, and he makes many innovations and improvements in which Anna takes an intelligent interest. Dolly comes to visit them. She has decided to visit Anna not merely because she and Anna are related and are good friends; Princess Betsy, Vronsky's cousin, was a friend

6*

of Anna's too, but this depraved woman is heartless to her now. Dolly is a real person, and follows the dictates of her heart, just as the Tolstoys did when they remained friendly with Princess Kozlovsky though she was living in an illegal union. Dolly who never knew a moment's peace at home, who was always either pregnant or nursing a child, trying to make ends meet, forgiving her husband both for running after other women and squandering the dowry that she had brought with her, Dolly now, on this journey, surveys her fifteen years of marriage: 'pregnancy, sickness, mental inadequacy, indifference to everything, and most of all, hideousness', and then the cruel memory of the death of her last little baby. All she can hope for is that her children will 'simply be decent people'. The Vronsky estate impresses her by its grandeur, and Anna looks beautiful and tells her that she is very happy: 'He [Vronsky] is very fond of this place, and, what I never expected, he has become intensely interested in looking after it. But he has such a rich nature.' Dolly takes a great interest and is very helpful. Once again, as in Italy, Anna and Vronsky are trying to arrest their precipitous run, clinging to the making of a home.

Vronsky takes the first opportunity to talk to Dolly alone: he wants her help. Their position in the world is terrible, he says, but that is not what worries him. 'You are happy and at peace,' Dolly says Anna had told her so, but as she says it a doubt enters her mind. 'But can it last?' Vronsky asks. He begs Dolly to persuade Anna to do everything to get a divorce, for the sake of their children, for the sake of a normal family life, ' "I am happy, happy in her love, but I must have occupation." ' Anna had told Dolly 'I'm inexcusably happy', but before the day is out she reveals that the reverse is true: she is not only terribly unhappy, she is hopeless. She does not believe that Lidya Ivanovna will now ever let Karenin give her a divorce, and anyway a divorce is no use to her for she will have to renounce her boy, and she only loves two people: Vronsky and her boy. She tells Dolly that she is not going to have any more children, that after her little girl was born the doctors had seen to that. ' "Think, I had a choice between two alternatives: either to be with child, that is an invalid, or to be the friend and companion of my husband – practically my husband,"

Anna said, in a tone intentionally superficial and frivolous.'
But how could the perceptive and sensitive Anna not know that
Vronsky wanted children and a normal family life with her?
All her reasons that her children would be unhappy do not
convince Dolly, or us, but what is tragic is that she should
think that her only way to keep his love was not to be pregnant.
When Dolly was leaving, only Anna was sad, 'no one else
would stir up within her soul the feelings that had been roused
by their conversation. It hurt to stir up these feelings, but yet
she knew that that was the best part of her soul, and that that
part of her soul would be quickly smothered in the life she was
leading.' Again 'smothered'. Dolly, an ageing, weary, anxious
woman, stirs up in Anna the 'best part of her soul' just as she had
in Karenin. When she was shown round the hospital Vronsky
had had built, and saw things she had never seen before, she
asked, 'And will you have a maternity ward? That is so much
needed in the country, I often . . .' In spite of his good manners
Vronsky interrupted her, and told her the place was meant for
infectious diseases. Just as in art Vronsky does not respond to
real life, but to the works of art of others, so in his charitable
work he is an imitator.

Why did Vronsky and Anna fail each other again and again?
In the moment of her greatest need, after the races, he failed to
say at once that they must run away, and so broke her back as
he had broken the back of his lovely horse. But now she had
failed him too, when she did not sense his longing for a normal
life, children and an occupation. How could she have agreed
to the doctor's preventing her from having more children, and
hope to keep Vronsky by sex alone, when he had already shown
signs of revulsion?

Driving home, Dolly has a wonderful feeling of relief. The
coachman, unasked, expresses his impressions, of the wealth
of her host, but of his meanness too. Still, the food was good, but
it seemed to him dreary there. Dolly thought the same, but
when she got home and described how well she had been received, the luxury and good taste of Vronsky's way of living,
she forgot her feelings of dissatisfaction and unease, and added
'One has to know Anna and Vronsky – I've got to know him
better now – to see how nice they are, and how touching.'

She was 'speaking with perfect sincerity': what she was saying was one aspect of the truth.

What is the impact of Anna on Levin? Stiva had invited him to come with him and meet his sister. She had been in the country, and was now back in Moscow waiting for a divorce; her position was very difficult: 'She does not go anywhere . . . she does not want people to visit her out of charity . . . So in such a situation another woman would not have found any resources,' Stiva tells him.

'But she has a daughter, so she probably looks after her,' Levin said. In this conversation with Oblonsky Levin expresses views identical with Tolstoy's. When Oblonsky says that she has written a children's book which a publisher thought was remarkable, Levin smiles ironically; when he hears that she is looking after an English family in distress, Levin is immediately put off. (Tolstoy had the most terrible quarrel with Turgenev when the latter told him about the English governess he had engaged for his daughter, and 'the good works' they did together. Tolstoy expressed his disgust and horror: to him such philanthropy was sham and hypocrisy.) There is nothing left for Oblonsky but to say 'Well, you'll see her'. Even before Levin meets her, the portrait of her by Mikhailov overwhelms him: ' "I never saw a better portrait." ' She makes a tremendous impression on Levin 'by her beauty, her brains, education and, at the same time, simplicity and sincerity'. We have never before seen Anna as we see her with Levin's eyes. She does not deceive herself: she says, à propos of her writing, that it is like work done by prisoners: 'those unfortunates achieve wonders of patience'.

Levin had judged her severely before, 'but now, following some strange trend of thought, he justified her and at the same time pitied her, and was afraid that Vronsky did not entirely understand her'. Levin is entirely captivated by Anna, and tells Kitty that 'She is very charming, very, very much to be pitied, and a good woman'. When Kitty weeps and accuses him of having fallen in love with 'that disgusting woman', he cannot calm her. Finally he manages it after acknowledging that, what with having taken too much drink, and a feeling of pity for her, he had fallen under her cunning influence, and that he would in future avoid her. Now we are told that Anna had been trying, though unconsciously, all the evening to arouse love in Levin: yet as soon as he left she stopped thinking about him. Suffering corrupts, and hopelessness even more so.

Levin and Kitty are, as we have seen very jealous people, but Anna's jealousy is of quite a different nature. Levin and Kitty had become one; Anna and Vronsky failed to achieve this, and she strives to possess him. It is that which makes her happy for a while in Italy. Anna and Karenin had never become one in marriage, but she had had with him a child she loved, the task of being a good mother, security and peace of mind. None of this is part of her relationship with Vronsky. Hence her mad jealousy. It sets ablaze a terrible battle of wills between them. Whenever she wins, has her way, she regrets it, sees how dangerous her victory is, and works for reconciliation. When he wins, he is frightened, and realizes how she suffers, but when he loses he feels angry and revengeful.

After one of the terrible scenes, which ends by her saying that he will regret it, he wavers for a moment, and then decides that there is only one way, not to take any notice, and leaves. She sends a note: 'I am to blame. Come home, we must have it out. For God's sake come back, I am frightened.' But Vronsky has already left the stable, and she sends a telegram: 'I must talk things over, come at once.' She also sends a messenger to his mother's, where he has gone. Then she goes off to the Oblonskys' but gets little consolation from Dolly and even less from Kitty. When she comes out of the Oblonskys' house, and the coachman asks her whether he should drive home, she says yes. Looking at two passers-by, she asks herself 'What can he be telling another person with such heat?' She had intended to tell Dolly about herself, but now she was glad she had not. 'How pleased my misfortune would have made her? She would have hidden it; but the main feeling would have been joy that I am punished for pleasure which she envied me.' Kitty too was jealous of her and hated her; and also despised her. Her unhappiness makes her feel, 'And we all hate one another.'

At home she finds a telegram from Vronsky: he cannot be back before ten o'clock; and the messenger is not yet back. She is in such a state that she fails to realize that the telegram is an answer to hers, and that he has not yet received her note. She decides to go to him, 'I'll tell him everything. Never in my life did I hate anyone as I hate that man.' And she tells the coachman to take her to the railway station.

Reading of Anna's last hour, I shudder to think how a lesser writer would have marred it. I will not go over it, except for a few points which complete her and Vronsky's story. Impressions come to her from outside: 'And Anna directed now for the first time that bright light, by which she saw everything, on her relations with him, which she had earlier avoided thinking about. "My love is becoming more passionate and more self-centred, but his is dying and dying, and that is why we are moving apart" – she went on thinking.' What she sees is an aspect of truth which she did not look at every day. 'The bright light' blinds her a little; but nevertheless, just as when she was delirious, or when she revealed her suffering to Dolly, the truth of it is consistent, and speaks for itself. ' "He says to me that I am senselessly jealous; but it is not the truth. I am not jealous, but I am not content. But . . . " she opened her mouth and changed her place in the vehicle, from the excitement roused in her by the thought which came suddenly into her head. "If I could have been something apart from a mistress who passionately loves only his caresses; but I cannot, and I do not want to be anything else." ' Of course, she says, she knows he will not be unfaithful to her, but if he is kind to her out of duty that is hell. 'He has ceased to love me long ago.' The streets are unfamiliar and there are so many people and 'they all hate one another'. She tries to think out what she wants in order to be happy: she gets a divorce, Karenin gives her the boy, and she marries Vronsky. As soon as she remembers Karenin 'she imagined him with unusual vividness . . . and remembering the feeling there was between them and which was also called love, she trembled with disgust'. Later, seeing some laughing schoolboys, she remembers her Seryozha. ' "I thought that I loved him too, and humbled myself before my own tenderness. . . . But I lived without him, exchanged him for another love and did not complain about the exchange so long as I was satisfied by that love." And she remembered with revulsion what she called "the other love".'

The last straw is another message from Vronsky 'Very sorry the note did not catch me. I shall be back at ten o'clock.' It might have been different, might have been full of love, and they would have come together again, but for how long? Death was the only end. After Anna's death, when Vronsky goes off to a useless war, says that he is a 'ruin', and weeps, we realize that his tragedy is greater than Anna's.

Tolstoy had begun with an Anna who was 'a revolting woman', and ended with one of whom Levin says 'what a marvellous, sweet, and unhappy woman'. Vronsky had come to love this woman, while her love for him was nothing but sexual passion. Anna became a possible Tolstoy no less than Pierre, but how did this happen? Tolstoy's imagination is always deciphering the 'book printed in him by reality': What do we find in that book to help us answer this question?

Tolstoy's 'joyful and innocent' childhood ended at fourteen; then began the 'terrible period' of twenty years, a period of greed, vanity, gambling, and, above all, lust. Day after day he poured out his regrets in his diary and made new rules, almost always broken the next day. Many of his affairs were casual; the most serious was with Aksynia, a serf, married and living some miles from Yasnaya Polyana. He was thirty at that time, she twenty-three. What she was like, how attractive, we know from the story *Tikhon and Malanya*. In May 1860 he noted: 'No longer the feeling of a stag but of a husband to a wife.' He fled abroad. He was running away not only from peasant women, but from some most eligible ladies. There were quite a number. A few years earlier he had nearly married Valerya Arsenev, but had fled abroad. There was one woman who was his equal in discernment, culture, depths of spirit: Alexandra Tolstoy, a distant relation. She had been a maid of honour, and remained close to the imperial family. He was falling in love with her, but alas, she was forty, and Tolstoy was not giving up his dreams of a family. Finally he fell in love with Sonya Bers, aged eighteen (he almost toothless, aged thirty-four), and they married.

There is such a vast amount of information about Tolstoy and his wife, that when two biographers set out from different points, they sometimes make you wonder in the end whether they are writing about the same man. This is what I felt after reading two recent biographies, by Troyat and by V. Shklovsky. Both are crammed with valuable information, but Shklovsky, as he says in his introduction, is guided (believe it or not) by Lenin's articles on Tolstoy; Troyat does not give one reference to them. So what two such biographers agree about is likely to be of considerable value. Troyat says that Tolstoy succeeded in writing *War and Peace* because, beyond any doubt, 'Sonya had succeeded in creating the atmosphere of peace and quiet that was necessary for the work to mature in him'; Shklovsky says that she took care of his labour: 'He chose the fate that he needed, and the woman that he needed was Sofya Andreyevna'. He says this without disguising his very definite dislike of her.

In Tolstoy's own words Sonya was good looking, intelligent, and pure when she married him, a depraved man. There were disagreements in the early months, but most of them were not anything out of the ordinary for two spontaneous people, honest with themselves. Some early moments were alarming, but Tolstoy buried them, as he had buried some shocks of his childhood. With his many diverse passions, his contradictions, his great complexity, he would not have achieved what he did without suppressing some of his experiences. (Dickens seems to have had the same gift.) And so in *War and Peace* he created the idyllic marriage between Pierre and Natasha.

Tolstoy's marriage was ten years old when he began *Anna Karenina*, and his splendid vision of childhood had faded into the light of common day: instead of Pierre and Natasha's marriage we have Levin and Kitty's. Kitty is as spontaneous, intuitive, able, as Natasha, but we discover that Kitty and Levin could not bear the memory of their honeymoon. Is this of very great significance? Perhaps Pierre and Natasha felt the same, but Tolstoy did not feel the need to mention it. Sonya Tolstoy disliked her first experience of sex very much, and years later warned her daughter of the degrading experience before her. But she was soon pregnant, and Tolstoy no doubt felt for her at that time just what Levin felt for Kitty: love without sensuality. Her care for the children, for the estate, her intimate companionship with her husband and, above all, the help she gave to the great writer, brought her much happiness. And so it did to him: 'a terrifying happiness'.

Sonya was having one child after another – thirteen pregnancies, plus the months of nursing. Her dislike of sex need not have menaced their marriage. The root of the disaster they were moving towards was in Tolstoy. The name Kitty holds a clue. It is a diminutive of Ekaterina, a common name in Russia. Kitty is a foreign form, only used by the upper classes. Levin's brother Nikolay, who dislikes class distinction, calls her Katya; but so does her father, the real aristocrat, occasionally; and so does Levin now and then. In *Childhood* the little girl to whom Nikolenka is attracted is called Katenka, another form of Katerina: the first stirrings of unconscious love. But before he wrote *Childhood*, Tolstoy had already been in love with a gypsy called Katya. In *Resurrection*, written very late in life, the girl whom Neklyudov seduced was called Katyusha. Katyusha, Tolstoy informs us, was adopted by two aunts; one treated her like a servant, the other like a ward, and as a result 'she was called by the intermediate name, neither Katka nor Katenka, but Katyusha'. A servant one would call Katka, a ward, or one's own child, Katenka. He leaves a clue when he informs us that Katyusha's father was a travelling gypsy. And so to Tolstoy, Ekaterina in all its different forms is the name for a woman (the gypsy he made love to, the child who stirred his feeling unconsciously, the girl he seduced, and the one Levin married) who attracts him sexually. In his vision of youth he was married to a Natasha, but that vision had faded and when a Natasha reappears in his late novel *Resurrection* she is a sister of Nekhlyudov.

Levin–Tolstoy's love story, his marriage, their quarrels, the birth of the first child, their jealousy, are experiences of a mature man, the memories of which usually live in the conscious mind. But what about Anna, who began as 'a revolting woman' and ended as 'a marvellous, sweet, and unhappy woman'? Tolstoy begins to write every one of his important books by fixing on some outside event; then he flaps about like a fish out of water, each time comes nearer and nearer to the edge, and finally he plunges in. In Levin and Kitty's love story he recollects the happiness of the early years of his marriage. The seed of

Anna's story came from outside, but it fell on the fertile ground of his early misgivings and fears that his wife was not of his kind, and that what he primarily wanted of her was sex. Anna's love for Vronsky is a sexual passion hidden in a poetic envelope. It immediately brings home to her that she detests Karenin physically. But as human beings Karenin and Vronsky are both of one kind: they lack imagination and are imitators. You need only think of Levin, Oblonsky, Dolly, Prince Shcherbatsky, even Levin's brother Nikolay, to see that they belong to a different kind of human being from the two Alexeys.

Just as Vronsky and Anna failed one another again and again, so did the Tolstoys in the last thirty years of their marriage; and just as Vronsky and Anna used to bury their fears and take up life again, so did the Tolstoys. Tolstoy used sometimes to express admiration for his wife, as Anna did for Vronsky to Dolly; and just as she, a few hours later, revealed to Dolly her deep unhappiness, so did Tolstoy to his brother Sergey, telling him that his marriage was a failure. Tolstoy again and again made plans to run away from his wife: when he did so in the end, what was it but suicide? His great intuition guided him to live the tragedy of the years he was approaching in a woman: a limited creature, and more of a piece than a man. When Anna saw to it, after her first child with Vronsky, that she should not have any others, she cut herself off, we are left in no doubt, from creative life. Her philanthropic acts were nothing more than a drug, as she herself knew. Anna's suicide is only on the surface due to jealousy, and hardly at all to the cruelty of society: her tragedy is that her love was nothing more than a sexual passion. Vronsky's tragedy, on the other hand, is that his sexual love evolved into a deep love for Anna, a desire for a wife, a mother, a companion. That is what Countess Tolstoy wanted of her husband, while all he came to want of her was sexual satisfaction.

From the moment Levin's beloved brother Nikolay died, he lost his peace of mind: whence did life come, why, and to what end? His attempts to find an answer are cursory: he tries studying the writings of great thinkers, reasoning, reading about the Church. He is content for a short while with the thought that an individual cannot attain divine truth, but that it is given to the community of men united by love – the Church. But when he reads the history of the Roman Catholic and the Greek Orthodox Churches he finds that each repudiated the other.

Not long after he finished *Anna Karenina*, all Levin's thoughts and the despair which made him afraid that he might commit suicide, Tolstoy expanded in the *Confession*. There is one experience in Levin's progress which transcends all others. Talking to the peasant Fyodor about a piece of land he wants to let, Levin asks him whether Platon, a rich peasant, would rent it for the next year. Fyodor says no, because the rent is too high: it would not pay Platon. How does Kirillov manage to make it pay, Levin asks? Quite simple: Kirillov will squeeze another man. ' "But uncle Fokanich [as he calls the old man Platon], do you think he would skin another man? . . . Fokanich lives for his soul. He remembers God." ' These words have a great effect on Levin: 'Undefined but significant thoughts seemed to burst out from where they have been locked up and, all striving towards one goal, whirled in his head, blinding him with their light.'

Just as Pierre was saved from despair by a peasant called Platon, so was Levin; but what a difference! Platon (Russian for Plato) is now plain Fokanich. Tolstoy does not even let us meet Fokanich, nor does he tell us the story of his life, as he told us of Platon's; he merely informs us that he was a well-to-do peasant who lived for his soul and remembered God. This fact alone fills Levin with thoughts which 'blinded him with their light'. It is very hard for us today to understand what 'living for one's soul and remembering God', in a man without any rights and privileges, meant to Tolstoy, and not only to him.

Levin's spiritual travail and the light that emanated from the existence of Fokanich are sketchy compared with the autobiographical pieces, *Confession* and *Notes of a Madman*, which were written not long after Anna Karenina. Levin is a great self-portrait: he searches for the meaning of life and he has the sensibilities of an artist, but writes only a book on agriculture! Anna is a possible Tolstoy. A possible self is often a greater achievement than a self-portrait, because the writer's imagination is tested to the limit.

When a future moment becomes a *now* we do not know if or

when it will happen, where and how; but the novelist creates the where, the when, and all the evanescent circumstances. Tolstoy was not the only great novelist to live in his imagination in the future: Dostoyevsky lived in the Stalin era in his novel *The Possessed.* I will go further, and say that the vision of the prophet is no more supernatural than that of the poet or the novelist. But in order to understand the prophet we must enter his frame of reference: he is not primarily concerned with his personal destiny or with that of his children, but with the destiny of the whole people. But if he can do no more than see that those who cry 'Peace, peace' when there is no peace are false prophets, or that they that run after Egypt will be destroyed by Babylon, he is no more farseeing than some statesmen. But the Hebrew prophet saw much further into the future. The expression of his vision was made within the framework of his faith, according to which the account is between the people and God, and the armies which march over the body of the land are nothing but instruments in the hand of God. The prophets differed from ordinary mortals not only in their un-concern with themselves, but also in resting on their faith in God, in daring to know their people's past and future. The prophet is deaf to the noise in the streets, for it would drown the voices of the past; he is blind to the 'obscuring daylight'. Since both past and future become present to him, his emotions are actual: he sees, he hears, he is tormented, his bowels yearn. He threatens, he implores. But he cannot, any more than any ordinary mortal, recall a moment of 'utter, utter misery', or live in a future of utter desolation, without immediately turn-ing to hope and comfort. 'I will destroy her vines and her fig trees' and in the next breath 'I will return to her her vineyards'. The cry of despair is followed by a jubilant chorus: 'I will answer, saith the Lord, I will answer the heavens, and they shall answer the earth; and the earth shall answer the corn, and the vine, and the oil, and they shall answer Jezreel.' Living in a future moment, unaffected by the vagaries of chance, for the prophet 'in today already walks tomorrow'. He sees the doom of his people, but almost immediately 'Not my people' becomes 'My people'. His hope keeps him young and saves him from the pessimism that often overtakes the artist.

Chekhov said that neither Tolstoy in *Anna Karenina* nor Pushkin in *Eugene Onegin* solved any problems: what they did was to pose them correctly. Tolstoy is everywhere in *Anna Karenina*, and at the same time least self-centred; he had put away all childish things, and though afraid of the future was yet taken out of himself. He was at the zenith of his powers.

# 4. The Fourth Period

In 1878, when *Anna Karenina* came out in book form, Tolstoy was fifty. In that year he recorded a few of his childhood memories for a publisher. Here is his earliest. 'I am bound; I want to pull out my hands, and I can't. I scream and cry, and I myself don't like my screaming, but I can't stop. Someone is bending over me, but I cannot remember who. And all this is happening in semi-darkness. But I remember there were two people. My screams affect them; it makes them anxious, but they do not untie me, and I scream louder. They think it is necessary (that is that I should remain bound), whereas I know that it isn't, and I want to prove it to them, and burst into more screams, disagreeable to me, but uncontrollable. I feel the injustice and cruelty, not of people, because they are sorry for me, but of fate, and I feel pity for myself.'

Babies in Russia were swaddled, not only in Tolstoy's time, but in our century, up to about nine months; but as Tolstoy says, he might have been a little older, and swaddled again to prevent him scratching a sore.

Such memories live in our mind as pictures, and as De Quincey said, we 'decipher what the child only felt in cipher'. Tolstoy tells us that this memory was the strongest impression of his life. Many, many people have recorded infant memories: compare Tolstoy's to one of St Augustine's: 'Gradually I came to know where I was, and I tried to express my wants to those who could gratify them, yet could not, because my wants were inside me, and they were outside, nor had they any power of getting into my soul. And so I made movements and sounds, signs like my wants, the few I could, the best I could; for they were not really like my meaning. And when I was not obeyed, because people did not understand me, or because they would not do me harm, I was angry, because elders did not submit to me, because freemen would not slave for me, and I avenged myself on them by tears.'

St Augustine, like Tolstoy, is deciphering his memory: to express their needs, all they can do is to make movements and sounds, and because these are not effective they scream. In neither memory are the adults unkind: Tolstoy felt that they knew he wanted to be untied but thought it was necessary that he should be bound, but St Augustine is not sure whether they fail to gratify his wants because they do not understand or because they think it would do him harm. They diverge in their final interpretations: St Augustine says that he was angry because they did not submit to him, while Tolstoy says, 'What is memorable is not my cry and suffering, but the complexity and contradiction of impressions. I want freedom, it would disturb nobody, but I lack strength, while they are strong.'

These interpretations come from the recurrence of the experience later in very different circumstances. At about the time he recovered this memory Tolstoy found his new faith and, convinced that all men were brothers, wanted to give away his property. His conflict with his family was very like the one in his infancy: the family were not unkind, but they would not let him be free and he 'lacked strength while they were strong', as he wrote in a letter to a friend.

From infancy to the end of his life his first demand was for his freedom, though in childhood and early marriage it did not prevent his conforming to rules and demands, out of love and respect for others. Throughout his childhood and the next twenty years, his aunt Tatyana Alexandrovna, his elder brothers, and his young sister teased him, laughed at him, warned him and were frankly critical of him when again and again he gambled or made a hasty decision. But he never felt he had to fight for his freedom, never felt that he was weak and they strong. Nor did he feel this in the early years of marriage. He had moods, he had misgivings, but he needed neither drink, drugs nor women to see him through an hour of depression. The first serious breakthrough of fear and despair happened at Arzamas, the year he finished *War and Peace*. The heart of that experience was the existence of death which made life meaningless: still that despair did not inhibit him from planning another novel and finally from creating Anna Karenina. It was not only the fear and horror of death that he experienced in the ten years between finishing *War and Peace* and *Anna Karenina*; there was also a fear that what he chiefly wanted of his wife was sex. But the artist triumphed, and uncovered a whole world for us. A quarter of a century later, looking back at that period – the first eighteen years of his marriage, during which he wrote *War and Peace* and *Anna Karenina* – he stated that it was 'perhaps the least interesting: I lived a correct, honest family life, not succumbing to any of the vices condemned by public opinion, but all my concerns were limited to selfish cares for my family, to increasing my property, to gaining literary success, and to all kinds of pleasure.'

This is an old man's summary but it is a guide in some ways. According to it he began a new period, the fourth, at the age of fifty-two. He ceased to be a nihilist, and found his new faith in God and his belief that we were all God's children, all brothers, and that the only way to live was to follow the man Jesus. He approves of this fourth period of his life, in which he had by then lived some twenty years, and says he hopes to die in it. 'From its point of view I see the whole meaning of my past life, and in this period I would not like to change anything, except the evil habits acquired by me in the preceding periods.'

This fourth period, which lasted thirty years, is more complex and full of contradictions than any of the other three. He failed to make his wife and his sons follow him, and of the three daughters who tried to live the life he preached, two married, exchanging, according to him, a higher spiritual life for a lower one. He could not coerce them, and did not want to. The heart of his first memory ('I feel the injustice and cruelty, not of people, because they are sorry for me, but of fate, and I feel pity for myself') is the heart of his conflict in that fourth period.

Can we accept his judgement of the fourth period, that he was a man who had found the meaning of life and was no longer afraid of death, but who was not free to live as he thought he should, to give away his property, and to follow the example of Jesus? If only his artistic creations of that period did not raise so many doubts!

Ten years after *Anna Karenina* was completed he wrote *The Kreutzer Sonata*. Though we know from all his earlier writings that he is always deciphering his real memories we are still surprised that nearly every landmark in Pozdnyshev's story comes straight out of Tolstoy's life.

Pozdnyshev is a landowner like Tolstoy. His age of innocence, like Tolstoy's, ended at fourteen; there follows a long period of depraved life. He is not a seducer or a pervert but he goes to women for his health, and never looks at any as a human being. At thirty he marries a pure and innocent girl. Their honeymoon is dismal and degrading, and they begin to quarrel. The quarrels are followed by reconciliations; both, Pozdnyshev asserts, functions of sex. The wife – she has no Christian name – is not well when the first child is born and listens to the wicked doctor's advice not to nurse the baby: Pozdnyshev takes an even gloomier view of this than Tolstoy did. After this she nurses all the other children until, unwell after the fifth child, she again listens to the doctor who tells her of means to prevent any more children. (This was something Countess Tolstoy longed to do but never did.) The quarrels grow worse, and there is about them a bitter hatred such as Pozdnyshev had never known in his quarrels with his brother, father, or friends. The children become weapons in their struggle, they take sides: he feels closer to his daughter Liza, she to her son Vasya. He is at times on the verge of suicide, and she takes poison but survives.

After she stops having children she recovers physically and takes up the piano again. A man Pozdnyshev had known in his youth, a musician, 'rather a rotten fellow', turns up, and now Pozdnyshev, jealous by nature, becomes a prey to a cunning, a terrible obsession. 'What a revolting feeling jealousy is' he says to himself. It ends in his murdering his wife. Tolstoy did not experience Pozdnyshev's jealousy of the musician till seven years after he wrote *The Kreutzer Sonata*, when his wife was attracted to the musician Tanaev. Not for the first time Tolstoy was living in his imagination in the future.

In *The Kreutzer Sonata* Tolstoy does not alter the bare facts taken from his own life even as much as he did in his other autobiographical books, but he transmutes his emotions, and the whole meaning of his experience of love and marriage, to a greater degree than in any of the other works of his imagination.

Pozdnyshev, recalling his first meeting with his wife, tells us that after years of depravity, he had found a young pure woman whom he thought worthy of him. The evening when they went out in a boat in the moonlight, it seemed to him that she understood everything, that he was feeling and thinking of higher matters, but what really happened was that the jersey she was wearing was very becoming, and so were her curls, and he wanted to be closer to her. Tolstoy transliterates the word jersey, and in Russian it sounds crude and almost obscene. Overfed and idle, Pozdnyshev says, like other men of his class, he had surplus energy and indulged in sexual excess, but this was a safety valve. When the valve was closed for a time, desires appeared which looked like love, and were accompanied by enthusiasm, admiration, poetry – all lies. Fact after fact out of Tolstoy's true story is distorted when it becomes part of Pozdnyshev's experience. Pozdnyshev, like Tolstoy, gave his fiancée before they married the diaries of his depraved past, but Pozdnyshev says that his diaries contained only 'a little' of his past, mainly about his last affair of which she would have heard from others, so therefore he thought it better to tell her about it beforehand. He says to the stranger to whom he is telling his tragedy in the train that towards the end 'all the preceding moments in my memory have taken on a sombre shade'. Not only the preceding moments, but the whole story, including the effect of music. Marriage is hell, he says: to an innocent girl the honeymoon is a nightmare; even when she is carrying a child, the man has not the decency of an animal. 'What were the first signs of my love? That I gave myself over to animal excesses, and not only was I not ashamed of them, but was, for some reason, proud of the possibility of physical excess.' He behaved in a 'swinish manner' to his wife. Their quarrels became more and more poisonous, and in each reconciliation 'mutual hatred hid under love, i.e. sensuality'. The man becomes a slaveowner, the woman a slave, and she revenges herself by subjugating him. It was only after he had murdered her that he saw 'a human being in her'.

*The Kreutzer Sonata* was a tremendous success. Its effect on

Chekhov is very interesting. To judge from the date of his first comment (1890), he must have read it, as so many other Russians did, before permission was granted for official publication. In his letter to A. N. Pleshcheyev, he expressed his admiration for *The Kreutzer Sonata*, in spite of glaring faults, such as statements about doctors, women's revulsion from sex, and so on: it enormously stimulated thought. But before the year was out he wrote to his friend A. S. Suvorin: '*The Kreutzer Sonata* has been an event for me, but now it is ridiculous, and seems without sense.'

*The Kreutzer Sonata* is not made out of Tolstoy's real memories, but of certain facts of his life. How right the autobiographers – Stendhal, Rousseau, Aksakov, De Quincey – were to insist that they were sure about the feelings of their memories, not the facts. It is true that the Countess was not very happy on her honeymoon; and, removed from Moscow, a home full of young affectionate people, to a spartan home in the country at Yasnaya Polyana, with so many elderly inmates, she felt lonely when Tolstoy was out for hours together, and there were quarrels. But it is not true that she felt a slave, or wanted to subjugate him. It is true that Tolstoy was very upset when his wife, for reasons of health, did not suckle their first child; but when Pozdnyshev says 'seeing how easily she threw aside the moral duty of a mother, I justifiably though unconsciously concluded that she would just as easily throw aside her duty as a wife', he is expressing a feeling which was not Tolstoy's.

We mistrust Tolstoy's imagination, and this is far more damaging than mistrusting the factual truth of an autobiographer. Pozdnyshev is pouring out his memories to a friendly stranger sitting in a semi-dark railway compartment, like a patient to a psychoanalyst. What makes his marriage ridiculous is our disbelief in his account: he has not given us the means to judge it for ourselves, no means to make comparisons, no means to tell that it is anything more than the account of a neurotic. If we believed that he was telling the truth, we should be making the same error as Freud when he believed for a time that his patients had been seduced by their fathers in childhood, as so many of them told him.

But just as we learn about human nature in general from the

aberrations of the neurotic so do we about a writer from his artistic failures. If one reads *The Kreutzer Sonata* immediately after *Anna Karenina*, Anna's tragedy sheds light on Pozdnyshev's and the other way round. Anna's love for Vronsky ends in tragedy because her love was founded on sex; Pozdnyshev goes straight to the heart of the matter: he tells us at once that his marriage was based on sex. Both Anna and Pozdnyshev suffer from the great curse of sexual love, jealousy. Sooner or later both come to a crisis which is not warranted by facts: neither Anna's nor Pozdnyshev's jealousies are justified. Anna throws herself in front of the train. Pozdnyshev, in his eight hours' journey by train, overexcited and driven mad by imaginings of his wife and the musician, thinks of getting out of the train and lying on the rails. Instead he turns home, and murders his wife; and only then, for the first time, sees that she was a human being. Vronsky does not need to see Anna dead to realize that ever since she was very ill his love for her as a person has been more important to him than sexual desires.

The quarrels between Pozdnyshev and his wife used to end in reconciliation, that is in kisses, embraces, and sex; but whenever he was satiated 'we again ceased to have need of one another'. In one of their terrible battles he cried out ' "I wish you were dead": I remember how my words terrified me!' He thinks of running away; so did Tolstoy. Already when he was writing *Anna Karenina* a battle of wills had begun to rage between Tolstoy and his wife, and without uttering the words he knew that he wished she were dead.

Pozdnyshev asserts that the court let him off because he killed out of jealousy, defending his honour, but 'I tried to make clear my meaning, but they failed to understand, that I wanted to rehabilitate the honour of my wife'. The public read *The Kreutzer Sonata* as if it were pure autobiography, and joked about the poor Countess who was carrying her thirteenth child. It is not an autobiography. It is an obsessional confession, full of fantasies. Pozdnyshev says 'Oh, I am frightened, frightened of railway journeys. . . . Ooh! what a terrible thing this Sonata is . . . And what a terrible thing altogether music is! . . . And most terrible of all is sex – not so much the physical act, but the illusions, lies, of love.' Pozdnyshev concludes: 'If I had known what I know now, all would have been different. On no account would I have married her ... I would not have married at all.'

The epigraph to *The Kreutzer Sonata* was 'If a man looks at a woman with a lustful eye, he has already committed adultery with her in his heart' (Matthew 5:28). And when a writer as serious as Tolstoy commits a murder in his imagination, is he not committing a crime? No! Tolstoy kills a faceless, nameless woman, 'a wife' who is no more than a generic term: he could not have murdered a person who lived in his imagination.

The year Tolstoy completed *The Kreutzer Sonata* he began the story *The Devil*. Once again a real happening started him off: as Antaeus needed to touch earth to renew his strength so Tolstoy needed to touch reality. A man named Fredericks, who worked as a jurist in Tula, not far from Yasnaya Polyana, had an affair with a peasant woman called Stepanida, and later married a woman from an educated family. His wife was very jealous of Stepanida. Three months after the wedding he shot Stepanida, was declared insane, and not long afterwards was found dead, run over by a train. In Tolstoy's story, the peasant woman is called Stepanida, and the hero Irtenev, the name of the Narrator in his first book *Childhood*.

Once again he had descended deep into his own experience, and brought back not just facts but memories of his affair with the peasant woman Aksynia who had borne him a son.

Irtenev was a well-educated man, with a brilliant future before him. After his father died, and he and his brothers found that he had left them nothing but debts, Irtenev gave up a government career and settled in the country to get the estate on its feet again. He had dreamt of marriage, and when the estate began to flourish he now felt that the time had come to marry.

He had begun to have sexual relations in boyhood, like Pozdnyshev, the Narrator in *Notes of a Madman*, and Tolstoy himself. But he did *not* surrender to debauchery, was never carried away, and never contracted disease. He needed sex for his health. Once again, as in *The Kreutzer Sonata*, there were no illusions about love: 'He fell in love because he knew he was going to marry.' This time the wife has a name, Liza Annenskaya, and moreover 'she had that something in her which constitutes the main delight of communing with a loving woman: she had, thanks to her love for her husband, an insight into his soul'. Developing this theme, Tolstoy shows her possessing some of the virtues of Kitty. In his bachelor days, Irtenev had lived with a peasant woman, 'for the sake of his health'; her name was Stepanida, and her husband was working away from home.

Before he married he made up his mind not to have any further dealings with Stepanida. She was living as before, having lovers. One day Irtenev, coming home in a contented gay happy mood, runs into Stepanida, who had been called in by his wife to help with the cleaning. She smiles with her eyes at him, and at once his old passion revives and he cannot take his eyes off her swaying, agile body, her bare feet, her arms and shoulders. On this occasion he sees his wife as 'particularly pale, yellow, long and weak'.

Whatever means Irtenev takes not to meet Stepanida, however much he struggles with himself, he knows that in the end he cannot escape from his passion; he murders Stepanida, and later becomes an alcoholic. This ending did not please Tolstoy, and he wrote a second: in this, instead of murdering Stepanida Irtenev commits suicide.

Pozdnyshev's marriage is tragic because it is entirely built on sex, Irtenev's marriage ends in tragedy because it is *not* based on sex. Pozdnyshev regrets bitterly that he ever married; so does Irtenev: 'I deceived myself when I married', but for the opposite reason.

Tolstoy secretly gave the manuscript of *The Devil* to his disciple Chertkov. Copies were made, and Tolstoy got one and hid it in his study, under the cover of an old chair. Twenty years later, in 1909, the Countess found the manuscript, and there was a terrible scene. They had been married forty-seven years, and Tolstoy had passed his eightieth birthday.

They were both undoubtedly very jealous people, but so was Proust and so was Dostoyevsky. Why was Tolstoy so conspiratorial about this story, and she so unhinged by reading it? Was she still suffering from the pain his description of his affair with Aksynia, in the diaries which he gave her before marriage, had caused her? We know she was distressed when she read the diaries, and later, at Yasnaya Polyana, was jealous when she used to see Aksynia. There is no evidence that Tolstoy was ever disturbed by Aksynia's presence, nor that he gave a thought to his illegitimate son who worked in the stables. Shklovsky, in his book on Tolstoy, quotes from his notebook of June 1909: 'I looked at my bare feet, remembered Aksynia's, that she is still alive, and they say that Ermil is my son, and I don't beg her forgiveness, have not repented, don't repent hourly, and dare to judge others.' Shklovsky points out that Tolstoy made a mistake about the name of his son: Ermil was the name of Aksynia's husband, Tolstoy's son by her was called Timofey. When he beats his breast about his sins, a doubt creeps into one's mind: was it not really regret that he had not stuck to his peasant woman, as his brother Sergey to his gypsy, and would he not have been then a free man, master of his mind, as Sergey was? Shklovsky seems to be impressed that Tolstoy had remembered the bare feet of the beloved woman, but Tolstoy remembered many things; he loved his memories more than he loved people. Surely the cause of the great suffering which the discovery of the manuscript of *The Devil* caused the Countess was that Tolstoy should have hidden it from her and conspired with Chertkov. There is general agreement among students of Tolstoy about Chertkov: he was an arrogant, fanatical person, and the evil genius in Tolstoy's family life. For years and years Tolstoy and his wife had been reading each other's letters and diaries, discussing all their problems, and his secrecy and conspiracy with Chertkov denied, annulled everything that she had lived for. Again and again in that fourth period one is amazed at the deficiency of wisdom, even ordinary common sense and a little charity in Tolstoy's dealings with his wife and children. He knew that too, he knew everything. Tolstoy wrote to Chertkov: 'I suffer because my wife does not share my convictions. When I speak to her under the influence of vexation about her repulsing me, I often speak coldly, even in a hostile manner; never have I entreated her with tears to believe in the truth, or told her it all, simply, lovingly, softly.' At that time he expressed his belief that all men, no matter what their premises, could follow Jesus's teaching. 'I believe that the fulfilment of that teaching is possible, easy, and joyful. All a man needs is to

keep five commandments: do not be angry, do not lust; do not
swear oaths, resist not him that is evil; and love your enemies.'
But was it not lust to live on memories of lust? some of his
disciples asked.

In 1889, the year he started *The Devil*, he also began *Resurrection*. He took ten years to finish it. And so he returned at last
to the form of the long novel in which he had created his
masterpieces. Two years earlier his friend Koni, a Petersburg
lawyer, visited him at Yasnaya Polyana, and told him of a
strange experience. A young nobleman came to him with complaints against the prison administration. It turned out that he
had been on a jury and had recognized in the defendant, a
prostitute accused of theft, a house serf in his parents' home
whom he had seduced when she was sixteen. She was in a
miserable state, physically, mentally and morally. He decided
to marry her, but before the marriage took place the woman
died of typhus in prison. Tolstoy asked Koni to write the story
for *The Intermediary*, the Tolstoyan journal. He promised to do
so, but did not, and Tolstoy then asked him if he could borrow
the plot. And so he began what he first called *The Koni Story*.
After a year he put it aside, not pleased with it, and did not
return to it for some years. He took it up again and again left it;
and so it went on for over a decade.

As so often before, Tolstoy had picked on an experience
which corresponded to one of his own, and after much trial and
error he descended into himself. Who is the chief character,
Dmitry Nekhlyudov? There is a Nekhlyudov in *Boyhood* and in
*Youth*, in *A Landlord's Morning*, and in *Lucerne*. The Nekhlyudov
of *Boyhood* and *Youth* is a portrait of his friend Dmitry Dyakov.
But in *A Landlord's Morning*, the Dmitry Nekhlyudov is a self-
portrait of Tolstoy. What is he in *Resurrection*? His experiences
are as often Tolstoy's as Levin's are. Tolstoy's need to use a
detail from his own life – an object, a name, a habit – is as great
as ever: we find Nekhlyudov, when accompanying the prisoners
to Siberia, using his 'leather cushion' (the one Tolstoy used
throughout his bachelor days, until he married and his wife
replaced it by proper pillows and linen); Nekhlyudov, like
Tolstoy, has an illegitimate brother; he has a habit of writing a
diary; of having, now and again, what he called 'a cleansing of

the soul'; of laying down rules for his future behaviour but
failing again and again. There are significant differences.
Tolstoy lost his innocence by the age of sixteen, while
Nekhlyudov remained virginal till nineteen, 'having been
brought up under the wing of his mother.' The importance
Tolstoy attached to this becomes clear when Nekhlyudov first
meets Katyusha. He had come to stay with his aunts, where she
was half servant, half ward, and his innocence makes this, his
first love wonderful. We know of no first love of Pierre, Andrey,
Levin, Pozdnyshev or Irtenev. Nekhlyudov, remembering his
love ten years later, describes thus the first stirrings: 'Everything became more interesting, gayer, more significant, life
became more joyful.' After this first encounter with Katyusha,
during the next three years, rich, serving in a smart guards
regiment, close to the Tsar's family, Nekhlyudov became corrupt and debauched. All that he believed in, cared for, the
desire for perfection and to do good to others, all was despised
by the society he lived in, and he succumbed to its influence.

It is a different Nekhlyudov who stops on his way to join
his regiment at his aunt's house 'dimly knowing, though hiding
from himself, what love consists of, and what it could lead to'.
At first his spiritual self struggles with his depraved self, and the
better self is in control on Easter Eve during and after the
church service, when his love for Katyusha is at its zenith,
'when there was nothing conscious, reasoned out, nothing
sensual'. During the service he feels that she is 'the centre of
everything', and that 'everything good in the world, all was
for her'. But after they return from church sexual desire takes
possession of him, and when she comes to call him to dinner it
seems to him that 'it was necessary that he should do something,
which all do in such circumstances'. 'It is spring, and the ice is
snorting and creaking and breaking, and his desire for Katyusha
is as uncontrollable as the thaw.'

When, ten years later, Nekhlyudov is by chance sitting on a
jury, and recognizes in the defendant prostitute the Katyusha
he had seduced and ruined, life enters into his memories of her.
He is now thirty-two, has left the army and tried to become a
painter, and has found, like Vronsky, that he is not one. He
has continued to live a debauched life, is in the middle of

7

an affair with a married woman which he wants to terminate, and thinks of marrying the daughter of Prince Korchagin. He desires marriage because it will free him from irregular sexual life, and give him a chance to live a moral life; but his chief hope is that a family and children will give meaning to his empty life.

Just before Nekhlyudov recognizes Katyusha in court he has almost decided to marry 'Missi' Korchagin. He explains that her name was Marya, 'and, as in all families of a certain circle, they gave her the nickname Missi'. Once again Tolstoy is leaving a clue. Before he married Sonya he, like Levin, had made up his mind to marry a peasant woman, and had told his peasant pupils and their teachers his intention, saying that 'to marry a miss [*baryshnya*] means to burden yourself with all the poison of civilization'. Now Nekhlyudov intends to marry a Missi.

At the end of the first day in court Nekhlyudov goes on to the Korchagins, where he is expected for dinner. He is late, but is made very welcome: he is a very eligible man. The old Prince Korchagin makes an unpleasant impression on him; the red face, the sensual lips, and the bull neck, but 'chiefly this fattened, military figure of the general', and Nekhlyudov cannot help remembering what he knows about this man's cruelty; 'God knows why, – he was anyway rich and distinguished, and had no need to gain by his service – he flogged and even hung people when he was the governor of a district'. Nekhlyudov feels the same disgust with the old Princess, hating her, body and soul. And Missi too repels him: her sharp elbows, and more than anything the broad nail of her thumb, which reminds him of her father's. The aristocrats, who had been 'comprehensible and dear' to Tolstoy when he was writing *War and Peace*, have become hateful, just as happened to Proust. The change in Nekhlyudov begins from the day he sees Katyusha in the dock: his past now appears evil to him.

He will not marry a 'Missi', there will be no wife, no large family, and he will give away his property – in short Nekhlyudov at thirty-two will reach the state of mind of Tolstoy in his sixties. He will not have to think of suicide or murder but will live the life Tolstoy longed to live.

But the artist has his say. Consider Nekhlyudov's relationship with his sister and brother-in-law. The sister's name is Natasha!

(No more wives of that name, only a sister.) She and her brother had much in common in their youth, she was even in love with Nikolenka Irtenev (the first possible Tolstoy, in *Child-hood*), Nekhlyudov's great friend. He is now dead. Nekhlyudov and Irtenev had had in common a faith in goodness and in per-fectibility, but Irtenev was an unbeliever, and his death is symbolic: Nekhlyudov, the believer, supplants him. After Irtenev's death Natasha had married a man who had neither name nor fortune, nor the sensibilities of her brother and his friend: Nekhlyudov hates him because his dear Natasha has 'a passionate, sensuous love for such a poor nature'. In his relations with his brother-in-law Nekhlyudov reveals all the contradictions in his character; he argues against him, putting forward Marxist views, offends him, and later regrets it. Sure that he is right to give away his land, Nekhlyudov nevertheless feels in the depths of his heart that his sister and brother-in-law have a right to his land, since he has no chil-dren. When he is leaving for Siberia Natasha comes to the train to say good-bye to him: he compromises and tells her that one of the estates he has not yet given away, and that it will go to her children in the event of his death. (Again Tolstoy cannot avoid using a real name: the estate is called Kuzminsky, the name of Tolstoy's brother-in-law who was married to Tanya, the model for Natasha in *War and Peace*.) Nekhlyudov, like Tolstoy, wished to give away all his property, but at the same time felt that his family had some right to it.

Talk about property and inheritance spoils their feelings for one another and Natasha is glad when the train begins to move. Being a sincere and spontaneous person she says the only words she can say sincerely to him: 'Farewell, well farewell, Dmitry.' He wants to free himself of her: 'He felt that there was nothing left of the Natasha who had been close to him, there was only a slave to a husband, to him an alien, unpleasant, black and hairy.' This becomes clear to him, he says, when he sees how glad she is when he begins to talk of matters that concern her husband, and of the property and her children's inheritance.

It is not difficult to prove that Tolstoy is deciphering his own experience: the unlaboured, spontaneous, sincere affection be-tween brother and sister, so like Tolstoy's relations with his

sister and brothers, Nekhlyudov's disgust with his sister's marriage, and the complexities of his feelings, so like Tolstoy's. It
is the relationship of Nekhlyudov and Katyusha Maslova which
makes us uneasy. When, for instance, Nekhlyudov returns
from Petersburg, where he had taken Katyusha's case to the
senate, he finds that she is no longer working in the prison
hospital to which she had been transferred thanks to his efforts.
He is told that she is back in prison because she was carrying on
with the medical orderly – he feels anger and revulsion. Only
much later he learns that this was not true. And then his anger
gives way to pity, and he says that he loves her not for his own
sake but for hers and for God's. He is not in love with her, and
tells his sister that if Katyusha does marry him there will be no
children, in other words no sexual relations. She is not yet
thirty and he is only a little older. Later in the story she gives
him up, because she loves him too much and thinks that she
will be a burden to him. Gorky once asked Tolstoy whether he
had read his story 'Foma Gordeyev', his first important piece
of work. Tolstoy was pitilessly frank: 'I began to read but
couldn't finish, couldn't get through it. Tediously thought up,
*"vydumano"*. Nothing of the kind has ever been and it could not
be.' This is just what we feel about Nekhlyudov's relation with
Katyusha Maslova.

Katyusha had been condemned for a murder she did not
commit. When Nekhlyudov takes up her case, he comes in
touch with the rulers and the revolutionaries, the corrupt social
order and the suffering prisoners. There are wonderful portraits of generals, judges, officials. They are as hateful as the
Korchagins: even a good man, Tolstoy shows, gets corrupted in
government service. There is Nekhlyudov's old friend Selenin,
who was a good man in his youth, and in *War and Peace* would
have belonged to the clan of the Bolkonsky–Rostovs. But he is
trapped in the system, and corrupted. The head of the district
in Siberia, a humane general, becomes an alcoholic. For the
prisoners Nekhlyudov feels sometimes admiration, or at least
pity. As he accompanies Katyusha to Siberia he gets to know a
great variety of people.

The many political prisoners, revolutionaries, differing in
class, education, and the reasons that have brought them to

revolt, all are marvellously delineated. There is the generous and virginal daughter of a general, Marya Pavlovna, with her protruding eyes; the sensitive Kryltsov, son of a rich landowner, well educated, who had been driven into the revolutionary camp by the utter injustice and cruelty of the rulers, which he had seen with his own eyes; Nabatov, a man from a peasant family, very able, who had chosen, instead of going to the university, to return to the people to enlighten them, an exceptionally practical, well integrated man. Simonson, a man of independent judgement who forms principles for himself and sticks to them, and, sexually pure, loves Katyusha platonically and marries her in the end; Novodvorov, ambitious to become a leader, who, devoid of moral qualities, never knows doubts or hesitation, to whom all other outstanding people are rivals whom he is ready to destroy, and who is only good to people who bow before him: a little Stalin.

Tolstoy was a great portrait painter: the Narrator Nekhlyudov's portraits of peasants in *A Landlord's Morning*, written in his twenties, are as good as those of Nekhlyudov in *Resurrection*. Peasants and aristocrats Tolstoy knew from childhood, but from his late forties he got to know new kinds of people: gentry in revolt against the regime, intellectuals searching for a meaning in life, and his own followers, the Tolstoyans, a great medley of types. Neither the ruling class nor the revolutionaries in *Resurrection* are caricatures. In the quarter of a century between *War and Peace* and *Resurrection* Russian society was entirely transformed: the hopes which had blossomed with the coming of Alexander II in 1855 had faded, and a bitter struggle between the rulers and the revolutionaries raged in the country and culminated in the assassination of Alexander II. The state of mind in the country when Alexander III mounted the throne, and Pobedonostsev, an arch reactionary, became his closest adviser, is best described in the *Memoirs* of V. A. Makhlakov, a friend of the Tolstoys and a great liberal lawyer. He shows the pessimism not only of the intelligentsia but of the aristocracy too, and the conclusion they had reached, about 1880, that there was no future for Russia except by way of revolution. Tolstoy's picture of Russia in the last decade of the century is true to life. But it is the truth not of a work of art but of a documentary.

The characters in *Resurrection* are, by and large, rooted in
Tolstoy's memories from about the age of fifty; but also in
pieces of acquired knowledge and many observations of yester-
day: of the penal code, the courts, the convicts. But the flaw of
the book is in the character of Nekhlyudov. After he has gone
through the long ordeal of taking Maslova's case to princes,
officials, lawyers, after he has followed the convicts to Siberia,
and she, in the end, is going to marry the good man Simonson,
he sits down and reads the Gospels. Imagine that after he had
first seen Katyusha in the dock, he had realized his guilt,
repented, undergone a change of heart and decided to marry
her, as really happened in the Koni story; and, just as in the
story, Maslova had died of typhus. Could not the end have
been the same? Could he not then have sat down at once to
read the Gospels?

What Nekhlyudov saw of the corrupted social order and the
revolutionaries, is not necessary to his story. Pierre's experience
as a prisoner of the French is absolutely necessary; so is Levin's
experience between Kitty's refusal of him and his finding her
again. The historian and sociologist will find Nekhlyudov's
picture of Russian life in the eighties closer to reality than
Pierre's experience of the Napoleonic Wars, but the picture of
society in a great novel (whether it be *Anna Karenina* or *Little
Dorrit*) is only important as a background to the characters.

To Tolstoy himself the entire social panorama in *Resurrection*
is of no great importance; he did not believe that the evils of
society could be eradicated by revolution. When Pierre, in the
Epilogue, confides to Natasha his hope of leading society, he
thinks of a revolt of all good people against the autocracy,
which was in fact beginning, and ended in the Decembrists'
rising: he would have taken part in that revolt against
Nicholas I. Tolstoy in fact began *War and Peace* by making
Pierre a Decembrist, and fifteen years later, after *Anna Karenina*,
he once again planned a novel about the Decembrists. But he
had long left all this behind him, and now believed in following the example of Jesus. The grand panorama in *Resurrection* is a documentary, written and produced by Tolstoy,
with Nekhlyudov as his photographer.

Tolstoy's aim in the fourth period of his life was to reach

saintliness. It was impossible for him to achieve it in his every-day life: most of his family refused to follow him and he felt too weak either to leave them or to coerce them. But his greater failure was to create in his imagination a viable character who reaches saintliness. One of Tolstoy's English disciples, John Bellhouse, wrote to him that he could not recommend *Resurrection* for distribution in Britain in aid of the Dukhobors: he was specially repelled by the scene of the seduction of Katyusha. 'I must say,' Tolstoy replied, 'I wrote the book hating lust with all my heart, and to give expression to my revulsion was one of the main aims of the book.' But he was an artist before he was a saint, and it is significant that in the same decade he wrote the story *Father Sergey*.

The time is the forties, in the reign of Nicholas I, the time of Tolstoy's own boyhood and youth. With great ease and elegance he brings the main character to life, a man of his own class, Prince Stepan Kassatsky. To his intimates he is not Stepan but Stiva: not that he is like Stiva Oblonsky, but we hear an echo, and guess that both belonged to the same club. He adores the Emperor, who took a personal interest in the pupils of his military school; later on he enters the Guards and has a brilliant future before him. He is very ambitious, a perfectionist, and whatever he is doing he must get to the top, whether as an officer, or in speaking French, or playing chess. Beginning to frequent society he realizes that he does not belong to the highest circle and, used to being first, he realizes that one way of reaching it is to marry a lady who belongs to it. He gets engaged to a delightful woman, and before long confesses to her that his first motive in approaching her was worldly but that now he has got to know her it seems insignificant besides his pure love for her. She returns his confidence by telling him that she has been the Emperor's mistress. He runs away, retires from the army, and enters a monastery. His sister, who is as proud and ambitious as he was, understands that he has become a monk 'in order to be above those who wanted to show him that they were above him'. But there was more to it. The disappointment in his fiancée, whom he imagined an angel, and the insult to him, brought him to despair, and despair to his childhood faith in God, 'which had never been violated in him'.

As a monk with a new name, Sergey, he remains true to his nature, that is he strives to excel, and being a very intelligent man he tries to excel in obedience. We have been told at the very beginning that he suffers from a hasty temper. It showed itself when he was still an officer, and it reappears now, when his pride is hurt. Quite effortlessly Tolstoy uncovers the complexity of his character. He is indifferent to the death of his mother and the marriage of his sister. But he sometimes regrets having broken with his fiancée and given up the life they might have had. That was in bad moments, when he not so much stopped believing, as ceased to see clearly what he lived by. In his seventh year at the monastery he begins to get bored: he has learned all that he was required to learn and there is nothing more to do. His superiors begin to promote him, and his monk's ambition, which used to disgust him in other monks, is rising in him. Pride is still powerful in him, and in order to master it his elder advises him to become a hermit. So he lives for six years more. What is hard is not fasting and prayer but an unexpected inner struggle with doubt and lust. Both rise together and though he thinks there are two enemies there is only one. No sooner is doubt exterminated than lust disappears. He is disgusted with himself when he realizes that he wants to be a saint. Imagining himself in glory, he shakes his head: 'No, that's not it. That is a lie.'

One remembers *A Landlord's Morning*: Tolstoy, fifty years younger, searching for the meaning of life, says again and again, 'No, that's not it.' When a society woman comes to Sergey's cell to tempt him, in his fight against his lust he chops off one of his fingers. She is so much affected by this that she becomes a nun. Father Sergey is pushed by his superiors, and by the people who come to him for help, into becoming a *starets*, a saint with power to heal people, and his fame spreads further and further. He is told that people need him, that he is fulfilling the law of Jesus – to love men, and that he cannot refuse them. But even as he surrenders to this way of life he feels that his inner life is becoming an outer one, that he is doing more and more for men, but not for God. And then a merchant brings to him his imbecile daughter: the girl tempts him, and he succumbs. His first impulse is to commit suicide, but he remembers a pathetic timid child, Pashenka, a relation, whom they used to make fun of. He sets out to find her. She lives in poverty, with her daughter and ne'er-do-well son-in-law, using all her strength to soften them so that there should be no rebukes, no anger. She is physically unable to bear unkindness between people: 'She simply suffered from the sight of anger, as from a bad smell, a shrill noise, or blows to the body.' Now he realizes that he had lived for men on the pretext of living for God, but she lives for God while imagining she lives for men. In the end he is arrested and, having no papers, sent to Siberia; and there he works in the vegetable garden of a well-off peasant, teaches children, and looks after ill people.

Do we believe that he will end his days living like Pashenka for God? Not really. She was humble, she judged herself but not others, she did not set out to reach holiness, was a mother and grandmother; she suffered from the sight of anger as from a bad smell. How well Tolstoy has transcribed the music of his life into the voice of Father Sergey! We have heard it all; the ambition and the urge to excel, the pride and hasty temper, doubts, unbelief, carnal passions; the desire for fame and the approval of men propelling him on the road to fame, and at the same time the freshness of his childhood faith and the feeling, as he became famous, 'that his inner life had become an outer one, and that he was doing more and more for men, but not for God'. But was Tolstoy's road the road to holiness?

After *Resurrection*, after *Father Sergey*, after his seventieth birthday, we find him not only still needing sex, but embarrassing Chekhov and even Gorky with personal questions about their sexual life and frank talk about his own. It was not done to interest these young writers, or come close to them; it was the curiosity of the artist. What would John Bellhouse have said to such talk? And might not Father Sergey, working humbly for the peasant in Siberia, if he had met with intelligent revolutionaries, have broken out in unseemly remarks about the Emperor, about women, about his own sexual desires?

The last decade of Tolstoy's life was as turbulent as any in his youth. The new Tsar Nicholas II was as autocratic as his father had been. Though Tolstoy preached against war, the defeat by

7*

the Japanese was terribly painful to him; the 1905 Revolution he rejected, but the repressions which followed appalled him. He was seriously ill, and plagued by conscience to the end. Biryukov records what Tolstoy told him in the last year of his life. One morning at Yasnaya Polyana, in the garden, Tolstoy began asking him about his work on the biography, and told him that he must not omit the 'bad things'. 'In my youth I led a very bad life, and two events of that time are a special torment to me ... Those events were: a liaison with a peasant woman from our village, before my marriage. There is an allusion to this in my story *The Devil*. The second is a crime which I committed against Masha, the parlour maid who lived in my aunt's house. She was innocent, I seduced her, she was dismissed and was ruined.' To begin with her name was not Masha but Gasha: Tolstoy had begun to forget names, like that of his own illegitimate son. But far more extraordinary is the fact that, contrary to his assertion, Gasha was not 'ruined': Tolstoy's sister Marie took her on as a chambermaid, and later, Gasha gained her confidence and brought up her children. He must have seen her many times when his sister and her family came to Yasnaya Polyana. She was the model for Katyusha Maslova, and when Tolstoy was beating his breast about ruining a young girl, he was thinking about the person who lived in his imagination!

It is not true that in the fourth period of his life he was still obsessed by the fact of death. He believed that every one could follow Jesus, and that this made life joyful; but to be with God a man should not live in memories of the past, nor in the imagination of the future, but only in the present, he said. It is true that he cleaned his own room, cut wood, and made shoes; but he could not give up his fight for his beliefs, nor his fight with his wife and sons for his personal freedom, nor could he stop writing. Before *Father Sergey* and *Resurrection* were completed he began *Hadji Murad*, a book without a moral. Introducing the story he wrote that it was 'partly what I had seen myself, partly heard from other witnesses, and partly imagined'.

Fifty years earlier, when he was in the Caucasus, he wrote to his brother Sergey that Murad had surrendered to the Russians: 'The bravest man in all Chechenya has committed an act of cowardice.' Tolstoy never forgot him, and used to tell stories about him to his peasant pupils.

To the old Tolstoy Murad is not a coward: he went over to the Russians because in his fight with his cruel overlord Shamil he had no alternative.

The tyrant Nicholas I, monstrously cruel to his own people, was subjugating the Caucasus. On the other side was Shamil, ambitious and equally cruel, the bitter enemy of Hadji Murad. Russians and Caucasians, fighting one another, are cogs in the great wheel of power. But everyone, on both sides, has a human face. Untroubled by sex and saintliness, the relations between men and women have the innocence, charm and shrewdness of the characters of *War and Peace*. The hero Hadji Murad, quick, ingenious, clever, dignified and very brave, is driven from one camp into the other, from his own people to the Russians. In the end the Russians murder him, not because he had turned traitor, but because he was trying to escape from them in a last attempt to save his family from the hands of his great enemy Shamil.

Biryukov records that he was working on Tolstoy's biography at that time, and asked him what he had been doing with himself while visiting his sister at the Shamardino convent. 'Very embarrassed, he whispered so that no one else should hear him, his eyes shining: "I was writing Hadji Murad." This was said in the tone (forgive the vulgar expression) of a boy confessing to his schoolmate that he has eaten the cake: he remembers the delight he experienced and is ashamed to own up.'

Writing Hadji Murad was not his only joyful experience. He wrote many short stories; his own favourite was 'The Prisoner of the Caucasus': once again he delights in the variety of life. Chekhov loved 'Kholstomer', the true story of a remarkable horse Tolstoy heard about. He began writing it in 1860 but finished it only in 1885. It is not like the usual stories of animals – not thought-up. It is full of surprises; whenever one returns to it one finds something new. The horse Kholstomer is one more possible Tolstoy.

Before Tolstoy had completed Hadji Murad, he began to record his memories of childhood for Biryukov. I have now completed the circle. Tolstoy re-read his first book *Childhood*, written more than fifty years earlier, and was not pleased with it. But at that time he was not pleased with any of his creative writings, and hoped to write an autobiography which would be more useful to people than 'my twelve volumes filled with chatter' (the edition of his work was at that time in twelve volumes).

*Childhood* was the creation of his imagination, and with his great artistic intuition he had begun with a Narrator aged ten, and had closed the door on his early years. Now and then he had fetched a memory from the dark room, but always a conscious memory, of which he knew where he had left it.

When Tolstoy recorded his earliest memory he was fifty, and he lamented bitterly when he found he had so few: only four before the age of five. Now, a quarter of a century later, he found he had very many memories from the age of five. This is not surprising, for it was then that he had to leave the nursery and join his three older brothers under the control of a tutor: it was like going to boarding school. He was very sad to leave his little sister, his aunt Tatyana Alexandrovna, his toys and his little bed – his first paradise. He was afraid, and did not respond to the tutor's enticements, but his feeling that it was his duty to go, that Tatyana Alexandrovna thought so too, though she was very reluctant to part with him, prevailed. There were very good reasons for his fears. He was a cry-baby, and in the nursery he could be both a baby and at the same time the eldest child. And now he was to keep up with three older brothers.

His memories of Nikolay and Sergey – Dmitry he did not remember till much later – were the most precious of his life. Nikolay was five years Leo's senior, and commanded the respect of all the brothers. Tolstoy says that for some reason Nikolay was addressed by the others as 'you', not 'thou'. He told them stories that he invented, three of which Tolstoy never forgot: 'Farfaron Hill' (Far far on? Nikolay was no doubt learning English), 'The Ant-Brothers', and 'The Little Green Stick'. He told them that if they fulfilled certain conditions he would lead them up the Farfaron Hill, and when they got to the top they would have any wish granted to them. But they had to swear to keep it a secret. The first condition was to stand in a corner and not to think of a white bear: Leo tried hard but could not

prevent himself from thinking of the white bear. The second
was to walk along the crack between two boards without stepping off it; the third, an easy one, Leo thought, was not to see
a hare for a whole year, alive, dead or fried. The second story
was 'The Ant-Brothers'. (The word *ant* in Russian is *muravey*,
and Tolstoy thought that his brother must have mixed up the
Moravian Brothers, a religious sect which flourished in the sixteenth century, with what he had read about Masons, their
mysterious ceremonies and their efforts to make all mankind
happy.) Nikolay promised that they would become 'muravey
brothers', and then there would be no more unpleasantness or
quarrels, and all would love one another. Leo loved that story;
it reminded him of an ant-hill. Nikolay's chief secret, he told
them, was written on a little green stick, it was the secret of how
to make people happy for ever, and the stick was buried on the
edge of the ravine in the old Zakaz forest. Tolstoy asked to be
buried in that place, in memory of Nikolay. The boys used to
play a game in which they and the little girls sat under chairs,
fenced around with pillows and covered with shawls, and pre-
tended to be 'ant-brothers'. 'Sometimes we talked about whom,
and what, each one loved, what is needed for happiness, how
we were going to live and love everyone.' Sometimes they sat
on the chairs, made them into a carriage, and turned into
travellers. 'That was very very good, and I thank God that I
could play like that. We called it a game, whereas everything
else in the world is a game except that.'

And so Tolstoy was fostered in early childhood by love and
fear, as Wordsworth was 'fostered alike by beauty and fear'.
Like Aksakov, De Quincey, and Proust, he had experienced
great love before the age of seven, a love that outlasted all other
loves.

Compare the old man's memories of games with these games
in his book *Childhood*. One day, after they had been out with
the hunt, the younger children wanted to play games, but the
eldest boy Volodya was condescending, and this spoiled
Nikolenka's pleasure. 'I knew myself that not only could one
not shoot a bird with a stick, but one could not even fire at all.
It was just play. But if one were to reason like that, it would
not even be possible to ride on chairs; and I think Volodya

himself remembers how in the long winter evenings we covered an armchair with a shawl to make a carriage of it; one of us sat in front as the coachman, another behind as the footman, the girls were in the middle, three chairs were the horses – and we started on the journey! . . . If one goes by reality there can be no games. And if there are no games – what will be left?'

The Narrator, Nikolenka, is ten years old, a big boy, not a child of five; the elder brother Volodya is blasé and makes Nikolenka sad by scorning games. A common enough experience in adolescence. The chief person in his real memories, the eldest brother Nikolay, is not there at all, nor are his wonderful stories. The young Tolstoy had no more access to his important early memories than Aksakov or De Quincey had. He had a conscious memory of the importance of games, but not the heart of the memories; nor the ability, at that time, to deal in fiction with the most unforgettable person in his life, his brother Nikolay. Uncorrected and unpolished, these memories are very important to us. But they are pale, because he has already lived in them and transmuted them: they are memories of memories.

The autobiography never got written nor could it have been. He had ploughed and harrowed the field of his memories thoroughly – a book, as Proust says, is a great cemetery – and Tolstoy had laid his memories in their graves. Wordsworth defines poetry as emotion recollected in tranquillity, meaning live emotions, new, not those which have been taken into the conscious mind, looked at again and again, rationalized, and expressed in words.

So Tolstoy wrote down only his early memories of childhood for Biryukov. He inserted some later ones, but these became rarer and rarer as the biography progressed. Tolstoy never stopped being amazed by the contradictions and complexities of life. He continued to feel, just as in his infant memory, that he was weak and 'they' were strong, even when to many Russians he was a second Tsar, because the Tsar dared not imprison him but only his followers. The contradictions in his opinions, on his writings, family life, religion, are only so bewildering because most people feel constrained not to change their views, or at least not to say so frankly.

De Quincey said: 'Man is doubtless *one* by some *subtle* nexus, some system of links, that we cannot perceive, extending from the new-born infant to the superannuated dotard: but as regards many affections and passions incident to his nature at different stages, he is *not* one, but an intermitting creature, ending and beginning anew; the unity of man, in this respect, is co-extensive only with the particular stage to which the passion belongs.'

When Aksakov was writing his last books, in the fifties of last century, and Tolstoy his first, Russian literature was only as many decades old as French and English were centuries. Aksakov was a contemporary of Pushkin, Tolstoy of Aksakov, Chekhov of Tolstoy. Perhaps the most remarkable phenomenon of that remarkable period was that Dostoyevsky was writing *The Brothers Karamazov* while Tolstoy was writing *Anna Karenina*. The common feature of all great periods – Italian Renaissance art, German music, Dutch painting, and science of our own time – is that even the humblest contributor has a purpose, and his work fits into the great edifice. When the old Tolstoy was very ill, Chekhov, half his age and with little time to live, wrote to his friend Menshikov in January 1900: 'I am afraid of Tolstoy's death. It would leave a great void in my life. I have loved no man as I have him . . . when there is a Tolstoy in the world of literature, it becomes a fine and easy thing to be a man of letters . . . Tolstoy's position is solid, his authority is immense, and as long as he is alive literary bad taste – pretensions and sentimental vulgarity, and all the frustrated little egos – will remain out of sight, hidden in the shadows.'

# PROUST

## 1. The Conception of *A la Recherche*

TOLSTOY, towards the end of his life, wanted to write his autobiography, the true story of his life. Proust began where Tolstoy ended: he started to write *Jean Santeuil* at the age of twenty-four, and claimed that it contained 'the very essence' of his life. The world did not know of this book till some thirty years after Proust's death, when Bernard de Fallois, who had been given free access to Proust's papers by his niece Mme Mante, discovered the manuscript and pieced it together. When, in addition, he edited Proust's *Contre Saint-Beuve*, he made a greater contribution to our understanding of Proust than all the memoirs put together.

Since *Jean Santeuil* is not pure autobiography but an autobiographical novel, Proust was not bound by facts, and at the same time could use his real memories. He was a homosexual, and before he started on *Jean Santeuil* he had had his first affair, with Reynaldo Hahn, which George Painter dates to 1894. But Jean is heterosexual. Proust was a half-Jew, and this had a profound effect on his life. Dreyfus had been accused of treason and condemned to life imprisonment before Proust began *Jean Santeuil*. Proust's father believed that Dreyfus was guilty, while he himself felt passionately about the affair and called himself the first Dreyfusard. His mother, a Jewish woman, was undoubtedly on her son's side but, being a loyal wife in the old-fashioned Jewish tradition, she kept her sympathies balanced between her husband and her son in this matter, as in many others. Jean is a pure gentile. Proust was a dedicated writer, but of Jean we are told in the introduction that he was 'without talent for any of the arts'.

Had Proust died before writing *A la Recherche du Temps Perdu* it is doubtful if *Jean Santeuil*, assuming that someone had pieced it together, would have achieved the fame of De Quincey's original *Confessions of an English Opium-Eater*, or of Tolstoy's *Boyhood and Youth*; not because Proust did not revise the book, but because he had attempted too much. If he had made a selection, as De Quincey and Tolstoy did, *Jean Santeuil* would have been a work of art. There are chapters in *Jean Santeuil* never surpassed in *A la Recherche*: his earliest memory of demanding his mother's kiss, for instance. The theme of involuntary memories is there: the young Proust already had a long experience of such memories, from childhood on, and felt no inhibition in writing about them. This theme is necessary for the understanding of the structure of *A la Recherche*.

Jean sometimes becomes 'I' in the middle of a paragraph, so it seems quite permissible to call 'Jean' Proust. One cannot claim with absolute certainty that all Jean Santeuil's memories are Marcel Proust's, but one can establish some of the factual truth with the help of a good biography like George Painter's. And here is what Proust himself wrote of *Jean Santeuil*: 'Should I call this book a novel? It is something less, perhaps, and yet much more, the very essence of my life, with nothing extraneous added, as it developed through a long period of wretchedness.'[1]

Proust's childhood was spent in an apartment in Paris, but in spring and summer the family used sometimes to go and stay at Auteuil, a suburb, with Mme Proust's uncle. But they spent many springs at Illiers, staying with Dr Proust's relations. These visits came to an end when Marcel was thirteen, because his father thought that the Loire district was bad for Marcel's health: he had been afflicted with asthma from the age of nine. May at Illiers (Etreuilles in *Jean Santeuil*) was a month in which there was hardly a garden without a lilac bush in flower. To the child they made every house magnificent. But even more than the lilac it was the pink hawthorn and the apple blossom which meant so much to Marcel, then and throughout his life. The reason why neither the white pear blossom nor the pink Pennsylvania rose could compare with the apple blossom, Proust says, 'lies deep in the heart'. The apple blossom to him was like 'an individual whom we love, for whom no one else in the world can act as a substitute'.[2] Flowers in his childhood memories are as precious as July sunshine in De Quincey's, or fishes in Aksakov's.

But Marcel was not content with his love for apple blossom: he felt 'that there is more hidden underneath, that our pleasure is something deeper'; he felt as if the flowers 'hold a message for the spirit, are, as it might be, the very form and body of some period in our lives with which we have just renewed a contact and can recognize'.[3] When he was at Etreuilles Jean 'felt happy almost before he felt awake, his eyes having caught sight of the sunlight's golden splashes on the table'. He would dress quickly, run into the garden to say good morning to the gardener, and delight in the glory of sunlight and flowers. Back at school in Paris, during a boring hour, the sunlight striking the blackened desks, scored by the penknives of innumerable boys, charmed him and he recovered for a moment 'all the sweet loveliness of childhood'.[4] This happened without his making any conscious effort to remember, 'without having first to see in memory our games, the garden in which we played, the health, that were then ours'.[5]

When the young Proust tells us this memory of childhood came to him, in the boring hour at school, without his making a conscious effort of the will and intelligence to bring back the sunlight and garden, he has already outpaced most auto-biographers' asides on the nature of involuntary memories. 'Why the gold and level beams on blackened desks so charm us, we cannot say'; but he does not leave it at that: 'The sunlight on all shadowed things, even on those that lurk in corners of mean rooms, can bring us just as much happiness as the colours on rich stuffs.' What he has not yet done is to connect the sun-light on the table at Etreuilles, the sensation in which the happiness of childhood was preserved, with the golden beams on the blackened desk. He makes further great progress when living in his memories of pink hawthorn at Etreuilles. 'There is something in us that lies more deep than aesthetic appreciation': though M. de Montesquiou could, by a remark about the flower in his buttonhole, 'set him on fire with passion for the moss-rose, the deep blue of the gentian, and the rich pig-mentation of the cineraria', his love for the pink hawthorn was something different, something which was part of him, 'embedded in a moment of the past which still lives on, intact and fresh, in some forgotten corner.'[6] He had so many different memories of the pink hawthorn: which particular experience, he asks, made the flower so special? The answer eluded him, but again it is the question he asks which is remarkable: was the pink hawthorn part of one of his painful, disturbing experiences? We have seen that the memories of Aksakov, De Quincey, Dickens, Tolstoy, all contained a disturbance, varying from a mild alert to a bad shock. When an autobiographer has recovered many early memories he generally recovers, as we have seen, the shock and the sensations in which each memory is preserved, but in some the shock is absent, and the memory is then only a precious fragment. This is what Proust's pink hawthorn was. It remained a fragment until he used it in *A la Recherche*.

Marcel's love of the pink hawthorn is part of a very important experience: in *Swann's Way* he is out for a walk with the others in Swann's park when he sees it, and he sees Gilberte also, for the first time. But she and Swann and the park are all creations of Proust's imagination. He uses his precious fragment as a jeweller a pearl which he places in a setting of his making. In *Within a Budding Grove* Marcel is out walking with Andrée when he comes across a bare hawthorn bush: he says he is 'touched by an exquisite memory of childhood'. No mention of Swann's park, or Gilberte, nothing of the setting his imagination had created earlier. He has gone back to his real memory, but unable to unveil the whole of it, and left with a precious fragment, he becomes, for once, sentimental, and starts a conversation with the leaves: 'I asked them for news of the flowers ... "The young ladies have been gone from here for a long time now" the leaves told me.'[7]

Aksakov's and De Quincey's memories are better written than Proust's in *Jean Santeuil*, but unlike them he is not content with passing observations about them, but applies himself to understanding them like a scientist. Here is an example. 'Jean, when he was quite old, expecting nothing more of life,' living in a city, 'sleeping badly, waking miserably', could recover the sweetness of childhood without making any conscious effort:

'he opened his eyes and saw the sunlight on the floor and it seemed, as of old, that happiness was something he could clutch and hold'.[8] On his way to work 'his smiling eyes were filled with the vision of the flowerdecked past'. And 'at such times, Jean knew so much happiness that he seemed about to faint. It was as though all life were standing still.'[9] The young Proust already knew the experience of regaining lost time, and that time in a memory appears to stand still, in other words is stretched compared to time measured by a clock. 'When he was alone in his room, and the distant sound of a hammer reached him, it seemed to him that he had just come back from a long walk at Etreuilles, and at such moments it was enough for someone to pass him a musty-smelling book, like the one that stood in the Curé's study, for his head to swim.'

This is not a unique experience: many an autobiographer living in his past knows it. Sitting in my room in London, my early childhood in Russia, more than forty-five years old, became more real to me than the sight of the room I was in; and one involuntary memory was followed by another, till they lit up a whole area. I was in my early fifties at that time, but Proust was in his twenties.

After working for four years on *Jean Santeuil*, Proust put it aside without revising it. But he did not stop working: he spent three years on another book, of which only a fragment is left. Before he began *A la Recherche* he had been working on yet another book: *By Way of Saint-Beuve*. It is as important to our understanding of *A la Recherche* as Tolstoy's last draft is for *War and Peace*. There is in it an expanding understanding of the nature of involuntary memories. The most important are the three memories in the Prologue.[10] In the first he dips, by chance, a piece of toast in his tea and this brings him back his childhood; in the second he steps on two uneven paving stones and the memory of Venice comes back to him; in the third a train journey comes back to him: the sound of a spoon knocking against a plate, which resembles the noise of the linesmen's hammers tapping the wheels when the train halted at a station, brings him back the whole journey. Add to these three one more, the feel of a napkin at the Guermantes's party which brings back Balbec, and you have the four memories which are the pillars on which the whole structure of *A la Recherche* rests, or at least did so in Proust's original conception of the novel.

The three memories of the Prologue did not come to Proust at the beginning of his work on *By Way of Sainte-Beuve*, but only after he had been living and working on the memories in that book for some time. This is very significant: I have shown that only after Aksakov had been working for some years on his boyhood memories, much earlier memories, completely new to him, came back. Proust laid aside *By Way of Sainte-Beuve* and within a short time he began *A la Recherche*.

How did Proust 'translate' his real memory (as he gives it in *By Way of Sainte-Beuve*) of dipping a piece of toast in tea into the madeleine? For the dry toast he substituted a plump little cake with a beautiful name, ' "petites madeleines" which look as though they had been moulded in the fluted scallop of a pilgrim's shell'.[11] In Proust's real memory this is what happened: 'as soon as I put it in my mouth . . . something came over me – the smell of geraniums and orange-blossom, a sensation of extraordinary radiance and happiness'.[12] He realizes that it is a memory of his uncle's garden at Auteuil, and remembers that when he used to go and say good morning to his grandfather he used to give him a piece of his toast soaked in tea. In the madeleine memory, for the garden at Auteuil is substituted Combray, and for the grandfather Aunt Léonie. The change from the real memory to the invented one is a change of evanescent circumstances. Every novelist does that. But it is when Proust begins to alter the heart of his memory that he makes one uneasy. In the memory of the piece of toast, the garden at Auteuil comes back as soon as he tastes the toast, but in the madeleine memory 'an exquisite pleasure had invaded my senses but individual, detached, with no suggestion of its origin'.[13] He takes another mouthful and a third, he analyses his feelings: 'I put down my cup and examined my own mind . . . I decide to make it reappear. I retrace my thoughts to the moment at which I drank my first spoonful of tea . . . I compel my mind to make one further effort, and follow and recapture once again the fleeting sensation.'

There is not one example in *Jean Santeuil* or *By Way of*

*Sainte-Beuve* of such a conscious effort. One cannot will an involuntary memory any more than an inspiration. Even today, when I know what made Proust depart from his real experience, I still say to Marcel: 'You'll never recapture that memory.'

The second feature of the madeleine memory is an exaggeration which is exasperating. Compare the expression of joy in Proust's real memory to Marcel's. Proust talks of 'the extraordinary radiance and happiness' which came with the taste of the toast: Marcel says, 'I had ceased to feel mediocre, accidental, mortal.' To Proust the memory restored only the garden at Auteuil, to Marcel the whole of his childhood at Combray.

We know that Marcel is an ageing man who has been living, through sleepless nights, in memories of his past – the whole of his active life – when the madeleine memory comes back to him and he is puzzled by 'this unremembered state'.[14] Just as a writer who has himself had many experiences of love from adolescence onwards may err when imagining an old man in love for the first time, by making the experience too different from his own, so did Proust err in imagining Marcel's experience of the madeleine. He made an involuntary memory, familiar to himself, indeed a universal experience, into a miracle.

A miracle did happen to Proust at that time, but it was not the experience of an involuntary memory bringing back a moment of childhood; it was the miracle of the conception of the original plot of *A la Recherche*.

'For a long time I used to go to bed early' is the opening sentence of the novel. Sometimes, waking at midnight, after a heavy sleep which completely relaxed his consciousness, he did not know where he was, and at first was not even sure who he was; but then memory 'would come like a rope let down from heaven to draw me up out of the abyss of not-being'.

At first it would be the memory not of the place in which he was but of places where he had lived, rooms in which he had slept. A room would be brought back by the position of his body, before the brain had collected enough impressions to identify it (for our memories are fixed in sensations) 'and my body, the side upon which I was lying, loyally preserved from the past an impression which my mind should never have forgotten, brought back before my eyes the glimmering flame of the night-light in its bowl of Bohemian glass': Marcel is back in childhood in his room at Combray.

Marcel tells us 'as a rule I did not attempt to go to sleep again at once but used to spend the greater part of the night recalling our life in the old days at Combray with my great aunt, at Balbec, Paris, Doncières, Venice, and the rest':[15] in fact his entire past. The memories did not follow a straight line; for instance, some memories of Combray, 'of melancholy and wakeful evenings' waiting for his mother's kiss came to life, while other hours at Combray did not. He could have brought them back, he says, with will and intelligence, but such memories would have contained little of the living past, and so would have been of no interest to him. After a long lapse of time, the accidental dipping of a piece of madeleine brought him back the memory of his Aunt Leonie who used to give him a piece of cake dipped in tea on Sundays, and out of it the rest of Combray sprang to life. And so, in his sleepless nights, he continued to live in the past 'remembering again all the places and people that I had known, what I had actually seen of them, and what others had told me'.

In the early pages of the novel, Marcel tells us that he would wake at night, sometimes in his bedroom at Combray, at other times 'I was in my room in Mme de Saint-Loup's house in the country'[16] – that is in Tansonville. You would have to read through thousands of pages to get to Tansonville – in *Time Regained*! After Tansonville he goes into a sanatorium.

The first version of the novel was completed in 1912, but only the first volume of three was published before the 1914 war. The second volume exists in proof, the third is lost. In the definitive version Proust made many additions to the unpublished parts of the first version. From Proust's original list of chapter headings, and other notes, we know that his visit to Tansonville, his entry to a sanatorium, and his visit to the Guermantes when he returns to Paris, must have occurred in the lost last volume of the original, as they do in the last part of the definitive version – *Time Regained*.

In the first version Proust's original plan is clear: he begins to live in his memories only after Tansonville, that is after the end of his active life. We are not told for how many years he has continued to live in his memories, or where he has been all the time. All we know is that when he returns to Paris from the sanatorium, having no more faith in himself as a writer, he finds an invitation to an afternoon party with music at the house of the Prince de Guermantes.

At the party, Marcel stumbles as he steps on two uneven paving stones, and immediately all his discouragement disappears. 'The happiness which I had just felt was unquestionably the same as that which I had felt when I tasted the madeleine soaked in tea.'[17] The madeleine had been an 'unremembered state', but this time he knows at once that his joy is due to a memory. 'Merely repeating the movement was useless.' But that is what he did when he tasted the madeleine: he took another mouthful, and another. What he needed now was to forget the Guermantes's reception, and to recapture the sensation which had accompanied the movement. And then, all at once he remembers that he had the same sensation of two uneven paving stones in the Baptistry of St Mark. And just as the madeleine had recalled Combray so the uneven paving stones recall Venice.

Next, a servant, in his effort not to make a noise, knocks a spoon against a plate. The sound brings Marcel the same sort of felicity as the uneven paving stones, but this time the sensation is 'entirely different: heat combined with a whiff of smoke and relieved by the cool smell of a forest background'.[18] The sound was similar to the sound of the linesman's hammer tapping the wheels when the train which was taking Marcel to Paris, stopped at a station.

Then a servant offers Marcel a napkin, and no sooner has he wiped his mouth on it than 'a new vision of azure passed before my eyes',[19] and this time it was the sea at Balbec that spread out before his eyes. The feel of the napkin was similar to that of a towel on which he had tried to dry himself before the open window on the first day of his arrival at Balbec, and the sensation brought him back that moment. 'The impression was so strong that the moment I was living seemed to me one with the past.'

To go back to my analogy: to Marcel, the ageing man, the experience of the madeleine, an experience of a first involuntary memory, was like a first love to an old man, an 'unremembered state', his feelings are exaggerated, and to all of us who have known love his attempt to grasp the phenomenon is jejune. But the experience at the Guermantes's party is quite different: he has earlier experiences with which to compare it, the madeleine, and other moments of inspiration, and is overjoyed to find that his past is still alive in him. If out of the taste of the madeleine, a fragment of a memory, the whole of Combray sprang, the three Guermantes memories, which are whole memories of widely different periods (Balbec of his youth, Venice of almost the end of his active life, the train journey of a recent event) assured him that his past contained the material of a work of art.

I have for years preferred the three Guermantes memories to the madeleine, if for no other reason than that they come closer to the involuntary memories of other writers. But only when I learned that they were written at the same time did it dawn on me what Proust was up to: he was drawing a pattern as clear as an architect's plan, the madeleine in the entrance, and the three Guermantes memories at the exit.

Proust makes the Guermantes memories even more of a miracle than the madeleine: they all come to Marcel by chance, in half an hour. But in *By Way of Sainte-Beuve* we find that his three involuntary memories came back to Proust in about a year. Nor must we forget that they came when he had been writing, translating memories, for some twenty years, unlike Marcel who had merely been remembering. And now – a miracle – Marcel is ready to start on a work of art.

But we have just read a work of art! Yes, but Marcel has not written it, he has not even tried to write one, he has not done any work: what we have read were memories in which he had been living in his sleepless nights.

Let us imagine what kind of book Marcel is going to write, after the Guermantes's party. Clearly he will not be content to transfer to paper the memories of those sleepless nights, even if it were possible. We know the material of his past life: now Marcel will try to 'translate' it into a work of art, just as Marcel Proust translated his memories, which we find in *Jean Santeuil* and *By Way of Sainte-Beuve*, into *A la Recherche*. If Marcel had ever written that book we might have had some surprises. For just as Marcel Proust, a homosexual, 'translated' his experiences into those of Marcel, a heterosexual, and just as Proust never stopped working while Marcel never got down to work, so Marcel might have created a Narrator who was a homosexual and who slaved away for years on a work of art!

But we are wasting our time: Proust had no intention that we should see Marcel's novel: Proust has reached his goal when Marcel is ready to write it.

## 2. *Swann's Way*

IN *Jean Santeuil* we have wonderful portraits of Proust's parents as the young artist saw them. When the family are planning to go to Etreuilles for Easter, M. Santeuil says: 'It won't be at all warm; Easter's early this year.'[1] And then something very important is revealed to us about Jean's parents: 'On hearing this Mme Santeuil, who had plenty of taste in matters of literature, much practical good sense in the ordinary affairs of life, a fund of humour which found expression in the telling of even the simplest story, a gift of tact, warm affections and considerable skill in the running of a household; but was ignorant in matters of meteorology, geography, statistics, and others of the sciences, was always amazed that M. Santeuil should know that Easter would be early in any given year and found in this evident proof of his superiority yet one more reason for silently renewing her admiring praise and for reaffirming that vow of docile obedience which she had once registered in the secret places of her heart.'[2]

M. Santeuil was a Permanent Assistant Director of Letters. 'If this position brought him honour, it was also a constant source of anxiety. No one was more frequently asked to exert his influence for persons anxious to have reserved carriages on the railways; no one was more often called upon to represent the Government at the funeral services of Marshals of France', and so on. Such distinction 'did more than impress his wife – it filled her with amazement'[3]; we are amused, but the child Jean was not: he was puzzled.

'I think Jean will have a feeling for poetry,' Mme Santeuil said with a timid look on her face. M. Santeuil was not interested in that, but later, watching the Newhaven boat going out, he said, ' "I should dearly like to have a little house at the seaside and spend many months of the year there" . . . "How you *do* love Nature!" said Mme Santeuil who, all this while, had been savouring the look of happiness in her husband's eyes, "I really do believe that if Jean turns out to have a feeling for poetry it will be because he takes after you!" '⁴

Proust was writing one book all his life, and what he tells of his parents in *Jean Santeuil*, he will not repeat later. There is realism and humour in the young Proust's picture of his parents and his relationship with them. The fun he makes of his parents comes out of a child's resentment. He was not very good at sharing his mother; neither was Jean: 'He longed . . . to hold prisoner for hours within his kiss . . . the whole existence of that being in relation to whom he saw all things.'⁵ Though the father and mother were very different people – M. Santeuil was 'weaker than his wife, more violent and yet softer'⁶ – they presented a united front to the child. He had conflicts with them. He had taken a virtuous decision and was on his way to bring his parents the good tidings, but as 'unfortunately not everybody thinks the same thing at the same moment'⁷ instead of a happy meeting 'there was a violent collision'. This happened after he had just completed a set of Latin verses and, delighting in his resolution, freely made, to do more work in future, bumped into an angry father and was told that he was going to be 'taken away from his school and sent to the Lycée Henri IV' – a prison to him. Misunderstood and discouraged, he shed tears of self-pity. ' "If life is like this," he said to himself, ". . . if human beings thus impose their decisions on those who have changed without their knowing it, while those decisions were in the making, if every moment is fraught with the danger of their being so far beside the mark, of their stifling a good intention . . . then this world is too complicated a place for me, and life too hard a thing." '⁸ After many decades, at the last party, Proust again returns to this idea: 'the internal time-pieces which are allotted to different human beings are by no means synchronized.'⁹

Proust was not sent to the terrible Lycée Henri IV: he was not bound by facts in writing an autobiographical novel, any more than Tolstoy was in writing *Boyhood*. There were other disagreements between Jean and his parents, but in the end, in a chapter called 'Parents in Old Age', Proust reveals profound understanding of them. M. Santeuil had been a very practical

man and had accumulated many honours, but in his old age
(when Proust was writing, his father was in his early sixties) he
turned more and more to people whom he had earlier regarded
as being 'slightly touched', people 'for whom admiration for a
poet, the table-talk of a novelist, and fondness for a favourite
son meant more than honours.'[10] He did not know what to say
to such people, and could do nothing but laugh; and when
Jean was young he easily 'shattered' his father's laugh – his
'poor little weapon' – in a moment of anger. But now he bitterly regretted it: the laugh had been his father's only weapon
'against follies and modernisms and an attitude to life which he
could not understand'; underneath it was kindness, 'surprise in
which there was no touch of arrogance, and pity for what he
considered to be pure folly, though he was never altogether
sure that it might not be a mark of superior ability'.

M. Santeuil 'developed a new delicacy in his attitude to his
wife'.[11] He was now more sensitive to her feelings, and the way
he remembered the days gone by, and especially her parents,
made his wife feel 'that what he had said had been a special
tribute of kindliness to her, and an act of piety to them'.[12] This
maturer Jean is no longer astonished at his mother's admiration
for his father: she had been right all along, and now felt
justified in adopting permanently an attitude of humility where
he was concerned.

There is not one thread of sentimentality or melodrama in
Jean's tribute to his parents. In his struggling youth and busy
practical maturity his father had 'had no time for the art of
dreaming. Old age was for him what youth is for others – a
time of illusion.'

Like all great writers Proust surprises us, and this is followed
by surprise that we have been surprised. This boring old M.
Santeuil, with his uninspired observations about nature, his
habit of precision, is still to all appearances the same, still
exhibiting his knowledge, still explaining to his wife everything
they saw. But these old conventional signs 'had become a
system of notations . . . for conveying the soft and almost poetic
sensations which he felt.' So the mother had not been far wrong
when she said long before that if Jean turned out to have a
feeling for poetry, it would be because he took after his father.

In *Swann's Way*, ten years after he had laid aside *Jean Santeuil* and after his parents had died, Proust did not go over the same ground again. There was not much he had to add to the portraits of his parents in *Jean Santeuil*. You will know a great deal about Combray before you learn that Marcel's father has much the same kind of knowledge as Jean's, and that the mother is as admiring. But Marcel is not puzzled, is not irritated; on the contrary he is delighted. Marcel has the understanding of the parents' marriage which Proust had reached at the end of *Jean Santeuil*.

*Jean Santeuil* began with Jean's memory of the evening when his mother, for the first time, did not go up to say goodnight to him in bed. Marcel's oldest memories are of the drama of going to bed at Combray. At once there is a striking difference. Jean's memory is of one particular evening, the first, when his parents had decided that they must stop mollycoddling him. Marcel's memory is not of a first occasion. Jean's parents had spoiled him because of his delicate health, but now that he was seven, they make a new rule, that the mother will not go up to say good night to him when he is in bed. We have here the characteristics of an early memory: the child is seven, and the first occasion when the mother is not coming to say goodnight is a very disturbing experience. We are not told how old Marcel is, but he is certainly older than Jean.

Compare the 'plots' of Jean's and Marcel's memories. At Combray, as the afternoons ended, Marcel's melancholy and anxious thoughts used to centre on his bedroom, where he would have to lie alone, unable to go to sleep. His sole consolation was that his Mamma would come and kiss him good night after he was in bed. But on the evenings when they had visitors she did not come up, and he had to kiss her good night before going upstairs. On that particularly miserable evening, which Marcel remembered always, they had their usual visitor, M. Swann, and as Marcel was waiting to give his kiss to his mother the grandfather remarked that he looked tired, and the father, in his usual arbitrary way, sent him off to bed without even that one kiss.

Jean used to feel, as soon as it began to grow dark, that the whole world was abandoning him, and his only consolation was

that his mother would come to say good night to him: her kiss
was a gift of peace. Then, and then only, could he sleep. On
this particular evening Jean had come for the third time to say
good night to his mother. His parents were entertaining an
important visitor, Professor Surlande, and he had been ill
received.

The evening that Jean remembered so well was a very special
one: it was the *first* evening that his mother was *not* going to
come up to kiss him good night. His memory has its beginning in
an external event: his mother's decision that 'A boy of seven
*must* learn to go to sleep alone.'[13] Very probably she had already
told him so, and to him her decision was harsh and, what is
more, he was afraid that he would be deprived of her goodnight
'on each succeeding night'.

Jean makes an attempt to go to sleep, and from the garden
they see the light go out in his room. But he cannot sleep, nor
can he help blaming his mother for causing him pain. His first
idea of calling her he drives away, afraid to displease her. He
feels responsible for his agitation, his sadness and tears, but
lacks strength to master them. He hears the old servant,
Augustin, and calls to him, but the man, used to the boy's nerves,
pretends he has not heard. Jean is now facing ordinary reality:
he gets suddenly annoyed and, afraid Augustin will go out of
earshot, calls him louder: 'Augustin, I may tell you in a moment
to fetch Mamma.' He does not dare to ask 'If I ask you to fetch
Mamma, will you?', in case he is refused. The servant says he
cannot disturb Madame when she has an important visitor,
that she would scold him. 'She would not scold you if it was I
who had told you to go,' Jean is quick to answer. Like Hamlet,
Jean is competent in dealing with the world though not with
his own conflict, and when the servant refuses to go Jean says
angrily ' "You will if I tell you, but for the time being I am not
telling you. Go away and let me try to sleep. Good night,
Augustin." "Goodnight, Master Jean." This final friendly
exchange did something to sweeten the bitterness with which
Augustin's obstinacy had filled Jean's heart.'

After Augustin has gone, Jean does not want to sleep. He
gets up and goes to the window: the moon like a lamp sheds
light on his mother, his father and the professor. 'All of a

sudden the guilty desire which had been haunting his loneliness, to call to his mother from the window, appeared to him in a different light, as something very simple and natural. His mother was down there; she could be with him in a moment. He made up his mind. He felt calm and the sense of his calmness reassured him though he fully realized the gravity of what he was about to do.' And then he opens the window and calls out to her, 'Mamma, I want you for a moment.'

Jean has just had a battle of wits and will with Augustin, and the grown-up man had been firm but not unkind. It was the child's contact with a manageable reality which freed him for a moment from irrational feelings, and that is how it came about, I believe, that his 'guilty desire . . . to call his mother' appeared suddenly 'as something simple and natural'.

His mother has been talking and thinking about her child all the evening; she believes that she must be firm because 'being spoiled will make life very hard for him when he is older'. She is annoyed when the light in the child's room goes on again; she decides to go up, but waits, hoping that Jean will put the light out. When, instead, he calls her, she rises in a panic. Her father M. Sandré, warns her not to give in, but her husband says: 'If she doesn't go up he'll never go to sleep, and we shall feel the disturbance much more in an hour's time.' And that is the last we hear of the father. The grandfather goes on arguing against her breaking the new rule, but she says to him: 'These prolonged nervous crises are the worst thing possible for his health. I'm sorry, I've got to go up.'

His mother comes, and 'in the warmth of her kiss, all his nervous agitation melted in sweetness and tears. "Oh, Mamma, my head's hot and my feet are cold and I can't sleep." She took his feet in her hands and rubbed them, though not too softly for fear of tickling him.' All is well, but just as she is going, and after he has already said 'Goodnight, darling Mamma, and thank you', an irrational fear of losing her, the fear 'that this time he could not make her come back', deprives him of all his self-control, and he runs after her, clings to her, and torn between his awareness of doing wrong and 'the despair which would follow her departure', bursts into a fit of sobbing. 'This time his mother was really angry, determined to go, determined to scold him. His sobs redoubled. He let go of her and lay rolling about on his bed with a feeling of tightness in his chest, uttering little cries and using the violence which remorse was turning against himself to bring his misdemeanour to a head. Then he lay down again beneath the blankets.'[14]

And this is the effect it had on his mother: 'And his mother, saddened by the suffering of her son, by the feeling that she could do nothing to cure him, by this relapse on the very day she had hoped that he would go to sleep without her, by the accumulated effect of all the years of his nervous ailments and vexed, too, at having to leave the doctor and her husband alone together, settled herself down beside his bed.'

Augustin comes in. 'Jean, who had wiped his eyes at the sound of the man's approach, glorying in the power he exercised over his mother, which Augustin seemed to have doubted . . . directed at the intruder a smile of happy triumph to which the feeling of dazzling and admitted superiority imparted a touch of affectionate good will.'

We are angry at the speed with which the little beast recovers, but we know that a child's survival is in this gift to change so rapidly; but above all we feel the real living relationship between Jean and Augustin. Augustin asks, 'Is there anything I can do for you, Ma'am, I trust Master Jean is not ill?' Before she answers, our attention is turned at once to the quick reaction of the child, his smile of triumph. And only afterwards comes the mother's answer: ' "You see, Augustin, Master Jean does not know what is the matter with him, nor what he wants," said Mme Santeuil, sadly. "He is suffering from nerves." '

Soon after Jean's little triumph over Augustin, and after his mother has stumbled on the ingenious way of taking off the child's sense of guilt, by blaming all on his nerves, Jean goes to sleep. When, years later, the sound of his childish screams echoed in his ears there mingled with them his mother's words to Augustin, 'he is suffering from nerves', words 'which had brought such happiness to Jean, because they had laid to the account of nerves . . . the sobs and screams which had caused him such feelings of remorse. That new sense of irresponsibility which his mother then had publicly recognized in the presence

8

of Augustin . . . had acted as a guarantee of his personal existence and assured his future.' This is beyond a child's understanding, this is what the grown-up Proust knew when he lived
in his memory and recaptured the child's relief and his
happiness before he fell asleep.

And now Proust reveals the vital reason for the importance of
this real memory to him. 'The cruel, the prolific struggles'
which Jean had waged against himself ceased on the day when
his mother recognized his fits as unfortunate but not criminal,
when she freed him of his sense of guilt; and not having to fight
himself so hard, 'and as a result of a constant effort, he did at
last force it [his will] to get the upper hand of his nerves.' Can
anyone who knows how Proust worked, in bad health, neurotic,
a homosexual, on a most difficult task – what he calls deciphering the book printed in him by reality – can anyone doubt that
the man had a will of iron?

Jean went on hearing for years the sound of his 'childish
crying which had once been so muffled yet so piercing'. We do
not wonder: we have seen, we have felt his desperate fear of
losing his mother again after she had come and granted his wish
and made him happy, his complete loss of self-control, his
violent fit, and the cruel defeat of the mother. No wonder that
he was never released from his wretchedness, 'for the basic
cause seemed to him always to be so inseparable from himself
that he could have got rid of it only by getting rid of his own
personality'. This 'basic cause', the Orpheus-like fear of losing
a person, places, things, made him later suffer agonies of
jealousy, keep young lovers as prisoners in his flat, and finally
find the solution in preserving people and things in a work of art.

This memory of a child of seven is as perfect as De Quincey's
and Aksakov's of the same age. The recovery of such a memory
greatly increases a person's self-knowledge, and what is truly
remarkable about Proust's feat is that he was only twenty-four,
while the others were old men.

Now let us turn to Marcel's memory, in *Swann's Way*. He had
climbed the hateful staircase against his heart's desire. Once in
his room the bed was like a grave to him, but before burying
himself in it he suddenly took a desperate decision, and wrote
a note to his mother, begging her to come upstairs for an

important reason which he could not put into writing. He was
afraid that Françoise, the maid, might refuse to take it and, to
give himself a chance of success, he tells us, he lied to her saying
that his mother had asked him to send her an answer to some
question. When she returned and told Marcel that his note
would be delivered later his anxiety at once subsided. 'Now I
was no longer separated from her; the barriers were down;
an exquisite thread was binding us. Besides that was not all,
for surely Mamma would come.'

She did not appear, and later sent a message by Françoise:
'There is no answer.' Marcel now felt that he could not go to
sleep without seeing her: telling himself to be calm only increased his agitation. And then, suddenly, all his anxiety had
gone: 'I had formed a resolution to abandon all attempts to go
to sleep without seeing Mamma.'[15]

He was well aware that this would be considered a very grave
fault, for he had been brought up to place at the head of the
list of faults 'yielding to a nervous impulse'. But happen what
might, he would wait up for his mother. Throughout, the
relationship between Marcel and Françoise is different from
that between Jean and Augustin. Jean battles with Augustin
with the cunning and innocence of a child. Marcel tells a direct
lie to get round Françoise. Augustin refuses the child's request
to take a message to his mother: he is firm yet he does not
defeat Jean, and that episode ends by their wishing each
other good night. Françoise takes Marcel's note, but walks out
'with an air of resignation which seemed to imply "what a
dreadful thing for parents to have a child like this" '.

Marcel's mother had never given a thought to the child
during that evening; she did not come after she had received
his note, 'but with no attempt to safeguard my self-respect
(which depended upon her keeping up the fiction that she had
asked me to let her know the result of my search for something
or other) made Françoise tell me, in so many words: "There
is no answer".' And even after the evening had come to an end
and the visitor had gone, and her husband said: 'Well, shall
we go up to bed?', she was not in any hurry: 'I don't feel in the
least like sleeping': she did not remember Marcel at all. But
remembering Françoise, who had been sitting up for her, she

said she would go and get her to unhook her while her husband undressed.

She was the first to see Marcel on the stairs, in miserable agitation, and when he threw himself upon her, she was at first astonished and then angry. But when she heard the father coming, to avoid the scene she thought he would make if he saw the boy, she said in 'a voice half-stifled by her anger: "Run away at once. Don't let your father see you standing there like a crazy Jane!" ' But the father was upon them and at once he grasped the fact of the child's unhappiness, and told the mother to go and stay in Marcel's room for a little. Even then she protested 'we must not make the child accustomed', but he interrupted her, and with his good pragmatic sense told her: 'There is no question of making him accustomed . . . you can see quite well the child is unhappy . . . stay beside him for the rest of the night.'

When Marcel was left alone with his mother he could no longer control himself, and burst into tears. The echo of those tears, he tells us, never ceased. His father had wronged him, when he sent him to bed without his mother's kiss, to which he had a right. But he knew his father 'paid no heed to "Principles" '; Marcel had adjusted himself to that, for he knew that though his father paid no attention to the 'Rights of Man', he was not inexorable; and as we have seen it was he who took pity on him and told the mother to spend the night with the child. Marcel had given way to a 'nervous impulse' on this occasion, to get his mother's kiss but there is no indication that he did not have such experiences many times, before and after that night. He tells us, 'I felt that I had with an impious and secret finger traced the first wrinkle upon her soul.' He talks of his mother having made 'a first concession', and 'that it was a first step down from the ideal she had formed for me, and that for the first time she, with all her courage, had to confess herself beaten'.

But she had only obeyed her husband, which she willingly and usually did; and in any case are we to believe that Marcel got through childhood and reached the age of writing notes and reading novels without ever defeating his mother? When, after settling down to spend the night with the child she is suddenly overcome by tears, and we are told that she 'had never allowed herself to go to any length of tenderness with me', and that 'her anger would have been less difficult to endure than this new kindness which my childhood had not known', we see quite clearly that Marcel's memory has very little in common with Jean's.

Marcel's memory is clearly not that of a child of seven, like Jean's: he might have been ten or eleven. Nor has it the special quality of a real memory of an event which overwhelms a child because it happened for the first time. It has not the artistic integrity of a child's memory. In *Jean Santeuil* Proust managed the disadvantage of writing about a child's memory in the third person by limiting the number of people in the garden to the parents, the grandfather, and one guest, and their conversations and thoughts to matters which intimately concerned the child and were not beyond his grasp. The picture is engraved on Proust's mind; the writing beneath it, as in most early memories, is in code, to be deciphered in maturity. But Marcel hears and remembers things on that special evening which, however precocious a child may be, he would not remember because they are not his concern. Take one example: just before the climax, when the parents are about to go upstairs, Marcel, tense and afraid, hears through the open window what this or that aunt says about matters entirely irrelevant to his experience. All this makes too many holes in the child's memory, like stones in a fishnet, which let the fish get away. It is only after one uncovers Proust's secret drive, which resulted in his transforming such an important memory as Jean's (Proust's) at the age of seven that one is ready to overlook the faults of Marcel's. The secret is in the part played by the grandmother.

In the very first lines we read that Marcel lay 'unsleeping, far from my mother and grandmother'. But we are never given a hint of the grandmother's reactions! Is it likely that on that particular evening she would have played only a walking-on part? Is it credible that Marcel never gave her a thought, as he was looking out of the window on all those present in the garden? I remember, once, going back to make sure that she was there, and reading that when the bell rang his grandmother would be sent out as a scout to see who the visitor was.

In Jean's memory there is no grandmother, and the mother is affected by her father's views, whereas in Marcel's memory the two women, mother and grandmother, who love one another and are so intimate, never exchange a word about Marcel. In the end I realized that the grandmother's dumbness in this memory is of special significance.

So long as I confined myself to the comparison of Jean's memory of his mother's kiss and Marcel's, I had no doubt that I preferred the real to the transformed memory. Proust could have said of this early memory what De Quincey said of his memory of the death of his beloved sister Elisabeth: 'the night which for me gathered upon that event ran after my steps far into life'. To evaluate Marcel's memory, one must first put Proust's own out of one's mind.

The young Proust, in *Jean Santeuil*, drew excellent portraits of his parents. He was primarily concerned with their effect on him, but towards the end of that book he revealed his deep understanding of them. He started *A la Recherche* from there. The father is essentially the same as in *Jean Santeuil*; it is the artist who has matured. He paints him with remarkable detachment, as if he had never been injured by him, nor has ever injured him. He seems equally detached and free to tell the truth about the mother in her relations to other people, whether real people like her husband or her maid, or imaginary like Swann and the Vinteuils. But the relation between the mother and Marcel is new: it is the relation of lovers.

Marcel had imagined, that night at Combray, that if Swann had read his letter to his mother he would have laughed at his anguish. But in due course Marcel learned that Swann had known similar anguish: 'to him that anguish came through Love, to which it is in a sense predestined, by which it must be equipped and adapted; but when, as had befallen me, such an anguish possesses one's soul before Love has yet entered into one's life, then it must drift, awaiting Love's coming, vague and free, without precise attachment, at the disposal of one sentiment today, of another tomorrow, of filial piety or affection of a comrade.'[16] In *Swann in Love*, Proust says that when Odette 'forgot Swann's very existence' she attached him all the more to her, for he was kept in a state of painful agitation. 'And he

did not have (as I had, afterwards, at Combray in my childhood), happy days in which to forget the sufferings that would
return with the night.'

And so the 'painful agitation' of Marcel on that night, when
he waited up for his mother, was the same as Swann's as a
lover. Like all Proust's lovers, the mother is heartless. To his
pleading note she sends the words 'there is no answer' and
during the evening she forgets his existence. Marcel is determined to get her kiss, but afterwards blames her as much as
himself. What made Marcel's suffering so acute was the feeling
that he was completely separated from her, that he did not exist
for her that evening. This must have happened often, for looking
back, he says he had known no kindness in his childhood.

We know that such important experiences as Marcel's long
distance telephone talk with the grandmother, and her death,
are based on his memories of his mother. But such knowledge is
if anything misleading. Undoubtedly his love of his real grandmother, and the close friendship between her and his mother,
helped him by providing a second model for the grandmother
in *A la Recherche*. But the inspiration out of which rose the
character of the grandmother was Proust's need for two
mothers: a mother-lover, who, like all Proust's lovers can be
heartless, and a mother-grandmother whose love reaches the
perfection he was always longing for. In Marcel's childhood
both mothers must be there, but when the mother-lover
dominates the hour, the mother-grandmother is dumb.

So far I have been dealing with Marcel's oldest memories,
contained in the first half of Combray. Here I must give vent to
my amazement that the translator, Scott Moncrieff, whose
translation is such a remarkable achievement, takes it upon
himself to call this part of the book 'Overture'. What audacity,
and how very misleading.

Apart from Marcel, Proust introduced in the first half of
Combray a number of characters of varying importance: the
parents, the maternal grandparents, the maid Françoise, all
very important; the grandfather's cousin, whom they used to
call great-aunt and with whom they used to stay at Combray,
a minor character whose only importance is that she is the
mother of Aunt Léonie; two aunts, sisters of the grandmother,

who are only mentioned in passing twice again in the rest of the book, and whose main function at the beginning is to shed light on Swann. He is the only character not a member of the family. Like Marcel himself, the family circle at Combray is the creation of Proust's imagination. Nothing could be less like Proust's family circle at Illiers.

It is very unlikely, as George Painter says, that the real maternal grandparents ever visited Illiers, on which Combray is modelled. For one thing it is known that the grandfather was very reluctant to spend even a night away from his home in Paris; and though, like many Jews, he may occasionally have made antisemitic remarks, it was quite a different matter to take hospitality from an antisemite, which Proust's uncle at Illiers was. There was plenty of antisemitism in the decade before the Dreyfus case, and it was one thing for a Jew to feel at home in Paris, and quite another at Illiers.

Neither Proust's maternal grandfather's or grandmother's relations had anything to do with Illiers. They were all Jewish people; the grandfather Nathée Weil, a wealthy stockbroker, came from Lorraine. None of them had changed their religion. Marcel's family at Combray belongs to one race, one religion, one class.

Proust's paternal grandfather had kept a shop, but he died long before Marcel was born. The grandmother kept on the shop for eleven years, and then retired and lived in an apartment over a shop in the market place, from which she could watch all the life going on in the town, as Aunt Léonie does from her bedroom. This grandmother he must have known very well, since she lived until Proust was a youth. The Prousts used to stay at Illiers with Dr Proust's sister and his brother-in-law, Jules Amiot. He was a draper, and his shop was in a prominent position in the market place.

Proust described this uncle in *Jean Santeuil* under the name Jules Sureau. He had lived in Algeria as a young man. He was comfortably off; his great passion was gardening. The garden adjoining the house at Illiers is very small, but he had a large pleasure garden, which he called Pré-Catalan, on a little hill on the outskirts of the town. It is still very impressive. It had a pond with carp in it, a great variety of flowers, fountains, fed

by a pump worked by a horse, Uncle Jules's summer house at
the top of the hill, and asparagus and strawberry beds. It was
separated from the lane which ran up the hill by a hedge of
pink and white hawthorn, Proust's most precious flower. This
garden was a great gift to the boy; he also shared his uncle's
passion for food. 'There are baked eggs for lunch today, fillet
of beef with bearnaise sauce and fried potatoes. Do you like
fillet bearnaise?' 'I should think I do, Uncle!' (*Jean Santeuil*).
As for the strawberries which he helped his uncle gather, they
were exquisite, as his mother said. To the man who showed my
husband and me round the garden M. Amiot still loomed large,
as he does in the photograph in the sitting room, with his
brothers: corpulent, strong looking men. 'The garden is not
what it used to be,' he told us, 'M. Amiot was a rich man.'

What a delight Uncle Jules's garden was to the child Proust
brought up in a flat in Paris; what a delight the whole town
must have been!

Illiers still has all the charm of an old small town. Neither a
very large town nor a village can be to a child what a small town
is: the village is not differentiated enough, the large town is not
a whole, it is reduced in the child's mind to one neighbourhood.
Illiers has everything to make it the hub of a child's universe:
a large church, a large market place, streets differing as subtly
as faces, all with gardens at the back, and some in the front as
well; beyond the town a river, a rolling plain, spires and towers
in the distance. With Illiers at the centre, Chartres with its
great cathedral not far off, and Paris on the periphery: it was
all a tangible universe, easily encompassed by a child.

In the streets lying near the market place lived the prosperous
tradesmen, and the notary and the doctor as well. It was in just
such a street that Uncle Amiot's house stood. It was a solidly
middle-class home, with a gardener, and a cook who produced
delicious food.

Proust had written his childhood impressions of Uncle Amiot
in *Jean Santeuil*, but when creating Combray the whole path of
that uncle's life lay before him.

When Proust's father went to Illiers in 1903 to preside at the
prize-giving at the boys' school, M. Amiot was deputy mayor.
Anticlericalism had succeeded his antisemitism. Proust, while

8*

not a political animal, had the sensibilities of an artist to the events of the time, and was as disturbed by anticlericalism as he had been earlier by antisemitism. He said: 'At the present time the socialists commit the same error by being anticlerical as the clericals in 1897 by being anti-Dreyfusard. They expiate their fault today; but we shall expiate ours tomorrow.'[17] This was the last visit of Dr Proust to Illiers: M. Amiot refused to speak to him, and the priest had not been invited to the 'prize-giving! There was no room for Uncle Amiot at Combray. Mr Painter suggests that Uncle Amiot disappears 'since his garden has been made over to Swann'. It is more to the point to connect his disappearance with the appearance of Swann himself.

What made Illiers specially precious to Proust was that his father's family had lived there for centuries. Here he was rooted in the soil of France, and its long history. As Marcel says, 'the name of Combray connotes to me not the little town of today only, but an historic city vastly different, seizing and holding my imagination'.[18] And when we read that Marcel, the child, never reaches the goal 'to which I longed so much to attain, Guermantes itself', we have here the root of Proust's longing to enter and be accepted by the French aristocracy, a need fed from the source of a child's imagination.

The three important characters at Combray which had their roots at Illiers were Marcel's father, Aunt Léonie, and the maid Françoise. This excellent cook and devoted servant, cruel and sentimental, was a 'medieval peasant' who had much in common with the medieval artist: their ideas came 'from a tradition at once ancient and direct, unbroken, oral, degraded, un-recognizable, and alive'.[19] With his Aunt Léonie Marcel had much in common. She was a bed-ridden invalid who 'attached to the least of her sensations an extraordinary importance . . . and, failing a confidante to whom she might communicate them, she used to promulgate them to herself in an unceasing monologue which was her sole form of activity'. In a volume written towards the end of his life, where Marcel has become Marcel Proust, he points out that 'I was beginning to resemble all my relatives'.[20] He was becoming more and more like his Aunt Léonie, and also like his father.

The other important members of the family, the mother, her

parents, Uncle Adolphe, had their roots in Jewish life; Proust turned them into Gentiles and planted them in Combray.

How deep has the assimilation of Marcel's mother and her family to French life gone? The nineteenth century saw the emancipation of Jews in Europe, and though the pace differed greatly from country to country, there were traits and tendencies common to all. Wherever a Jew was given some civil rights, and could get out of the ghetto, the first thing he did was to learn the language of the country. Men needed such knowledge to enter business and the professions, but to women it meant something quite different. In the ghetto the Jewish woman was the rock on which the family was founded, and very often the breadwinner, but she was almost entirely uneducated. While there was practically no illiteracy among men, and every boy was taught Hebrew (even the poorest and quite uneducated people taught the boys at least to read), the women were considered not to need more than to be able to read the prayer book in Yiddish, the spoken vernacular used in the home. As soon as women learned the language of the country they absorbed its literature with passion. Love of literature was characteristic of emancipated women everywhere in Europe, Jews and Gentiles alike, before the universities and the professions were open to them. Literature led a Jewish woman to a double emancipation, as a woman and as a Jewess. It led to an earlier assimilation of women than of men. Moses Mendelssohn and his family are a great example. His was the first generation to come out of the ghetto. He was a Hebrew scholar, and acquired a thorough knowledge of German; he became a friend of Gentile writers, and Lessing portrayed him in his *Nathan der Wise* (later anathema to the Nazis). At home Mendelssohn was a Jew, outside it he was a citizen of Germany. His daughters became passionate lovers of German literature; they made friends with German writers, married Gentiles, and became Christians. The emancipation of Proust's mother did not go nearly as fast or as far: this obedient wife did not give up her religion when she married the Catholic Dr Proust, nor, as far as we know, did he urge her to do so.

We know from biographical sources that she mourned her parents for a whole year, following the Jewish tradition. It was a serious matter with her. When her husband died she kept the three days of his illness and death sacred every month! On these days Proust stayed at home with her. Proust discovered after her father's death that it had left his mother broken-hearted. We learn from *Jean Santeuil* a great deal about her relationship with him. M. Sandré had very strong views on how the grandson should be brought up. He was a very forceful person, had 'a vehement temperament' and a loving heart, and was devoted to his daughter and her family. He dreaded the idea of his grandson becoming a poet. 'To see a young chap dissipate a fortune, amassed honourably by his intelligent and successful father, to see him dragging a name universally respected into the mud, ending up by starving among a lot of good-for-nothing scribblers, was a terrible thought.' Why even the best 'are either spendthrifts like Lamartine or old skinflints like Victor Hugo'.

The mother said, 'Even if I wanted to make him a poet – which God forbid! I am pretty sure that I should not succeed.'[21] She argued that good books would provide food for the boy's mind and refine his feelings. She was trying to pacify her father on this subject, as on many others. It was with her mother that she shared her love of literature: the letters of Mme de Sevigné meant a great deal to them both, and we know that she read Victor Hugo's *Les Contemplations* and Corneille's *Horace*.

The different attitudes to literature of men and women continued into our century, not only in Jewish but also in Gentile families, and not only in the middle class but in the aristocracy as well. Two of my friends in Berlin shared with their mothers the love of poetry and art, which were despised by their fathers, who were Prussian generals and read only military science and history. Marcel's grandfather and grandmother share many of the virtues and prejudices of their class, whether Gentile or Jew. Proust states in *Jean Santeuil*: 'The ideas in which she [the mother] was bred up were those still lively in the mind of M. Sandré, even when he was old.' To a home like his 'no poet would ever have been admitted there, still less, it is needless to point out, an actor . . . One never went to evening parties, nor came home in a cab, any more than one changed one's clothes several times a day. One spent as little money as possible.'

So far we have been dealing with the morals of the thrifty middle class everywhere in the industrial countries of Europe. But when he continues: 'A lovematch, that is to say a marriage based on love, would have been considered a proof of vice. Love was something that came after marriage and lasted until death',[22] we feel there is something unusual in the pattern. No doubt many marriages in the France of 1870, when Proust's mother was married, were still arranged by the parents, but would such a middle-class Frenchwoman, hearing of a married woman that she had a lover, been as appalled as if 'she had heard that her old butler had been guilty of murder'? The pattern becomes even more distinct when Proust goes on to tell us: 'No woman ever stopped loving her husband any more than she would have stopped loving her mother. Not to consider that one's husband was intelligent – even if he wasn't – would have been looked upon as being as barbarous as not to want to kiss one's mother because she was ugly.' This is not the tradition of the middle classes of Europe: it is a very old Jewish tradition.

Proust knew another kind of Jewish woman: Mme Straus, for example. He may have had her in mind, or some other Jewish woman who kept a salon, when he asked, in *Jean Santeuil*: would, to a woman who fills her house with English furniture and admits only people who share her aesthetic tastes, who will not entertain anybody who is not a countess or a painter, 'husband, father, mother, child be all in all'?

Mme Proust was probably as well educated, intelligent, and well-off as Mme Straus, but she did not keep a salon. All her interests were centred on her parents, husband and children. She mothered them all. She was not disturbed by her husband's exertion of authority, his insensitiveness, his dullness; by her father's interferences, disapproval, sullenness; she put up with her son's nerves, ill-health, and endless demands on her time and energy, and the infinite number of defeats by him. Most probably Mme Proust, like Mme Santeuil, made constant endeavours to keep her father and husband from quarrelling; and in the end her husband comforted her by his loving memories of her parents. She was very young when she married Dr Proust, and 'love was something that came after marriage and lasted until death'.

But she took for granted quite a number of things: her father's 'immensity of love' for her and her family; that her husband was neither a profligate, gambler, or drunkard; that her son would be like his father and that vice would never touch him. What she asked of all of them, without putting the request into words, was the freedom to make room in her life for her parents as well as for her husband and her children, to share her love between them all. The root of her love was contentment, and a certainty that this love made a woman's life meaningful and, in spite of all hardships, blissful. She was not only essentially Jewish, she was a thoroughbred!

What affects a child, especially a very sensitive one, is the living tradition of a parent, something the parent is hardly conscious of, something he goes on living without knowing why, something he does not express in words still less in clichés, as the boy Aksakov was affected by his father's passion for field sports.

Mme Proust used sometimes to make critical remarks about Jews, a well-known Jewish characteristic which some Jews resent. The Jew who has completely destroyed his Jewishness does not make such remarks: he either keeps silent from a sense of guilt, an invisible finger pointing at him, or he becomes an active antisemite. We know of Jews who played an important role in the Spanish Inquisition. It is the Jews who still care about their tradition who are specially sensitive to the short-comings and vulgarities of other Jews; as an Englishman abroad is often disturbed by the behaviour of his fellow-countrymen, out of a sense of belonging, while he is quite indifferent to the unbecoming behaviour of other nationals.

Proust's mother's ancient, uncompromising and narrow Jewish moral code caused Proust much suffering. By and by his influence on her grew. He tells us in *Jean Santeuil* that 'the son, whose mind and ways of life she had been so eager to form, had imposed upon her his own conception of mind and ways and life'.[23] She had become more tolerant of his friends and followed her son 'in imagination, into the great world, into the society of tainted women and vicious men whom Monsieur Sandré would have driven from his door'. She knew them through her son 'as characters in a novel. It was not that Mme Santeuil's moral values had altered, but only her view of the

moral values of others.' Nothing could be plainer! But such
acquired tolerance by an ageing loving mother could not abate
the flood of guilt that covered Proust's life. He re-created his
sense of guilt in fiction, wrote a story about a daughter whose
sexual vices are the cause of her mother's death, of a son who is
a parricide. The cry of the mature Proust, when writing of
inverts, pierces the heart: 'sons without a mother, to whom they
are obliged to lie all her life long and even in the hour when
they close her dying eyes'.[24] How he dealt with his suffering in
life, and far more profoundly and significantly, in art, is a
fascinating story.

There is a remarkable passage about Jean's mother in the
chapter called *The Marie Scandal*. Mme Santeuil became a
devoted friend of Mme Marie. She, 'who would have thought
it very wrong to give any considerable portion of her heart to
anyone other than her father' (there is no grandmother in *Jean
Santeuil*), 'her husband or her child, feeling as she did that they
were her appointed responsibility and the persons whom God
had put in her charge so that she might keep them good, happy,
and strong, had had one great woman friend – perhaps because
Mme Santeuil's affection for that woman's husband did in some
sort sanction her devotion. That woman was Mme Marie, an
exquisite creature, ravishing and intelligent, a wonderful wife
and mother, who had died of consumption at the age of thirty.
She had been a Jewess, and only the irresistible effect of her
charm and an intimate knowledge of her virtues had made it
possible for Mme Santeuil, who had come of a family in which
a dislike of Jews had been prevalent, to regard her as it were
as a sister.'[25]

I have quoted this passage in full for two reasons: first
because it is an excellent picture of Proust's own Jewish mother,
and secondly because he makes her not only a Gentile but one
of an antisemitic family! And just as significant is the fact that
she felt towards a Jewish woman as to a sister. What Proust
needed was to put Jean at a double remove from Jews, as from
homosexuals. Tolstoy, too, needed such removes, and so did
Dickens. Marcel, like Jean, comes from a purely Gentile family.
The Jew Swann, 'though much younger than my grandfather
was his best friend, and that in spite of my grandfather's dislike

of Jews.' But it is really rather funny to read about the family at Combray teasing the grandmother. She is out in the garden, after dinner, and the one thing which brings her back to the house is when they call out to her 'Bathilde! Come in and stop your husband from drinking brandy!' They used to make him take a few drops 'simply to tease her (she had brought so foreign a type of mind into my father's family that everyone made a joke of it)'.[26] The grandmother did not see the joke: 'My poor grandmother would come in and beg and implore her husband not to taste the brandy; and he would become annoyed and swallow his few drops all the same': nor would Freud's, Weizman's, or Mandelstam's grandmothers have seen the joke, and like Mme Amedée, would have suffered torment. Proust puts his remark about the grandmother's 'foreign type of mind' in a bracket, but he went further. Talking of Bloch, in *Within a Budding Grove*, a Jew who in later volumes becomes more and more objectionable, Marcel says 'he was not altogether a bad youth, this Bloch; he could be, and was at times, quite charming. And now that the race of Combray, the race from which sprang creatures absolutely unspoiled like my grandmother and mother, seems almost extinct – ':[27] that race was not that of Marcel's father or his Aunt Leonie, not of the French who had lived for generations at Illiers, but the race of Jewish women.

Precious as Proust's holidays at Illiers were to him, much as he had in common with his father and aunt, it was his imagination which created the 'race of Combray'. In *Time Regained* we are not surprised to be told that 'Combray for me had a shape so distinctive, so impossible to confuse with anything else, that it might have been a piece of jigsaw puzzle which I could never succeed in fitting into the map of France'.[28] As Proust says of a painting by Elstir that it 'gave the impression of harbours in which the sea entered into land, in which the land was already subaqueous and the population amphibian, the strength of the marine element was everywhere apparent', so Combray enters into Paris, and becomes the element everywhere apparent in *A la Recherche du Temps Perdu*.

Many a writer who creates a character in his own image, takes from him the crosses that he himself has carried. Proust

treats Marcel like a father who has suffered a lot and is trying
to spare his son the same suffering. You do not have to be half
a Jew, it is enough if your family has a Jewish friend who has
influenced your life. You do not have to be a homosexual,
enough if you get acquainted with inversion by watching others
through a window. You do not have to work for twenty years
on a book, nor to struggle, to go through ordeals of doubt and
despair; it is enough if you live through sleepless nights in past
memories, and that in the end that past springs miraculously
into life and you feel ready to start upon a work of art.

Had Proust merely taken his crosses from Marcel without
imagining characters in which lived all his own 'great convulsions', *A la Recherche* would not have been a great novel. He
created the Jew Swann, the only outsider present on the evenings at Combray, and in Swann he probed his own suffering
during the Dreyfus trial, his relations with the aristocracy,
uncovering both what he hated and what he loved. This and
many other sides of his nature he lived out in Swann. A far more
difficult task was to live his life as a homosexual in created
characters.

Go back to Proust's true story. Jean passionately loved
his mother. He was irritated by her deference and love for
her husband. Both Jean and Marcel are only children. But
Proust had a brother, Robert. Imagine Marcel Proust, aged
about seven, calling his mother again and again and getting
himself into a terrible state, while Robert, aged five, had probably gone to sleep without any need for a second kiss! Robert,
who was like his father and later followed in his footsteps,
became a Professor in the Faculty of Medicine, married, and
had a child. What a jealous person Proust was we know: the
fact of his making both Jean and Marcel only children points
to an act of Cain in the imagination, the killing of Abel whose
gifts pleased the father so greatly.

Proust's first love was for Marie de Benardaky. He makes
Jean a boy of thirteen when he meets Marie Kossichef, two
years younger than Proust had been when he met his Marie.
Turgenev, writing the true story of his first love, makes the boy
a year older than he had been. How right Turgenev and Proust
both were, one to make the boy older, the other younger!

Though intellectually and emotionally precocious, Proust was a child where love was concerned, and what kept him a child in this was the great love between him and his mother. Turgenev was much more mature; he feared and hated his mother.

Jean's mother plays a prominent part in the boy's love for Marie Kossichef. Jean went to bed every night with the thought that he would see Marie tomorrow in the Champs-Elysées. When it was snowing in the morning, when there was doubt that he would be able to go to the Champs-Elysées, it was not the nursemaid's objective comment on the bad weather that upset him, but the mother's irony. She was sure that 'there will be nobody in the Champs-Elysées today' while the maid only said 'one never knows'.[29] The mother was sure that anyway Marie would not be allowed to come out and dirty her pretty frock, and she said it as though it was of no great importance. Jean could have struck his mother. That the boy's passion should be violent, making him ill, is not surprising; nor is his parents' anxiety. According to the mother and the grandfather, M. Sandré, the only way of restoring the boy's health and peace of mind, was to separate him from the girl. The father, 'in whose flabby heart love for his son lived on equal terms with love of his own ordered and placid existence, had constantly put off, for fear of "causing the boy distress" ', putting an end to the meetings. The mother, on the other hand, 'with gentle severity and with a sad look on her face,' asked the boy to give up seeing Marie. 'Jean, however, who as a rule was so submissive to her and could so easily be reduced to tears by a kind word' saw towering over him 'the life and death threat which now confronted him'.

But even more than his mother's actions, her words, her attitude to his love, affected the boy deeply. While his love was blazing, 'fanned by the fury of his despair', the mother tells him that nothing will come of it, 'because he was far too young to think of marrying Mlle Kossichef' and she was 'vehemently seconded by M. Sandré'. 'In ten years time you will feel quite differently.' Loving one's parents is more than just a desire to hug them, and crying when one is separated from them, his mother said. 'That is not loving, but something one does in spite of oneself, because one is sensitive and a victim of one's

nerves. It has nothing to do with true goodness of heart . . .
Even Nero could suffer from nerves.' And she told him that if
one wants to do a thing hard enough, one can always do it, and
left him with the feeling that 'there was nothing good in him
except a sensitiveness that had nothing to do with his will'. She
finally brought the matter to a head by arranging for Jean to
go and have lessons with a M. Jacomier at two o'clock, the hour
he used to go to the Champs-Elysées. He screamed at her that
he would kill M. Jacomier, and to the grandfather, who came
near, that he hated him. There was a terrible scene; the mother
called her husband. The boy was beside himself, and shouted,
'Papa, dear Papa, they want to hurt me, mamma is persecuting
me – you must protect me, you *must*!' M. Santeuil said,
'Nonsense! your mother is perfectly right.'

He did go that same day to his lesson, crying all the way. In
the evening he did not hang back, but went into supper,
'though the words he had used to them in the morning had
exceeded in violence any he had ever spoken in the worst of his
nervous crises'. He wished everyone a good evening, and of the
three it was his grandfather, who as a rule was much sterner
with him than his parents, who answered his greeting. It was
M. Sandré, who had always urged his daughter and son-in-law
to separate the boy from Marie, who now, after the parents had
left the room, spoke gently to his grandson, took him on his
knee, and pressed his dry old lips to the boy's cheek, 'salty with
all the silent tears that they had drunk since morning'.
' "Darling Grandpapa, Grandpapa darling," said Jean, clinging to the thin neck, while his small body was wracked with
sobs.'[30]

He continued to go every day to his lessons, and learnt that
'our sorrows never last as long as we expect'. That is what
Proust thought in his twenties, but the longer he lived the more
clearly he became aware that if some sorrows do not last as long
as we expect, the effect on us of people we have loved, and our
sense of guilt, lasts for ever.

The mother's reason for demanding that he should give up
Marie 'since nothing will come of it', was part of her uncompromising attitude to love: 'Love was something that came
after marriage and lasted until death', and a love-match was

'a proof of vice', ideas which dated back to the Jewish life of the Middle Ages, and which had made of the family a tower of strength which greatly helped the survival of the Jews. It was an attitude, he knew at the time of writing, which was absolutely incompatible with homosexuality. Proust kept his homosexuality a secret from her, and remained a 'son without a mother'. He made Jean heterosexual, and Marcel too. His imagination solved the problem, dictated by prohibitions far, far stronger than the climate of opinion at that time.

One of the cornerstones of Combray is the story of the musician Vinteuil and his lesbian daughter. For the time being I ask the reader to take this assertion on trust: it only becomes fully justified in the volumes Proust was working on at the end of his life. M. Vinteuil belonged to a good family and had once been music-master to Marcel's grandmother's sisters. He had retired to the neighbourhood of Combray and lived in a house called Montjouvain. He used to be invited to Marcel's home, but had given up coming because he did not want to meet Swann who had made 'a most unsuitable marriage'. He was very modest and little was known about his music. A widower, he devoted his life to his daughter. Throughout the Combray period and through much of the rest of the novel the most memorable impressions of a character are the grandmother's. 'My grandmother had drawn our attention to the gentle, delicate, almost timid expression which might often be caught flitting across the face [Mlle Vinteuil] dusted all over with freckles, of this otherwise stolid child. When she had spoken . . . one would see, in clear outline, as though in a transparency, beneath the mannish face of the "good sort" that she was, the finer features of a young woman in tears.'[31] Marcel and his parents often met Mlle Vinteuil driving her dogcart at full speed, but we never hear any talk between them; we hear nothing about her life until her friend, a girl older than herself 'with an evil reputation in the neighbourhood', installs herself permanently at Montjouvain. Rumours about them began to spread. The father continued to adore her, for 'The facts of life do not penetrate to the sphere in which our beliefs are cherished'; but when he saw his daughter and himself from the point of view of the world, he condemned themselves as much as the inhabitants of Combray condemned them. In a matter of months he changed into an old man, and died.

It was after his death that Marcel found himself, purely by chance, outside Montjouvain, whence he could watch every movement of Mlle Vinteuil through the window which was partly open. (He could not get away because she would have heard him, and thought that he was hiding there to spy on her.) There was a photograph of the dead father on the table and Mlle Vinteuil, to draw the attention of her friend to it, exclaimed 'that is not the proper place for it'. 'This photograph was, of course, in common use in their ritual observances, was subjected to daily profanation, for the friend replied in words which were evidently a liturgical response: "Let him stay there. He can't trouble us any longer. D'you think he'd start whining, d'you think he'ld pack you out of the house if he could see you now, with the window open, the ugly old monkey?"[32] Proust makes a supreme effort to prove to us that Mlle Vinteuil, 'a girl leading her friend on to spit upon the portrait of a father who had lived and died for nothing and no one but herself', was not evil. The appearance of evil was strong, for ' "Sadists" of Mlle Vinteuil's sort are creatures so purely sentimental, so virtuous by nature, that even sensual pleasure appears to them as something bad, a privilege reserved for the wicked. And when they allow themselves for a moment to enjoy it they endeavour to impersonate, to assume all the outward appearance of wicked people, for themselves and their partners in guilt, so as to gain the momentary illusion of having escaped beyond the control of their own gentle and scrupulous natures into the inhuman world of pleasure.'[33]

However this escape was 'impossible' for her to effect; what prevented her from enjoyment of these pleasures, what stood between them and her, 'was the likeness between her face and his.' And 'it was not evil that gave her the idea of pleasure, that seemed to her attractive; it was pleasure rather that seemed evil.'

Mlle Vinteuil 'came at length to see in pleasure itself something diabolical', and did not realize either in herself or others 'that indifference to the sufferings they cause which, whatever names else be given it, is the one true, terrible and lasting form of cruelty'.

Proust says 'The function and the task of a writer are those of a translator'.[34] The translation of himself, the invert, into Mlle Vinteuil, and his mother into the musician Vinteuil, a man of genius, is a wonderful achievement. To Proust his mother was a genius. Among a number of questions which he was asked at thirteen, one was: 'Who are your favourite heroines in real life?'; when he answered: 'A woman of genius leading an ordinary life', he undoubtedly had his mother in mind. In the Vinteuils, Proust lived out in his imagination his own predicament of an invert son to the bitter end: Vinteuil's terrible last years might have been his mother's had he taken a male lover into their home. She would never have stopped loving her child, any more than Vinteuil did. When Proust tells us what Marcel's mother felt about the Vinteuils, his imagination is extracting profound truth. She 'had not forgotten the sad end of M. Vinteuil, his complete absorption, first in having to play both mother and nursery maid to his daughter, and, later, in the suffering which she had caused him'; she shuddered to think of the remorse Mlle Vinteuil must be feeling 'at having virtually killed her father'. Did she understand what the rumours meant? We cannot tell. She used to say: 'he lived for his daughter, and now he has died for her, without getting his reward. Will he get it now, I wonder, and in what form? It can only come to him from her.'

Proust had begun the defence of Mlle Vinteuil in 'Combray': she was virtuous by nature, and pleasure seemed to her evil. And then, a decade later, defying all realism, he again defends her, as if he is defending himself before the throne of the Almighty. The musician will get his reward: Mlle Vinteuil's lover saves his work, left scattered on poor little pieces of paper, which she transcribes in fair copy. Proust might have said about himself, like De Quincey, 'and the crime which *might* have been was in my eyes the crime which *had* been' (*The Affliction of Childhood*). And he rewarded his mother by writing *A la Recherche*.

Proust, as Mr Painter thinks, probably remained ignorant of the existence of homosexual love in his teens, just as did Gide. The profaning of a dead parent's portrait did not occur in Proust's life till after his mother had died, that is when Proust was in his thirties. Marcel's experience of the lesbian lovers at

Montjouvain is not a boy's experience, nor, as we have seen, was Marcel's experience of demanding the mother's kiss, Marcel Proust's as a child. Dickens in *The Pickwick Papers*, Tolstoy in *War and Peace*, created adults with the minds and hearts of remarkable children. Proust created a boy with the mind and heart of an adult.

The lack of any dialogue between Marcel, his mother, his grandmother, and Mlle Vinteuil, as if they belonged to different nations, makes the translation perfect: it fits Proust's original conception of Marcel to whom inversion is totally foreign.

Proust, like Tolstoy, usually needed more than one model for a character. Tolstoy *was* Ivan Ilich (in *The Death of Ivan Ilich*), and at the same time had as a second model a judge in Tula. When biographers give us new information about them it is certainly helpful, as when Mr Troyat tells us that the judge was the brother of the famous Russian scientist Mechnikov. Mr Painter suggests that the musician Vinteuil 'resembles César Franck and no other'. I dare say M. Vinteuil resembles no other musician, but as a man of genius and the parent of an invert he *is* no other than Proust's mother.

At the end of 'Combray', and before the beginning of 'Swann in Love', Marcel states that, lying awake till morning and dreaming of his past, he lived in three different kinds of memories: of the wakeful evenings at Combray, which he calls 'my oldest memories'; of other days at Combray, recently inspired by the taste of the madeleine; and lastly of Swann's love story, which happened before he, Marcel, was born, memories of another which he had acquired at second hand. All these memories, he tells us, had coalesced into a single substance, but he could still discern the different kinds, 'the strata', as Scott Moncrieff calls them, could tell the difference of origin, age, and formation.

Since *we* cannot know the difference of origin, age, and formation, what was the point of this statement? I thought at one time that this page might have strayed into the novel out of one of Proust's notebooks. But the more one knows of *A la Recherche* the more certain one becomes that no statement is there without a purpose.

Proust was pursuing two objectives: to decipher the book

which had been dictated to him by reality, and to reveal the process of this deciphering. For some twenty years his instinct had driven him to write autobiography, and in the end he had rejected the fruits of his great labour, *Jean Santeuil* and *By Way of Sainte-Beuve*. In 1909 he conceived the novel which would consist of many strata. Every one of these strata is the work of Proust's imagination. I have shown that his 'oldest memories' of the wakeful evenings at Combray differed in important ways from his real memory. The second stratum, the other memories of Combray, is no less a work of the imagination than was Tolstoy's *Childhood*: he invented Swann, his park, his maternal grandmother, M. Vinteuil and his daughter; every important experience of Marcel is created. The third stratum, Swann's love affair, is no less a work of imagination as we shall see. All three 'strata', though described as 'memories', involved acts of creation.

The second objective, to reveal the nature of the process of 'deciphering', he pursued relentlessly, though in ways not always obvious to the reader, throughout the novel. He had already expressed his interest in this pursuit in the Introduction to *Jean Santeuil*: the 'friends of the writer C.' tell us that they were profoundly interested in 'the secret relations, the necessary metamorphosis, which exist between a writer's life and his work'. Proust throughout attends to this metamorphosis. I have shown that at the age of twenty-four he recorded his real 'oldest memory' as perfectly as De Quincey did his. In an anthology of real memories it would occupy a place of honour. But in *A la Recherche* this memory is transmuted into memories of a mother-lover. After that, Marcel gives us no memories of Combray, though he assures us that other hours and scenes existed: he could have brought them back, but only by the exercise of will and intelligence, and little of the past would have been preserved in them. Anyone who has recaptured childhood knows that this is true, that collecting one's conscious memories with 'will and intelligence' leaves one with a collection of pressed flowers. It is when the feelings of a past moment are transfused into a present moment that life enters into memories. But inspiration achieves the same. I defy anyone who does not know Tolstoy's real past to distinguish between real and created memories in his *Childhood*.

Proust, of course, had not forgotten what he had written of Etreuilles in *Jean Santeuil*. He had not destroyed the manuscripts of *Jean Santeuil* and *By Way of Sainte-Beuve*, just as Tolstoy never destroyed his early drafts. The holidays at Etreuilles are a collection of conscious memories in which little of the past is preserved. Let us take the example of Jean's memory of Ernestine, the maid at Etreuilles, and compare it with Marcel's of Françoise, the maid at Combray.

We are given a great deal of general information about Ernestine: what a good servant she was, how she ruled the household and reduced the kitchen-maid to tears, and how different was the smiling Ernestine in the dining-room: how Jean worried about the way she treated animals, but could not help taking sides with her because she was the only person who knew how to make his bed, and produced his favourite dishes. All this is background memory. Anyone staying at Etreuilles might have informed us as well.

But what Marcel tells us of Françoise, the maid at Combray, is his experience of individual events. He was in the habit of going downstairs to find out what there was for dinner: on a particular occasion he came into the kitchen and saw Françoise killing a chicken. She was already a bit late because the kitchen-maid was ill, and the bird's resistance put her into a terrible rage; as she attempted to slit its throat beneath the ear she uttered shrill cries of 'Filthy creature, Filthy creature!' And even when it was dead, and she was mopping up its streaming blood, she did not let her rancour die down, but burst into a rage again and, 'gazing down at the carcass of her enemy, uttered a final "Filthy creature!"'[35]

Marcel crept out of the kitchen 'trembling all over. I could have prayed, then, for the instant dismissal of Françoise. But who would have baked me such rolls, boiled me such fragrant coffee . . . And, as it happened, everyone else had already had to make the same cowardly reckoning.'

Marcel says later, in *The Sweet Cheat Gone*: 'Things, people, did not begin to exist for me until they assumed in my imagination an individual existence.' This statement is repeated many times in the novel. Françoise killing a chicken assumes an individual existence for Marcel, and through him for us. We all know in general what Jean tells us, that a cook can be rough in killing a chicken, and very different from the smiling person who brings it into the dining-room; we also know that children early learn to do what their elders do, that is to forget the seamy side of life. But what Marcel, that incredibly sensitive child, felt when he saw a primitive peasant murdering a chicken is new to him and to us, and his emotion is transfused to us. What made him tremble was a recognition or, perhaps, only an inkling, of the universal murderous nature of human beings. Later, Mme Verdurin, who sets out to destroy Swann's and Odette's relationship which she has herself fostered, abusing Swann to her husband, inarticulate with rage, screams 'the filthy creature': the very words, Marcel reminds us, of Françoise, 'which the last convulsions of an inoffensive animal in its death agony wring from the peasant who is engaged in taking its life'.

Combray is far closer to Tolstoy's *Childhood* and the childhood of *David Copperfield*, than to Aksakov's or De Quincey's childhoods, which are built out of real memories.

The third stratum, which contains Marcel's 'memories' of Swann's love story before he was born, was 'acquired' by Marcel. But Proust has told us again and again that we only know another person from impressions he has made on us, from our own memories of moments of him. So how did Marcel acquire his 'memories' of Swann, with an accuracy 'which it seemed as impossible to attain as it seemed impossible to speak from one town to another, before we learned of the contrivance by which that impossibility has been overcome'?[36] What is the contrivance he is hinting at? Determined throughout to give us clues to the metamorphosis, Proust describes, towards the end of *Swann in Love*, a dream of Swann's in which there are two Swanns. He comments: 'like certain novelists, he had distributed his own personality between two characters, him who was "the first person" in the dream, and another whom he saw before him, capped with a fez.'[37] This is just what Proust did: he distributed himself between two characters, Marcel and Swann, creating two possible selves. So did Tolstoy, so did Dickens, but they did not let us into their secrets; we do not even know that they were conscious of them themselves.

My hypothesis that Marcel and Swann are two possible

Prousts is confirmed by the links between them and Jean. Jean's apple-blossom and pink hawthorn, his involuntary memories, his love for Marie Kossichef, all become experiences of Marcel. Jean's memories of music, his love for a Mme S., all become experiences of Swann. If you have any doubt, read Jean's dream about Mme S.; it is similar in minute detail to Swann's about Odette. But there are not two Jeans in the dream, as there are two Swanns: Proust had not yet conceived two possible selves.

In one of the Notebooks Proust wrote: 'Monsieur Swann . . . as I knew him at first hand, and, still more, as he seemed to me later, when I had supplemented my personal knowledge with the various odds and ends that I heard about him from others, was a man *to whom I felt myself to be peculiarly akin,* a man whom I could have loved very dearly. M. Swann was a Jew' (Maurois, *The Quest for Proust*).

Proust had other models for Swann. The existence of a Jew like Charles Haas, a man who had fought with distinction in the Franco-Prussian war, a member of the exclusive Jockey Club, accepted in the highest society, a modest man who carried his position with dignity, was a welcome bit of reality. Proust borrowed only the shell of Haas; he filled it with his own substance. Writing about the Jew in himself, at a distance, his imagination was free and his intuition sure.

Only someone who has never written novels could think that Charles Haas, whom Proust hardly knew, could be the prototype for Swann, whom Proust knew as well as he knew Marcel, as well as he knew himself. He was irritated when people tried to find the model of one of his characters, just as Tolstoy was, and used to say that there were many. He used Emile Straus's devotion to his wife's social career for Swann's to Odette's. Another Jew he used was Charles Ephrussi. All he was doing was to borrow 'the various odds and ends that I heard about him [Swann] from others'. Moreover he deliberately tried to throw his contemporaries off the scent, and with his love of teasing alluded several times to Charles Haas in the novel, as if he were his model.

He did not direct our attention to the fact that Swann was the son of a rich stockbroker, a refined sensitive man and a lover of art, easy to imagine as the son of Proust's Jewish grand-father, and even easier as the brother of Proust's mother. Proust informs us that Swann was a young militiaman in 1870, the year when his mother was twenty-one. The parallel of Tolstoy's Prince Andrey, whom he made the brother of his mother, is most striking. And just as the primary object of the opening chapter of *War and Peace* is the meeting of Pierre and Andrey, Tolstoy's two possible selves, so is the object of the opening of Combray the meeting of Swann and Marcel. Very deliberately Proust does not give Marcel a surname anywhere in the novel. But there was a person who either learned the truth from him, or who guessed it, and that was Proust's lover and secretary Agostinelli, a clever man according to Proust. He ran away from Proust, and enrolled in an aviation school, under the name of Marcel Swann! We shall come later to the evidence of a deep relationship between Swann and Marcel. 'I began to take an interest in his character', Marcel tells us, 'because of the similarities which, in wholly different respects, it offered to my own.'[38]

When Swann was first introduced to Odette he was rich, cultured, and accepted, indeed sought after, by the highest society of the Faubourg Saint-Germain. He was a very 'ardent lover' and 'once they [the women of the aristocracy] had taught him all that there was to learn' he became more and more attracted towards 'illiterate and common women'. Indeed he was eager to shine in the eyes of 'the fair unknown of humble circumstances, and a man who was at his ease when with a duchess, would tremble, for fear of being despised, and would instantly begin to pose, were he to meet her grace's maid'.

Swann the Jew, son of a stockbroker, accepted by the Faubourg Saint-Germain and taken as one of them, paid for this success, we are told, by debasing his erudition in matters of art, using it to advise society ladies what pictures to buy, and had given up working on his book on Vermeer. Being both well off and intelligent, living a life of idleness, he put 'life' above the attainments of art and learning: not the first idle and intelligent man to find an excuse in such an idea.

Proust succeeds in convincing us that Swann was a remarkable man, if for no other reason than that the point of his

becoming a member of the highest society was that he enjoyed
advantages even over men of intelligence and refinement who
had never gone into society: the reason being that men who
have gone into society 'no longer see it transfigured by the
longing or repulsion with which it fills the imagination but
regard it as quite unimportant'. And such men 'freed from all
taint of snobbishness' grow independent. This profound truth
about Swann is the truth about Proust himself, as so much of
Anna is the truth about Tolstoy: truths which a writer can only
embody in a character who is at some distance from himself,
but which, if stated by an autobiographer, only make us uneasy.
Swann was not like those people who 'remain moored like
house-boats at a certain point on the bank of the stream of life,
abstain from pleasures which are offered to them above and
below that point'. In this he resembles all the rich and idle
aristocrats, like the Guermantes, and aristocrats the world over:
independent and free to be eccentric. Only artists share this
privilege of the aristocracy, and just as some aristocrats mature
and come to feel responsibilities towards other men without
feeling that their freedom is impugned, so do some artists. We
shall see later a different Swann, responsible towards his wife
and child, towards his race and towards what was best in French
society.

Odette was a courtesan. Her style of beauty left him indifferent; more than that, it repelled him. It was she who at first
made advances to him, but then he began to fall in love. Swann
says 'in his younger days a man dreams of possessing the heart
of the woman whom he loves; later the feeling that he possesses
the heart of a woman may be enough to make him fall in love
with her'. In order to delay her desire for him reaching the
point of satiety, Swann tries to make her feel that there are other
pleasures that he prefers to her company. He prefers to Odette's
style of beauty that of a little girl 'as fresh and plump as a
rose' with whom he is simultaneously in love, and with whom
he spends the first part of the evening, sure of seeing Odette
later at the Verdurins' to whom she had introduced him. He
used to meet her and drive her home, 'a privilege which he
valued all the more because . . . no one else would see her, no
one would thrust himself between them, no one could prevent

him from remaining with her in spirit, after he had left her for the night'.

They were strange drives; on the one hand, he felt, she must on no account read in his eyes 'the first symbols of desire' because then she would no longer believe in his indifference; on the other hand, he must, without betraying his concern, make sure that he would find her next evening at the Verdurins, and so to 'prolong for the time being, and to renew for one day more the disappointment, the torturing deception that must always come to him with the vain presence of this woman, whom he might approach, yet never dare embrace'. Why not? He has had innumerable love affairs, and she is a courtesan. Mme Verdurin says of Odette 'As she has no one else at present, I told her that she ought to live with him. She makes out that she can't: she admits that she was immensely attracted by him at first, but he is always shy with her, and that makes her shy with him.'

One evening Swann, 'irritated by the thought of that inevitable dark drive together' with Odette, stayed out longer than usual with the 'little girl', and when he arrived at the Verdurins' Odette was gone. She had left word with the butler that she would probably stop at Prevost's, and Swann set out in search of her.

She was not there, but now there was no question of his going home: he must find her. 'A great gust of agitation' swept over him and this is the most efficacious method 'by which love is brought into being' for 'All that is necessary is that our taste for her should become exclusive'. He was now overwhelmed by 'an anxious torturing desire – whose object is the creature herself, an irrational, absurd desire . . . – the insensate, agonizing desire to possess her'. Swann's search for Odette that night ended in his finding her and taking her home. On the way the horses suddenly started, and she and Swann were thrown forward from their seats. He used that moment to put his arm round her shoulder. 'Whatever you do, don't utter a word; just make a sign, yes or no, or you'll be out of breath again. You won't mind if I put the flowers straight on your bodice.'

His stratagem, which is new to Odette, for she was not used 'to being treated with so much formality', appears very artificial, and Proust makes it plain that not only on that evening, which ended in her complete surrender, but even afterwards, 'he was so shy in approaching her' that he used 'the ritual pretence of an arrangement' of her flowers, the cattleyas she always wore. And so Swann, to make love, needs a ritual, just as Mlle Vinteuil had done.

This loveless love story bewildered me more than the perplexing love stories in Dostoyevsky's *Idiot* and *The Brothers Karamazov*; boredom blocked my way for a long time, and I did not appreciate it until after I had read all the 'fresh personalities' added to Swann in later volumes.

I had failed to understand that Swann's love was like that of an adolescent whose main concern is the impact another person makes on him, not the person himself. 'Other people are, as a rule, so immaterial to us that, when we have entrusted to any of them the power to cause us so much suffering or happiness to ourselves, that person seems at once to belong to a different universe, is surrounded with poetry, makes our lives a vast expanse, quick with sensation, in which that person and ourselves are ever more or less in contact.'[39]

Love was precious to Swann because he 'was finding in things once more, since he had fallen in love, the charm that he had found when, in his adolescence, he had fancied himself an artist'. The inspirations of his boyhood, which he could feel reawakening in himself, all now bore 'the reflection, the stamp of a particular being'.

The adolescent, like the child, is a 'particular being', but the difference is that the adolescent is conscious of fighting for his separate identity, while the child is not. The adult is very often nothing more than a creature of habit: experience no longer causes him great happiness or suffering, and he has fewer and fewer new impressions, and consequently lays down fewer memories of moments. But when a man is in love he becomes an adolescent again, and his life 'une étendue émouvante'. Swann in love is a test of Proust's general belief, which he already held in his twenties: 'When we are in love we find again that lovely gift of childhood, so that each day becomes for us something feverishly looked forward to, the unknown goal of all our hopes.'[40]

Swann 'became gradually himself again'. He had heard that Odette was a 'tart', a 'kept woman', but what was that to him, when he saw that 'Odette, so good, so simple, so enthusiastic in the pursuit of ideals, so nearly incapable of not telling the truth'. At the Verdurins, in their little clan, they knew that Odette was a courtesan, and quite uneducated, and they could hardly think that Swann believed in her virtue; 'And yet, you never know: he seems to believe in her intelligence ... but really – to expound theories of aesthetic to her – the man must be a prize idiot.'

He does at times appear 'a prize idiot': when Odette became 'the body of her whom he loved', and henceforth 'the only one capable of causing him joy and anguish', he went so far as to proclaim that Mme Verdurin was 'a great and noble soul'. But remember that he had fancied himself as an artist when he was a boy and love had made him a boy again: again he looked, as the real artist always does, with his own eyes, the eyes of the imagination, and was blind to what others saw. Did he not know from experience 'that an educated, "society" woman would have understood them [a decadent piece in the theatre or an impressionist painting] no better (than Odette), but would not have managed to keep quiet about them so prettily'? He saw that Odette was vulgar, but he tried 'to find satisfaction in the things that she liked, and did find a pleasure not only in copying her habits but in adopting her opinions'. He had always been sceptical about the absolute value of the objects that we admire, and considered that vulgar fashions are worth just as much as those which are regarded as refined.

He had been sending Odette a lot of money, but 'he had never imagined for a moment that she could have taken a penny from anyone else before'. Is it possible that this man of the world, the son of a stockbroker, who is quite capable of looking after his financial affairs and those of Odette, could be so naive? He is not naive, he is not posing as the Verdurins suggest. In love he is once again a boy, an artist. A 'kept' woman, indeed! – 'that Odette upon whose face he had watched the passage of the same expressions of pity for a sufferer, resentment of an act of injustice, gratitude for an act of kindness which he had seen, in earlier days, on his own mother's face, and on the faces of friends'. Is it not this seeing with one's own eyes that makes both the boy and the artist capable of greater understanding of human nature – both its good and its evil – than the adult who is ruled by habit?

Here I will put aside Swann's love story until I reach the point at which I saw it in a new light, and move on. Swann's love story belongs to the time before Marcel was born. In his childhood at Combray, he knew Swann, who was a friend of the family. There were two 'ways' Marcel and his parents used to take on their walks: one was called 'Swann's way', and passed by Swann's estate, Tansonville, the other was called the 'Guermantes way'. Marcel's parents had ceased to visit Tansonville since Swann's marriage to Odette; but one day, hearing that Swann's wife and daughter were away, they walked by Swann's park, and that was the occasion when Marcel saw Gilberte for the first time.

The last chapter of *Swann's Way*, 'Place-Names: the Name', begins with Marcel telling us that among the rooms which used to take shape in his mind during his long nights of sleeplessness was one in the Grand Hotel de la Plage, at Balbec. But instead of living in imagination in that room he recollects what the name Balbec had meant to him as a boy, and thence passes to other place-names. He was in Paris, a schoolboy, when his father decided that they should go for Easter to the north of Italy, and Marcel lives in imagination in the names of Florence, Venice, Parma. But he had fallen ill before they started, and the doctor had assured them that, even when the boy recovered, the idea of travelling must be given up for at least a year. His parents had to be content with sending him out to walk in the Champs-Elysées, with Françoise the maid in charge. There he saw Gilberte Swann again, and fell in love. One day she invites him to join in a game: from then on we have the boy Marcel as we know him already from Combray; the same Marcel who tells us, in *Time Regained*, that his past was 'immured within a thousand sealed jars, a colour, a scent, a temperature, hunger, desire for pleasure', absolutely different from one another, but all memories of moments. But the ageing Marcel, who lives in his memories of his first love, does

9

something more than recover all these various sensations. He is working hard to penetrate the nature of love. 'I still believed that Love did really exist, apart from ourselves.' Even in those moments when Gilberte gives him pleasure, there is not much joy. His passion for her overspills into passion for her parents, both her father and mother. To meet Mme Swann he goes to the Allée des Acacias, and once again he fills many 'jars' with his impressions of her clothes, her carriage, her behaviour to others and that of others to her.

The chapter concludes with Marcel bringing us back to the present, to a November day 'this year', when he revisits the Bois de Boulogne. When 'this year' was we cannot tell, except that he had long been living in memories of his past active life, and that it was a long time since he had walked in the Allée des Acacias with Mme Swann. Now instead of carriages there were cars; the 'little hats' which were in one of those jars in his memory were now replaced by immense hats; and in place of the lovely gowns in which Mme Swann walked like a queen, appeared Greco-Saxon tunics ... or sometimes, in the Directoire style, "Liberty-chiffons" sprinkled with flowers like sheets of wallpaper'. 'The reality that I had known no longer existed.'[41]

## 3. The Addition of New Personalities

*Swann's Way*, the first volume of what was to have been a three-volume novel, was published in 1913: the second volume did not appear until after the war, in 1918. Proust continued to work on the later volumes until the last days of his life, and several did not appear till after his death. Professor Feuillerat was very perplexed when he compared *Swann's Way* in substance and style with the volumes published after the war. It was known that the second volume of the original version was already in proof when the war began. Feuillerat discussed the matter with Proust's brother Robert, who confirmed that the second volume had been in proof, but he did not know what had happened to it. Feuillerat set out in search of it. With perseverance, luck, and the kindness of a number of people, he ended in finding it. With the help of the chapter headings of the original second and third volumes, which were printed opposite the title page of the 1913 edition of *Swann's Way*, he made a thorough comparison of the original with the final version. What he found was an enormous increase in the size of the novel; it was three times as long as Proust had originally intended. The alterations in the final version varied enormously: there were both small and great additions, very important new episodes, and the transference of all important chapters, such as the death of the grandmother, from the projected third volume to earlier parts. All this Mr Painter acknowledges in his biography, but nevertheless dismisses Professor Feuillerat's book *Comment Marcel Proust a composé son roman* (1934) in a footnote, alleging that his 'prejudiced and destructive fallacies . . . have done lasting harm to Proustian scholarship'. What Painter disliked was Professor Feuillerat's attempt to show that the originally projected version was one book and the definitive version quite another, that in the many years which lay between them, Proust changed greatly as a man and as a writer. Feuillerat tried to show that the first version was a novel in the French tradition, while the definitive one was more like the journal of Saint Simon, which Proust greatly admired.

I am profoundly grateful to Professor Feuillerat. First I must remind you that he wrote his book without the knowledge we now have of *Jean Santeuil* and *By Way of Sainte-Beuve*, and when many facts of Proust's life were still unknown. Had he known all this he would have realized that Proust was all his life writing one book, and this would have helped him to understand the many ambiguities and contradictions in *A la Recherche*.

Partly because I was very interested in Proust's theme of memories, partly because I admired him 'this side of idolatry', I could not ignore, or just get round the contradictions: the more I knew about him the more intolerable they became. Why did Proust make Marcel's experience of the three Guermantes memories miraculous? Why did Marcel think, after the Guermantes memories, that he was ready to start on a work of art, while many writers who have had the experience of involuntary memories hoped at best to record them? But these questions were of little significance beside the following: Marcel was having many involuntary memories throughout the long novel, so why had he not discovered long before that his past contained the material of a work of art? Proust realized that he could not get away with this. If he is to be believed about the Guermantes memories, then the involuntary memories of childhood and youth of Doncières, Rivebelle and Combray, must have had a similar effect. This is how he explains their failure to do so: 'I felt on perceiving them an enthusiasm which might have borne fruit had I been left alone and would then have saved me the unnecessary round of many wasted years through which I was yet to pass before there was revealed to me that invisible vocation of which these volumes are the history.' And the reason why the revelation did not come to him was that his friend Robert de Saint-Loup joined him! When Coleridge tells us that 'persons from Porlock' interrupted and terminated a moment of inspiration, we believe him, but if he had said, like Marcel, that they prevented him from discovering his vocation as a poet, we should not have been convinced.

By the time I read Professor Feuillerat's book I was already well aware of the impossible contradictions in *A la Recherche*; when I found in his book the evidence that Proust had added to the definitive version of *Within a Budding Grove* a new involuntary memory of the boy Marcel which was absent in the original second volume, I held the end of the thread which led through the labyrinth. What made Feuillerat's book specially valuable to me was that he did not direct attention to this or any other involuntary memory: he does not concern himself with the theme of memories at all, whether because he did not realize their significance to Proust, or just because he did not understand them.

The new involuntary memory which Proust added comes to Marcel when he meets Gilberte Swann in the Champs-Elysées; he is still being accompanied by the maid Françoise. It is a boy and girl love story. Gilberte tells him, with a laugh, that her parents can't abide him; she returns the letter he had sent to her father and repeats her father's words: 'All this means nothing.' Marcel is in despair. At that moment Françoise calls him, and he has to leave Gilberte and accompany Françoise 'into a little pavilion covered in a green trellis' which had lately been turned into a lavatory. The old damp walls 'emitted a chill and fusty smell' which at once relieved him of all his anxieties and 'pervaded me with a pleasure' quite unlike ordinary pleasures, one 'on which I could lean for support, delicious, soothing, rich with a truth that was lasting, unexplained and certain'.[1] We know that the child Marcel was in the habit of puzzling about his impressions: now he would have liked 'to descend into the underlying reality which it had not yet disclosed to me'. But the elderly dame who kept the establishment talks to him, and takes his mind away from his impression. When he returns to Gilberte she reminds him that he must take the letter that she had brought back. Feeling irresistibly attracted to her body, he uses the letter as an excuse for wrestling with her, suggesting that she should try and stop him from getting his letter, and see who is stronger. They embrace and fight: 'I held her gripped between my legs like a young tree which I was trying to climb . . .' She likes the wrestling so much, that, when he does snatch the letter, she says they can go on wrestling if he likes. After he leaves Gilberte, and is walking home, it suddenly comes to him that the fusty smell of the lavatory was the same as the smell of his Uncle Adolphe's sitting room at Combray.

The boy's memory, like the madeleine, is the creation of Proust's imagination, but it is closer than the madeleine to Proust's real experiences as we know them from his autobiographical books, and closer, also, to other writers' experiences. The boy's memory is not presented as miraculous, as the madeleine is: he describes no exaggerated joys, no revelations. He does not say, as the ageing Marcel says in *Swann's Way*, 'I had ceased now to feel mediocre, accidental, mortal'. Without making him feel that it was a miracle, the memory pervades him with a pleasure that contains a lasting truth, unlike the pleasures of love 'which leave one more unstable than before'. This intimation of an inner life, the life of a poet, of which there are some proofs in Combray (such as Marcel's experience of the steeples of Martinville), is now apparent in this earliest involuntary memory.

This memory of the boy Marcel is the beginning of Proust's abandonment of his original plan. From this first volume of the definitive version onwards Marcel is writing a novel like other writers, has ceased to be a man who still has to discover his vocation. For lovers of Proust who are fascinated by the many scenes in which beams of light glitter on the surface of deep waters, the proof that the Guermantes memories have lost all their meaning in the definitive version, may not seem of much importance. But unless one first understands that Proust formed and then abandoned the plan of the book, that *A la Recherche* is a novel *im werden* (in process of becoming), one ends by describing the Emperor's clothes.

My second debt to Professor Feuillerat is for showing that some characters in the definitive version are not the same as in the original, though they bear the same names. Odette de Crecy is mediocre, uneducated and vulgar; Mme Swann is distinguished, well-informed, a friend of the writer Bergotte, whom she helps with his work, and even wants to control it! The first

Odette 'played vilely', while the second Odette played the Vinteuil sonata so well that she 'enchanted' Marcel. 'Her touch appeared to me (like her wrappers, like the scent of her stair-case, her cloaks, her chrysanthemums) to form part of an indi-vidual and mysterious whole.'[2] Clearly Proust changed his model, but so did Tolstoy in *War and Peace*: Natasha before her marriage was mainly modelled on Tolstoy's sister-in-law Tanya, and in the Epilogue she is modelled on his wife. But Proust's change of models was a far far harder task than Tolstoy's. The first Odette is not a woman, but a man: this first came to me from Feuillerat's book, which lists the pages in the definitive version which are absent from the original second volume. On one of these additional pages we read: 'Aesthetically the number of types of humanity is so restricted that we must constantly, wherever we may be, have the pleasure of seeing people we know ... Thus it happened that in the first few days of our visit to Balbec I had succeeded in finding Legrandin, Swann's hall porter, and Mme Swann herself, transformed into a waiter, a foreign visitor whom I never saw again, and a bathing superintendent.'[3]

I can give at least three examples of my own experience of these startling resemblances, and I know that others have had similar experiences. I believe that, like involuntary memories, it is a universal experience. These are the salient features of my own: I suddenly saw in the fishmonger who was serving me a publisher I knew, in an agricultural labourer's wife from whom I was buying vegetables a lady of a very distinguished family, and in an assistant at John Lewis's in Oxford Street a famous professor of physics. I could be pretty certain that there was no blood relationship, at least not for the past hundred years. In any case, what struck me were not family resem-blances: it was like looking at a print taken from the same plate, whereas family likenesses are like different sketches made of the same person. Proust continues: 'And a sort of magnetism attracts and retains so inseparably, one after another, certain characteristics, facial and mental, that when nature thus introduces a person into a new body she does not mutilate him unduly.' His generalizations have the same stamp of authenticity as his impressions, but what he says

next comes as a surprise: Mme Swann was a *male* bathing
superintendent. 'Legrandin turned waiter kept intact his
stature, the outline of his nose, part of his chin; Mme Swann,
in the masculine gender and the calling of a bathing superintendent, had been accompanied not only by familiar features,
but even by the way she had of speaking.' In my own experience
the barriers of class, education, even nationality (the professor
of physics was a German) all vanished, but there was not one
case of a change of sex. Proust tells us that not only had the
masculine bathing superintendent the same features as Mme
Swann, but also her way of speaking. To appreciate Proust you
have to connect: in *Time Regained* he says 'The writer must not
be indignant if the invert who reads his book gives to his
heroines a masculine countenance.'[4] I will show that Swann in
love with a masculine bathing superintendent makes the love
story more understandable. But before we come to that I must
remind the reader that Proust was in the habit of leaving clues
like this. Painter gives some examples, and even says that it was
Proust's 'usual practice'. I have shown that Tolstoy left clues
in the names of some of his characters, and could give others.
These clues bring to mind the pictures which hang on the walls
of rooms in Vermeer's paintings.

Once Odette de Crecy's feminine trappings are removed, and
you see the male bathing superintendent, much that was incomprehensible appears in a new light. Why did Swann, who
had had many love affairs, while driving Odette home – a
courtesan – never dare to embrace her? Why did his 'great gust
of agitation' sweep over him on the evening when she was not
waiting for him at the Verdurins and he set out to find her,
why was he only then filled with the 'agonising desire to possess
her', and succeed in doing so? And why did he need 'the ritual
pretence of an arrangement of her cattleyas', so that even after
they had become lovers, to 'do a cattleya' stood for making
love?

I do not know whether such behaviour was necessary to
homosexuals then or is now, but I follow Proust's own instruc-
tion: 'Every reader,' he says, 'is the reader of his own self.'
'Look for yourself, and try whether you see best with this lens
or that one or this other one.' The writer, he says, must leave

the reader the greatest liberty. I saw better when I thought of Odette as a male bathing superintendent. I returned to *Jean Santeuil*: Jean's love for the widow Françoise S. is a poor sketch of what Swann's love for Odette will be.[5]

Jean did not dare to kiss the respectable widow, as Swann will not dare to kiss a courtesan. Even more tantalizing is the statement *à propos* of Jean's passion that 'complete realization is wholly impossible, as we retain within our bodies those primitive organs for which no use can be found in a civilized state': Swann's anguish is 'an irrational, absurd desire, which the laws of civilized society make it impossible to satisfy and difficult to assuage – the insensate, agonizing desire to possess her'.

Jean did not take long to realize that he could not go to bed 'with this young, independent but eminently respectable widow' and 'that he could not even as much as give her a kiss'. Françoise 'received him every night from ten o'clock until two in the morning, and more than that he only faintly desired'. Jean lived in hope to possess her one day, 'waiting to see in what fashion, at present unknown, our possession of the beloved will be fulfilled'. It did happen, but we are not told how. Jean says 'Love is more a subjective sensation than anything else'. and Swann 'one seeks in love before everything else a subjective pleasure'.

Love and jealousy, Proust wrote in *Jean Santeuil*, 'which subordinate the life of our mind and spirit to a single person' give him 'an individual character with the result that every detail in that person's life becomes of great interest, and curiosity, even espionage, become the means of knowing her.' And so Jean is eager to know 'what she really has been doing', and a chance visit to Françoise, one afternoon, very similar to Swann's to Odette (including that vital minute detail that it was the first occasion of such an afternoon visit), lays open 'a tiny portion of real life'.

Françoise's phrase 'if you had left something of yourself as well, I would have kept and treasured it', becomes, when Odette writes to Swann when he has left his cigarette case in her house, 'Why did you not forget your heart also? I should never have let you have it back.' And yet Swann's love story is to Jean's like a finished work of art to a preliminary rough sketch.

9*

I knew from biographical sources that Proust had had a homosexual love affair before he wrote *Jean Santeuil*. To the critic who says it is not legitimate to bring such knowledge to one's appreciation of a work of art, my answer is that it is as legitimate as using one's self-knowledge.

Proust discovered everything through suffering. He suffered inordinately from jealousy. Through suffering Swann discovered the evil that there was in Odette. She had brought the Comte de Forcheville to the Verdurin's, just as she had earlier brought Swann. When Forcheville, one evening, cruelly reduced his harmless brother-in-law Saniette to tears, Odette gave Forcheville 'a malicious smile', 'a look of complicity in the crime'. Swann intercepted her expression, and just as an expression of pity on her face lived inside him, so did this new one of malice.

For a long time Swann 'knew nothing of how she spent her time during the day, any more than he knew of her past'. He was not in the habit, as we have seen, of paying attention to gossip. Even when he did listen to it, it was 'the most commonplace part of his mind that was interested; at such moments he felt utterly dull and uninspired'. But it was quite different when he was in love, and he became curious to know the least detail of Odette's daily occupations; his thirst for knowledge was the same with which he had once studied history. This happens because when we are in love 'the personality of another person becomes so enlarged, so deepened. . . .'

Since everything that Odette told Swann was a mixture of lies with a few truths, he felt it legitimate, in his search, to tell lies himself. More than that, 'actions, from which, until now he would have recoiled in shame, such as spying tonight, outside a window tomorrow for all he knew, putting adroitly provocative questions to casual witnesses, bribing servants, listening at doors, seemed to him now precisely on the level with deciphering of manuscripts'.

The truth he discovered was terrible: she had lied to him on that evening when he was searching for her; she was a lesbian, she had dealings with procuresses, who knows what else. So long as his mistrust remained vague and uncertain it had not the power to cause him great suffering, but when he extracted

from Odette the details of what happened on one particular
evening in the Bois, when a woman invited her to come with
her behind a rock, he was in agony. What made the pain even
more excruciating was that it had happened on an evening
quite recently – he remembered it so well – 'which he had lived
through with Odette, of which he had supposed himself to have
such an intimate, such an exhaustive knowledge, and which
now assumed, retrospectively, an aspect of cunning, deceit and
cruelty'. Following the various stages of Swann's malady of
jealousy, we fully realize the price he paid for finding, when
in love, the same charm in things as when he was a boy. And so
Swann 'became gradually himself again, but himself in
thraldom to another'.[6]

Mme Verdurin at first welcomes Swann, and later turns
against him. It is enough for her husband to tell her that Swann
'poses' to make her go stiff with rage: it 'seemed to imply that it
was possible for people to "pose" in her house, and, therefore,
that there were people in the world who "mattered more" than
herself'. Swann had committed another sin against her: 'he had
failed to take Mme Verdurin daily into his confidence' about his
feelings for Odette. And when Odette brings another man to the
Verdurins, the newcomer, Comte de Forcheville, a crude and
vulgar man, is soon preferred to Swann. That Mme Verdurin
should set out to destroy Swann's and Odette's love is perfectly
in character, later confirmed by her efforts to ruin the love of
Baron de Charlus for Morel. As Proust tells us, other people's
happiness caused her grief, and her one consolation was to
destroy it.

That Odette should meekly take orders from Mme Verdurin,
not to go home with Swann but to come and sit with de
Forcheville, is credible, but only partly. Odette is such a con-
summate liar that it does not seem likely that she is under
Mme Verdurin's thumb. Anyway she has a child with Swann:
was it an accident, or did she arrange to trap him that way?
What were they like together while she was carrying his child?
All we learn, through others, is that she blackmailed him into
marriage by the threat that she would not let him see their
child.

In the first part of 'Combray' Proust focused our attention on the similarity between Swann's suffering and Marcel's child-hood anguish; 'to him [Swann] that anguish came through Love, to which it is in a sense predestined . . . but when, as had befallen me, such an anguish possesses one's soul before Love has yet entered into one's life, then it must drift, awaiting Love's coming . . . at the disposal of one sentiment today, of another tomorrow, of filial piety or affection for a comrade.'[7]

Later, when Odette began to give Swann much cause for jealousy: the moments when she did not give him a thought, forgot his very existence (just as Marcel's mother forgot her child that special evening), 'Swann was kept in that state of painful agitation which had once before been effective in making his interest blossom into love'. Proust runs straight on: 'And he did not have (as I had, afterwards, at Combray in my childhood) happy days in which to forget the suffering that would return with the night.' Even more arresting is the fact that the words in which Swann's desire is described: tortur-ing, irrational, absurd, agonizing, fit more closely Proust's own memory of when he was seven (in *Jean Santeuil*) than Marcel's.

At the beginning of *Within a Budding Grove* there are several pages which were not in the original second volume. Marcel's father says that 'Swann with his ostentation, his habit of crying aloud from the housetops the name of everyone that he knows, however slightly, was an impossible vulgarian', not fit to be invited to dinner with the Marquis de Norpois.

Swann, married to Odette, ceased to be jealous of her. He had hoped that when he ceased to love her he would revenge his sufferings, but now he no longer cared: in love with another woman, he takes precautions so that Odette shall not discover the existence of a rival.

Odette, too, changes: after her marriage she is a new Odette. Impossible for Mme Swann to resemble a male bathing superin-tendent! Proust has now a new model, Laura Hayman, 'the lady in pink', a famous courtesan whose many lovers included Proust's uncle, Louis Weil. The first Odette, according to Swann and others as well, was stupid, uneducated, and vulgar: Mme Swann, like Laura Hayman, was intelligent, witty, cul-tured, and though she was not accepted by Marcel's parents,

her model was accepted by Marcel Proust's. Mme Swann's
wonderful clothes, her flowers, her furniture, her interest in
literature, her fine piano playing, all are part and parcel of the
woman, not the mere wrappings and trappings which Proust
used in vain as the feminine disguise of the first Odette.

Swann's new personality was that of Odette's husband, and
the father of Gilberte; and since Odette was not accepted in
high society, Swann became a vulgarian, a social climber.
Marcel explains that 'like certain other Israelites, my parents'
old friend had come to illustrate in turn all the stages through
which the race had passed, from the crudest form of snobbishness up to the highest pitch of good manners'. Proust knew this
from his own experience; he had himself behaved like a vulgarian when he wanted to enter high society, and asked Robert
de Montesquiou to introduce him.

Swann a vulgarian! The man who, as we have heard, at the
beginning of 'Combray', already occupied a brilliant position in
society' 'one of the smartest members of the Jockey Club, a
particular friend of the Comte de Paris and of the Prince of
Wales,' a man so modest that he kept his friends in utter
ignorance of his position in the world? Marcel gives an answer:
'What had happened was that, to the original "young Swann"
and also to the Swann of the Jockey Club, our old friend had
added a fresh personality (which was not to be his last), that of
Odette's husband.' Odette was not accepted in the highest
society; it was astonishing to hear Swann who 'would so
gracefully refrain from mentioning an invitation to Twicken-
ham or to Marlborough House, proclaim with quite unnecessary
emphasis that the wife of some Assistant Under-Secretary for
Something had returned Mme Swann's call'.[8]

In pursuit of their pleasures a Baron de Charlus, a Saint-
Loup, a Prince de Guermantes, would go after a Morel, a
Rachel – all of the common people; but rooted in their feudal
past they would never in any circumstances have attempted to
gain a position in a lower stratum of society. Like Charlus they
knew 'that one cannot with impunity lose one's heart to a
servant, that the lower orders are by no means the same thing
as society, that in short he did not "get on" with the lower
orders as I [Marcel] have always done'.[9]

Marcel compares Swann to a great artist, modest and generous, who, if he turns in the end to cooking or gardening, is grateful for the compliments paid him, and will not listen to criticism which he had heard unmoved when applied to his real achievement.

To Swann, in his 'fresh personality', people are no longer immaterial as they had been before his marriage : he no longer needs to fall in love to feel, once more, 'a particular being'. Gilberte now matters more to Swann than Odette. According to Marcel, Swann thinks his daughter is 'quite perfect', and she reciprocates his love. 'How can one ever forget a person one has loved all one's life?' she asks Marcel; she will never, she says, want to know Mlle Vinteuil, of whom she had heard that she had given her father much trouble. But before long Gilberte shows how little she considers her father's feelings. He took the anniversary of his father's death very seriously, just as Mme Proust did, but Gilberte rejected his appeal not to go out to some entertainment on that day. Marcel does not understand how she, so loving, so thoughtful, can resist her father's appeal in 'so trifling a matter'. Marcel cannot understand: Marcel Proust did not leave his mother on such anniversaries. Swann has become as Jewish as Mme Proust. More significant still is Swann's form of belief in immortality, a Jewish belief as old as the patriarchs: 'in their child they believe that they can feel an affection which, being incarnate in their own name, will enable them to remain in the world after their death'.[10] Long after Mme Swann's death, when Gilberte for snobbish reasons changed her name to Mlle de Forcheville, her stepfather's name, Marcel remembers how Swann, hugging and kissing her, used to say: 'It is a comfort, my darling, to have a child like you; one day when I am no longer here, if people still mention your poor papa, it will be only to you and because of you.'[11] Gilberte's act is no venial transgression: she is breaking an important commandment, like Jessica, the daughter of Shylock, and forfeiting the blessing of a long life which comes to people who 'honour their father and mother'. Marcel, like Marcel Proust, never did anything of the kind; and even though he spat on his dead mother's portrait, prostrated himself before the 'dark idol' of inversion, as De Quincey prostrated himself before opium, he later expiated his sin in art, pleading for Mlle Vinteuil, the invert, who embodied his sin and his predicament.

What brought out the Jew in Swann even more strongly than family life was the Dreyfus case. Swann feels deeply involved and becomes, like Proust, a Dreyfusard. Mme Swann, 'fearing that her husband's racial origin might be used against herself, had besought him never again to allude to the prisoner's innocence'. Like Mme Verdurin, she had become a furious antisemite and anti-Dreyfusard, had thereby gained entrance into various societies, and had even succeeded in making friends with members of the aristocracy. One of Swann's great ambitions when he married was to present Odette and his daughter Gilberte to the Duchesse de Guermantes. She had been once a good friend of his, at the time when she was still Princesse des Laumes, but she changed greatly: in passages added to the original second volume we learn that she refused her great friend Swann the favour of meeting his wife and daughter, and showed herself quite heartless to the dying Swann. Professor Feuillerat's opinion is that the Duchesse de Guermantes of the original version could not have become as rotten as she is in the definitive version. But the mature Proust, recollecting the Dreyfus case, felt a hatred of the aristocracy greater than he had felt at the time.

Proust was as little a political animal as Tolstoy. Both Jews and Gentiles who felt as strongly as Proust about Dreyfus's innocence must have been angered by his refusal later, to support the anticlericalism which succeeded Dreyfusism, as Lenin was by Tolstoy for rejecting the 1905 Russian Revolution. To Proust the Dreyfus case was a personal experience of the same order as a love affair, and in Swann's he re-created it perfectly.

The description of the party at the Princesse de Guermantes's house, which Marcel attends (*The Cities of the Plain*), is on first reading bewildering if you are not a Proust addict. Though the time is the end of the nineteenth century, this aristocratic society seems far more remote from us than the Russian society of 1805 at the party given by Anna Pavlovna Scherer, with which *War and Peace* begins.

Swann has now his 'fresh personality', Dreyfusism – a further loss of caste, 'better described as a recasting, and ... entirely to his credit, since it made him turn to the ways in which his forbears had trodden and from which he had turned aside to mix with the aristocracy'.

The Duc de Guermantes, a cousin of the Prince, had doubted whether Swann would be invited, now that he was a Dreyfusard: his cousin the Prince, 'falls in a fit if he sees a Jew a mile off'. In fact, according to the Duc, the only reason the Prince had been friends with Swann was his belief that Swann was the natural grandson of the Duc de Berry, and thus not a Jew at all. However, Swann is at the party. When the Prince is seen having a long talk with him, the gossip spreads that the Prince 'gave Swann a dressing down . . . that he was not to shew his face in the house again, seeing the opinions he flaunts'.[12] We shall learn in time that this was nothing but 'spontaneous generation of falsehood' as Swann calls it.

Proust makes marvellous use of the form he has invented: on the one hand, Marcel is a Gentile from an antisemitic family and can take a detached view of Swann's Dreyfusism; on the other hand, Swann is his friend, and only to him reveals a great deal of his conversation with the Prince, and of his feelings on many other subjects. We have now the intimacy, the communication between two characters, which a writer achieves only between two possible selves. It is the intimacy of Pierre and Andrey, Anna and Levin.

The Duchesse de Guermantes tells Marcel that she is not very anxious to see Swann, as she has been told that he would like her, before he dies, to make the acquaintance of his wife and daughter. She is determined not to, and she sticks to her decision. Both she and the Duc are uncompromising in their anti-Dreyfusism. The Duc says 'I have always been foolish enough to believe that a Jew can be a Frenchman, that is to say an honourable Jew, a man of the world. Now, Swann was that in every sense of the word. Ah, well! He forces me to admit that I have been mistaken.' Or again: 'Oh! I have been greatly deceived . . . but if only for Oriane's [the Duchesse's] sake he ought to have openly disavowed the Jews and the partisans of the man Dreyfus.'[13]

In every work of art, Proust says, 'we can recognize the men the artist has most hated, and, alas, even the women he has most loved', because 'They indeed have quite simply been posing for the artist at the very moment when, much against his will, they made him suffer most'.[14] Proust hated the Duc and Duchesse de Guermantes. When trying to understand how he came to hate so many of the aristocrats, after allowing for his resentment against Count Robert de Montesquieu's anti-semitic remarks, and his regrets for having wasted so much time on climbing into that society, it is as well to remember how Tolstoy, without Proust's reasons, came to hate high society, with what hatred he wrote of them in *Resurrection*.

We get Marcel's first impression of the Prince de Guermantes: he immediately tells us that he is entirely different from the Duc de Guermantes 'who spoke to you at your first meeting with him as "man to man" ' but was fundamentally disdainful, while the Prince in his reserve, though not treating one as an equal, showed a consideration such as may be found in all strongly hierarchical societies, concealing 'more kindness, true simplicity, cordiality beneath their traditional aloofness than their more modern brethren beneath their jocular affectation of comradeship. "Do you intend to follow the career of Monsieur, your father?" he said to me with a distant but interested air.'

Swann reveals to Marcel that the Prince has told him that he has discovered that Dreyfus is innocent, and that his wife, the Princesse, quite independently, has discovered the same. The Prince was known to be a convinced Royalist and an anti-semite. He and the Princesse were not at home even to a Rothschild or a Baron Hirsch, who were accepted by the highest society. He was at home to Swann, and had been his friend since boyhood, but only because he believed that Swann was the natural son of a royal duke. Marcel informs us that this was false. In *The Sweet Cheat Gone*, the last volume to be written, on which Proust was working till the day he died, Marcel and his mother are talking of the latest news: Robert de Saint-Loup is marrying Gilberte Swann. ' "And yet, can you imagine for a moment," my mother said to me, "what old father Swann – not that you ever knew him, of course – would have felt if he could have known that he would one day have a great grand-child in whose veins the blood of mother Moser, who used to

say 'Ponchour Mezieurs', would mingle with the blood of the
Duc de Guise?" ' And so we discover that Swann's mother
could not speak French properly. Proust's grandmother most
likely spoke French with a German accent.

It is at the Prince de Guermantes's party that we see Swann
for the last time. He had begun to look very Jewish, his nose
now seemed enormous; at the same time a feeling of solidarity
with other Jews, never experienced before, was now revived by
'his mortal illness, the Dreyfus case and the antisemitic propa-
ganda'.[15] 'Thanks to the gifts he had inherited from his race'
he perceived a truth still hidden from people of fashion, but 'he
showed himself nevertheless quite comically blind'. His views
on politics, even literature, were all affected by his Dreyfusism.
His marriage to Odette, and his consequent loss of caste, had
made him even welcome a visitor like Mme Bontemps, and
think her intelligent; but now her anti-Dreyfusism made him
think her a fool. Clemenceau, of whom he used to have a very
low opinion, he now declared, since he was on Dreyfus's side,
a very great fellow. To Marcel's father he seems inconsistent and
comically blind, as he had earlier appeared a vulgar snob, but
the artist knows a deeper truth. Swann loved the army as
dearly as the Prince de Guermantes, as Marcel's grandfather, as
Marcel Proust himself, did. Deeply committed as he is to the
Dreyfus cause, he will not turn against the army.

Bloch, the ardent Dreyfusard, whom Swann used to avoid,
he now found intelligent. When Swann told him that the Prince
de Guermantes was now a Dreyfusard, Bloch immediately
wanted to make use of this, to ask the Prince to sign an appeal
for Picquart. But Swann thought this wrong: 'The Prince would
compromise himself with his own people, would be made to
suffer on our account.' Swann even refused his own signature:
'he did not wish to be mixed up in the anti-militarist campaign.'
And so, while some people considered Swann a fanatical
Dreyfusard, Bloch 'found him lukewarm, infected with
nationalism, and militarist'.

Swann, the son of a well-off stockbroker, educated and
artistic, had fought in the Franco-Prussian war. He had
adopted the aristocrat's best quality, modesty, based on taking
an unassailable position in the world for granted. But such

grandeur as a position among the aristocracy is transitory for a Jew, like the possession of a fortune: if he loses either, and is not lacking in energy and purpose, he sets out with determination and diligence to acquire a new position, if necessary in a lower social group. That is what Swann did. It was a worldly end for which worldly means were appropriate. But what he really cared for was not his own position in French society before he married Odette, but a man like the Prince de Guermantes, whom the aristocracy sometimes produced. 'If only you knew him [the Prince] as I do', Swann says to Marcel, 'if you could realize the distance he has had to traverse in order to reach his present position, you would admire him as he deserves. Not that his opinion surprises me, his is such a straightforward nature.' But whatever Swann's rationalizations may be, what matters are his feelings: 'I must tell you that this speech of the Prince de Guermantes moved me profoundly.'

Love of justice made Swann a passionate Dreyfusard; love of truth made the Prince and Princesse de Guermantes, in spite of their antisemitic background, acknowledge their error about Dreyfus's guilt. The dying Swann, according to Marcel, had 'arrived at the age of the prophet'. Here are Swann's last words to Marcel who had asked him about his health: he admits that he is worn out, 'and I accept with resignation what ever may be in store for me. Only I must say that it would be most annoying to die before the end of the Dreyfus case . . . I should like to live long enough to see Dreyfus rehabilitated and Picquart a colonel.'

Like all religious prophets he has known despair but is not a pessimist. Looking back, Swann states again that love is a disease, which brings one little pleasure. And yet he says, 'I have been very fond of life, and very fond of art.' Now he has become too weary to live with other people, but 'the memory of those sentiments is, we feel, to be found only in ourselves; we must go back into ourselves to study it'.[16]

Swann had not got it in him to create a work of art, as Marcel will, but he has the nature of an artist. Even now, nearing his end, his memories are very precious to him: 'Even when one is no longer interested in things, it is still something to have been interested in them; because it was always for reasons which

other people did not grasp.' With the creation of Swann
Proust laid down one of his crosses – of being a Jew, as Dickens
laid down his – his parents – when he wrote *Little Dorrit*. Free
of all fanaticism, Proust felt able to create the complicated and
unpleasant Jew, Bloch.

That the theme of homosexuality was not written into the
original version on the scale that it was into the definitive
version nobody would dispute. On 18 July 1918, Proust wrote to
Bernard Grasset that the two volumes of *Sodome et Gomorrhe*
were written since the beginning of the war: not quite exact,
according to Professor Feuillerat. But one thing is certain: the
changes, and above all the additions, made by Proust in the last
few years of his life were 'enormous'.

The additions made to the second volume of the original
version, concerning Morel and Jupien, the important actors in
the Baron de Charlus drama, show how the theme had grown.
That Proust had conceived Charlus as a homosexual in the
first version, we know from his note to the *Nouvelle Revue Fran-
çaise* written in 1912: 'C'est un charactere que je crois assez
neuf, le pédéraste viril.' For my purpose it is enough to know
that Proust added a fresh personality to Charlus as he had to
Swann.

Proust's model for Baron de Charlus was Count Robert de
Montesquiou, whom, unlike Charles Haas, he knew intimately,
and for very many years. Proust made Charlus as conceited,
snobbish, arrogant, and mad an aristocrat as the Count himself
was. But the depths of Charlus's feeling, as well as his vices, are
all the creation of Proust's imagination.

Marcel discovers that Charlus is 'a woman'. The grandmother's impression of him, much earlier, that he had a
feminine sensibility (an addition to the original second volume),
takes on a new meaning: Marcel, from childhood on, had been
seeing many things and people with her eyes. She was completely unsnobbish, humble and naive, and 'heard the tones
of truth'.

The Baron de Charlus is the brother of the Duc de Guermantes and has the family features, but in him they have taken
on 'a fineness more spiritualized, above all more gentle'.[17] As
Marcel watches him unobserved, he sees that the features are

those of a woman, and the pride of his virility, a mask. It is
very likely that even the conception of Charlus as 'a woman'
was not part of the original version. It is important to realize
that Charlus was created in the last period of Proust's life; for
not only is he one of Proust's greatest creations, but his love
stories are more human than either Swann's or Marcel's.

Odette, Albertine and, we must not forget, Françoise in *Jean
Santeuil*, were all in love with both sexes. Morel, too, the young
violinist whom Charlus loved, 'was sufficiently fond of both
women and men to satisfy either sex with the fruit of his experience of the other'.[18] But Swann, Marcel, Jean, all love only
one sex, and suffer most of all from their lovers' homosexual
loves for others. Charlus deplores, among other changes in
society, the change in the nature of homosexuals: in old days,
he says, they 'never kept mistresses except to screen themselves',
while 'nowadays they are recruited also from the men who are
the most insatiable with women'.[19]

In Swann's and Marcel's case jealousy is a terrible malady,
and love is nothing more than a byproduct of jealousy. Charlus
has plenty of reasons for jealousy, but his feelings for Morel are
not different from a heterosexual's: he wants to make a home
for Morel, 'a little nest for him to which he would often return.
For during the rest of the time he wished him to enjoy his freedom, which was necessary to his career as a violinist.'[20] Charlus
sets out to make Morel, who was only a virtuoso on the violin,
into a real musician. Morel is 'modest in regard to his true
merits, but possessing talents of the first order': Charlus con-
trives to educate his artistic sense. Later in the story we learn
that people said Charlus had intended to adopt Morel: the
invert felt the need 'to keep a lover . . . to settle down, to marry
or form a permanent tie, to become a father'.[21]

Morel was the son of Marcel's uncle's valet, and we know
from Marcel that though Morel had a charming side to him he
would not 'shrink from any act of meanness, was incapable of
gratitude'. But 'this youth who set money above everything,
above, not to speak of unselfish kindness, the most natural
sentiments of common humanity, this same youth nevertheless
set above money his certificate as first prize-winner at the
Conservatoire'. At the evening party given by the Verdurins

when Morel plays the violin Charlus behaves as if it was he who
was giving the party. He had been as blind to the evil of Mme
Verdurin as Swann had once been. In the old days, when a
peal of laughter came from Odette talking to Swann, it 'gnawed
her [Mme Verdurin's] heartstrings', and she now felt the same
about Charlus and Morel. 'She found one consolation alone
to her griefs which was to destroy the happiness of other people.'
Swann had been blinded by his desire to meet Odette every
evening at the Verdurins, but Charlus was unaware of danger
primarily because of aristocratic arrogance, the same arrogance as his model's Count Robert de Montesquiou, who used
to tell people that he was connected with all the most important
aristocratic families in Europe, which was a fact.

Now Mme Verdurin, by a word to Morel suggesting that his
relationship to Charlus threatens his reputation at the Conservatoire, turns him against Charlus. When Charlus advances
to congratulate Morel after the performance: ' "Leave me
alone, I forbid you to come near me," Morel shouted at the
Baron. "You know what I mean, all right, I'm not the first
young man you've tried to corrupt!" '

Mme Verdurin has torn off Charlus's aristocratic pride and
trampled it underfoot. The execution is masterly, tragic, and
yet not without comedy, but above all we understand Charlus as
never before. Marcel's 'sole consolation lay in the thought that
I was about to see Morel and the Verdurins pulverized by
M. de Charlus'. The extraordinary thing that happened was
that he was 'dumb, stupefied, measuring the depths of his
misery without understanding its cause . . . he had been seized
and dealt a mortal blow at the moment when he was unarmed
(for, sensitive, neurotic, hysterical, his impulses were genuine,
but his courage was a sham; indeed, as I had always thought,
and this was what made me like him, his malice was a sham
also.'[22] Proust succeeds in rousing in us the same feeling of
pity for Charlus as Marcel feels and, like him, we would have
liked to run away before 'the execution of M. de Charlus
occurred'.

When Charlus is tormented by Morel, one part of him wishes
he would never return, for (we remember) he did not really get
on with the lower orders as well as Marcel. But his other self,

when there is no answer from Morel to his appeals, is so disturbed that he lies awake all night, 'had not a moment's peace, so
great is the number of things of which we live in ignorance, and
of the interior and profound realities that remain hidden from
us'.[23] It is very likely that on just such a night there had ripened
in Charlus the decision to murder Morel, of which he writes in
a letter to Marcel. Before he sees this letter, Marcel, meeting
Morel one day, asks him why he does not go and see Charlus,
who is old and likely to die, and who has been good to him.
What were Morel's reasons, Marcel wants to know: 'Is it
obstinacy or indolence or perversity or ill placed pride or virtue
(be sure that won't be attacked) or is it coquetry?'

   It was none of these: Morel was afraid. The letter reached
Marcel only after Charlus's death, but it had been written at
least ten years before, when he was very ill. Charlus tells him
that it was Providence which had intervened: 'God counselled
him [Morel] prudence to preserve me from crime. I do not
doubt that the intercession of the Archangel Michael, my
patron saint, played a great part in this.'[24]

   When Swann suffers agonies of jealousy of Odette, and
Marcel of Albertine, we are interested, we are curious, but we
do not feel pity for them. We have been shown Swann's many
memories of moments of Odette, and Marcel's of Albertine,
just as a great artist shows us a large number of sketches of a
model made over a period of time. When Marcel tells us 'My
love for her [Albertine] had not been simple: to a curious
interest in the unknown had been added a sensual desire and
to a sentiment of an almost conjugal mildness, at one moment
indifference, at another a jealous fury', we recognize the tune:
it is the same as Swann's love story, only played on a different
instrument. And after all, neither Odette nor Albertine have
independent existences for Swann or Marcel, and in consequence they have none for us; although Proust has created them
out of a large collection of moments, which makes them vivid.
'But the infinitude of love, or its egoism, has the result that the
people whom we love . . . are only a vast and vague place in
which our affections take root . . . And where I had gone
wrong was perhaps in not making more effort to know Albertine
in herself.'[25]

Call them what you will, Swann's and Marcel's feelings are not love. M. de Charlus's feeling for Morel is.

When Marcel shows us the Baron de Charlus and his brother the Duc de Guermantes, 'so different in their tastes', the latter, an old dodderer having a last love affair with Odette, 'imitating his own earlier proceedings', and the former, quite blind, making love to a boy, could we have taken it from a homosexual that there was nothing to choose between the brothers, and that 'the normal proclivities of the one and the abnormal habits of the other' degraded both? It is only because Marcel is like ourselves that we can overcome our aversion as through his eyes we watch M. de Charlus and the tailor Jupien discovering one another, and hear them making love, and when we are told that it was a bit of good fortune for the Baron to meet Jupien, 'the man predestined to exist in order that they [men like the Baron] may have their share of sensual pleasure on this earth; the man who cares only for elderly gentlemen', we feel compelled to put aside our intolerance and, like Marcel, to tell ourselves to have courage 'when the theatre of operations is simply the human heart'. But Proust achieves more than this. The infuriating Baron, the Germanophil and anti-Dreyfusard, grotesque, maddening, at best a dilettante, is loved and cared for by Jupien, who provides him with men, treats his crazy demands as if they were the most ordinary matters, and continues to take care of him to the end. We see him with Charlus at the end of the story, arriving for the last Guermantes party: Charlus is convalescing from an attack of apoplexy, the locks of his hair and beard 'clad the aged and fallen prince with the Shakespearean majesty of a King Lear'.[26] We are given a masterly picture of the Baron with one foot in the grave: 'The Baron's humble and obsequious greeting of Mme de Sainte-Euverte proclaimed the perishable nature of earthly grandeurs and all human pride', while at the same time 'his intelligence survived'. Jupien and Marcel take a few steps together, and Marcel learns what has been happening to Charlus. 'Excuse me for telling you this, but as you once by chance entered the temple of impurity [i.e. walked into his homosexual brothel], I have nothing to hide from you.' And so to the very end Marcel remains an outsider. But not merely a listener, an observer; he is a student of the human heart, and like the scientist who selects a particular phenomenon only in order to get at a general truth, so Marcel fixes on a singular impression which he illumines within himself: 'Since every impression is double and the one half which is sheathed in the object is prolonged in ourselves by another half which we alone can know.'[27] ' "Oh, my God," called Jupien, "I had good reason not to want to go far away. There he is starting a conversation with a gardener boy. Good-day sir, it's better I should go, I can't leave my invalid alone a moment: he is nothing but a great baby." '[28]

We do not doubt Jupien in his role of devoted nanny; he had really meant it when he had said earlier of the Baron 'he's too good-hearted'; and he certainly needed looking after. We are the more convinced because Jupien is not a simple good servant; he had been after all Charlus's lover, had kept a brothel for him. M. de Charlus is a ruin: we feel pity for him when we remember that he adored his mother, that she was a beautiful woman, that he was like her, that what was feminine in a woman became effeminate in a man. The writer is not bound by the art of the possible; on the contrary he often must attempt the impossible. A life is tragic if after a long struggle a man is still no more than 'a great baby', and it is a relief to us to think there is someone like Jupien to care for Charlus.

These 'fresh personalities', added to Swann and Charlus, make the definitive version, as Mr Painter says, superior to the original.

Swann's concern for his wife's position in the world, his love for his daughter Gilberte, his courage in the Dreyfus case, his love of France and her army, all that had brought ripeness to him; but many of the fruits of his labour, during his life and after, were bitter. Odette was an antisemite and an anti-Dreyfusard; Gilberte changed her honourable name of Swann for mundane reasons to de Forcheville. Dreyfus was acquitted, but the anti-clericalism that followed would have made Swann, had he lived, as apprehensive as it did Proust. The Baron de Charlus, the arrogant, gifted, idle aristicrat, will never create anything new, never bring a child into the world, like Swann; never reach the point when he feels, like Marcel, ready to start on a work of art. But he is not immune to suffering: did he not love Morel with a deeper and more human love than Marcel's for Gilberte or Albertine, or Swann's for Odette? The Baron de Charlus achieved ripeness by his love for Morel: he had worked hard to make him into a musician – more purposefully than he ever did to create anything. He had hoped to make a home for him, to have a permanent tie with him, and to give him freedom at the same time. His hopes were betrayed, and he was driven nearly to murder.

But Swann and Charlus, Proust's possible selves, are not the only great characters he created. There is the grandmother. Once again he had two models: he used his real maternal grandmother as the outer shell, and filled it with the substance of his mother – not the heartless mother-lover of his 'melancholy and wakeful evenings' at Combray, but that other mother whose love is perfect. This grandmother is present from the beginning. After dinner Marcel was usually obliged to leave his mother; she stayed with the others in the garden if it was fine, but if it rained they sat in the little parlour – 'Everyone except my grandmother'. She alone would pace the deserted garden, run up and down the soaking paths, 'with her keen jerky little step regulated by the various effects wrought upon her soul by the intoxication of the storm, the force of hygiene, the stupidity of my education and of symmetry in gardens',[29] rather than any anxiety to save her plum-coloured skirt from spots of mud.

All the things which affected her soul we shall find affecting Marcel's. We see her alone and apart from the others, whom she joins only when called to come and stop her husband (who was forbidden liquor) from drinking brandy – to them a joke, to her a grave matter. She begs and implores, but he does not listen, and she goes out again discouraged, 'but still smiling, for she was so humble and so sweet that her gentleness towards others, and her continual subordination of herself and of her own troubles, appeared on her face blended in a smile which, unlike those seen on the majority of human faces, had no trace in it of irony, save for herself, while for all of us kisses seemed to spring from her eyes, which could not look upon those she loved without yearning to bestow upon them passionate caresses'. The great-aunt, who teased her, and who knew that the grandmother never agreed with her, expresses the opinion that she would say anything 'just to seem different from *us*'.[30] But then the great-aunt is a crude person.

The character of the grandmother grows unobtrusively but very convincingly: she does not play a main part in 'Combray', and yet there are few things or people which impress Marcel which we do not see with her eyes as well as his. It comes as a relief to see the church with her eyes, after Marcel's elaborate description. We are glad that she does not know anything about architecture. Proust knew a great deal, and once again he is lending his adult experiences to the boy Marcel. We take it from her that the church had 'a natural air and an air of distinction'. She liked a garden which was not trimmed by a gardener; she could not allow herself to give her grandchild a book that was badly written. Distinction to her was entirely independent of social position and she easily confused the names and titles of the aristocracy. When she tells us that Swann had plenty of taste, doubts the sincerity of Bloch, or has noticed a delicate and timid expression of Mlle Vinteuil's face, we shall never forget, however much we learn about those characters later.

The people she loved most were her daughter and her grandson. We surmise that she was a good wife, though we are not told much about her marriage, and nothing of her love for her husband. Different as Proust's sexual nature and experience were from Tolstoy's, they both came to worship the immaculate woman. How delighted Tolstoy was when he discovered that his relation Tatyana Alexandrovna, whose goodness and perfection, he had to admit, radiated not from love of God but from love of one man, his father, had refused the offer of marriage he made her some time after he became a widower! She did not want to spoil 'her pure and poetic relations', Tolstoy says.

It was with the grandmother that the youth Marcel went for the first time to Balbec. The first night at the hotel, in a new room, he was tormented. The journey had fatigued him, partly because he was ill, partly because he was so open to impressions. 'I was utterly alone; I longed to die. Then my grandmother came in, and to the expansion of my ebbing heart there opened at once an infinity of space.'[31] He confessed to the grandmother that he was not feeling well, and thought that they would have to return to Paris. She did not protest, and went out to buy a few things which would be useful whether they stayed or left. He took a turn in the streets, but got no pleasure from this, and returned to the hotel. He needed his grandmother more than ever, now that he was afraid that his state of health must have discouraged her. Going up in the lift, he addressed a few words to the liftboy, 'I did more than display curiosity, I confessed my strong attachment. But he vouchsafed no answer.' He entered the room, half dead with exhaustion, and the unfamiliar objects tormented him.

I was glad to learn from Feuillerat that all this, and the experience of that night and the following morning, apart from a few unimportant additions, were in the original version. The whole is almost pure autobiography. This is Proust, attached and dependent on his mother, asthmatic, interested in liftboys, but not yet fully conscious of the significance of his interest, suffering because he had to assimilate new things, and tormented by the mortality of all things and all people.

The grandmother returned, in her loose cambric dressing-gown which she always wore whenever anyone was ill, 'her servant's livery, her nurse's uniform, her religious habit'. 'The trouble that servants, nurses, religious, take, their kindness to us, the merits that we discover in them and the gratitude that we owe them all go to increase the impression that we have of being, in their eyes, someone different, of feeling that we are alone, keeping in our own hands the control over our thoughts, our will to live.' But Marcel knew that when he was with his grandmother, however great his misery 'it would be received by her with a pity still more vast; that everything that was mine, my cares, my wishes, would be, in my grandmother, supported upon a desire to save and prolong my life stronger than was my own; and my thoughts were continued in her without having to undergo any deflection, since they passed from my mind into hers without change of atmosphere or of personality'. He kissed her cheek, her brow: 'I drew from them something so beneficial, so nourishing, that I lay in her arms as motionless, as solemn, as calmly gluttonous as a babe at the breast.'[32] She would come whenever he wanted her: he had only to give three little taps on the wall as a signal; she at once replied with three little taps, repeated twice, telling him plainly, 'Don't get excited, I heard you; I shall be with you in a minute.'

Never did the kiss of his mother at Combray, even on those occasions when she did come up to his bedroom after dinner, give him such satisfaction and peace. He always longed to say to his mother 'kiss me just once again', but knew that she would be displeased because his father disapproved of her habit of going up to kiss him goodnight. But nobody stood between him and his grandmother. She never gave him any cause for the agitation, the wretchedness, that came over him that evening when he had been sent off to bed without his mother's kiss, and had been as determined to get it as Swann to find Odette on that night when she had left the Verdurins before he got there. Marcel did not need to force his grandmother's love, she gave him joyfully all he wanted; he did not need her kiss: he kissed her.

But even though the grandmother was ready to come at once, and came often, she did not save him from the agony of that night, which returned after she had left him: she could not save him from his own nature. Just as the child at Combray examined his conscience again and again, so now Marcel takes a near-fatal dose of self-knowledge. De Quincey, as we have seen, often did this. Tolstoy sometimes did the same, but from boyhood on he could always get away to riding, hunting, gambling, womanizing.

Next morning Marcel felt a boy again, and as he tried to dry himself on a stiff towel his eyes were on the 'ocean green and blue like the tail of a peacock'. That fragmentary memory came back to him years later, at the last Guermantes party, but in the week that followed he used often to knock for his grandmother: he had no sense of guilt, as he had had when calling his mother.

Not only do we see many people and things that mattered to Marcel with his grandmother's eyes, but we find also that many important experiences in his life begin with the grandmother. Meeting the Guermantes, for instance: it was the grandmother's friend, Mme de Villeparisis, who introduced Marcel to her great-nephew Saint-Loup and her nephew Charlus. She was staying at the Grand Hotel at Balbec at the same time as Marcel and his grandmother, who had known her for years but, because of the 'caste theory', had not cared to keep up any degree of intimacy. That Mme de Villeparisis should have renewed her friendship with the grandmother at Balbec, and that she showed kindness to Marcel, is in character. She was modest, shrewd, of independent mind and judgement. Late in life she wrote her *Memoirs* and became well known. Though born of a famous house, she was not quite the exclusive, conventional aristocrat: the main reason for this, Proust informs us, was because she had an intellect. Marcel's grandmother was not her only friend who came from the middle class: she had many others.

When Marcel, through his grandmother, meets Mme de Villeparisis, who introduces him to the Guermantes, Marcel Proust removes yet another cross from his created character: Proust asked Robert de Montesquiou, as a favour, to introduce him to high society – and then suffered a rebuff. The grandmother 'lived shut up in a little world of her own': the worldly advantage of renewing her friendship with Mme de Villeparisis did not exist for her. But to Marcel it mattered a lot: 'the drives with Mme de Villeparisis made it possible for him to cross in a few moments the infinitely wide (at least, at Balbec) social gulf'.

But, as so often with Marcel, we discover that in the midst of a worldly experience he hears the small voice of the artist. Just as during the disturbing experience with Gilberte in the Champs-Elysées the fusty smell of the lavatory brings him a memory of Combray which holds a deeper happiness than his wrestling match with Gilberte, so, on one of his drives with his grandmother and Mme de Villeparisis, as the carriage approaches Hudimesnil the sight of three trees fills him with profound happiness, resembling the happiness which the spires of Martinville gave him. Why the trees affect him so deeply he cannot tell: he is sure that he has never seen these particular trees before, and realizes it must be a memory which is bringing him such happiness. This is Proust's own experience, described in the Prologue to *By Way of Sainte-Beuve*: the universal experience of a fragment memory which brings us great emotion, while the memory itself, except for the precious sensation, eludes us. Marcel cannot penetrate his impression because he is not alone. All the same, apart from worldly reasons, the drives with the Marquise de Villeparisis become an important experience for the artist. She tells the coachman to take them back by the old road to Balbec, and 'At the time, I found no great attraction in it, I was only glad to be going home. But it became for me later on a frequent source of joy . . .' This is just what Aksakov says of the nightingales in the spring at Aksakovo when he was seven.

The same Marcel who loved his grandmother so much, and who took all his impressions of life to her, 'for I was never certain what degree of respect was due to anyone until she had informed me', was at times blind and heartless to her, as growing people often are. Once when his friend Saint-Loup was going to take a photograph of the grandmother, he saw 'that she had put on her nicest dress on purpose, and was hesitating between several of her hats', and he was not only surprised but asked himself whether he had not been mistaken in her, 'whether I had not esteemed her too highly . . . whether she had not indeed the very weakness that I believe most alien to her temperament, namely coquetry'. He was cross with her, he 'added a few stinging words of sarcasm' and 'succeeded at least in driving from her face that joyful expression which ought to have made me glad'. This was the intolerance of youth, springing from his need that she should be perfect, should not deviate an inch from his idea of her. Years later, after her death, he learnt from the maid Françoise, that she was a very ill woman at the time, and because she had not one photograph of herself had asked Saint-Loup to take one of her, so as to leave Marcel some likeness of herself: she had tried to hide her illness under a smile and a magnificent hat.

Once when Marcel was at Doncières he had a long conversation with his grandmother on the telephone. He 'discovered for the first time how sweet that voice was', 'but also how sad it was . . . fragile by reason of its delicacy, it seemed at every moment ready to break, to expire in a pure flow of tears; then, too, having it alone beside me, seen, without the mask of her face, I noticed for the first time the sorrows that had scarred it in the course of a lifetime'.[33] We know from *Jean Santeuil*, and from Proust's letters, that this telephone talk was with his mother, when he was in Fontainebleau and she was in Paris, and that it had just such a profound effect on him. He was twenty-five at the time, still living with his parents, making demands of his mother like a child; and she still taking care of him as if he were a child.

But besides learning so much about the grandmother, during this long distance telephone talk, Marcel discovered in her a new attitude to himself. 'The orders or prohibitions which she addressed to me at every moment in the ordinary course of my life, the tedium of obedience or the fire of rebellion which neutralized the affection that I felt for her were at this moment eliminated, and indeed might be eliminated for ever (since my grandmother no longer insisted on having me with her under her control, was in the act of expressing her hope that I would stay at Doncières altogether, or would at any rate extend my visit for as long as possible, seeing that both my health and my work seemed likely to benefit by the change); ... This freedom of action which for the future she allowed me and to which I had never dreamed that she would consent, appeared to me suddenly as sad as might be my freedom of action after her death (when I should still love her and she would for ever have abandoned me).'

So far we have seen how good a 'translation' Proust has made of his own experience into Marcel's. No doubt Proust, earlier in his youth, had felt robbed of his freedom of action by his mother, and the 'tedium of obedience'. But how could the grandmother have given Marcel such feelings, with the mother living? From what we know of these two people, the mother and the grandmother, of their mutual understanding and love for one another (both in real life and in the 'translation'), is it likely that the grandmother would have usurped the mother's rights?

These pages are missing from the original volume. Proust is putting the creation of the grandmother's character before realism. But so he had done earlier, in the description of that melancholy evening at Combray when he was determined to get his mother's kiss: he had kept the grandmother, who was there too, completely out of it. Whenever anything puzzles me in *A la Recherche*, I look for the answer elsewhere in the book. 'This work of the artist, this struggle to discern beneath matter, beneath experience, beneath words, something that is different from them, is a process exactly inverse to that which, in those everyday lives which we live with our gaze averted from ourself . . .'[34]

When Marcel returned to Paris from Doncières, and entered the drawing room, he found his grandmother there reading. She was not aware of his presence, and for a moment he looked at her as a stranger would, 'the photographer who has called to take a photograph'. And: 'I saw, sitting on the sofa, beneath the lamp, red-faced, heavy and common, sick, lost in thought, following the lines of a book with eyes that seemed hardly sane, a dejected old woman whom I did not know.'[35] He had never seen her like this, 'I who had never seen her save in my own soul, always at the same place in the past, through the transparent sheets of contiguous, overlapping memories', he saw her now as an observer, a photographer would. 'We never see the people who are dear to us save in the animated system, the perpetual motion of our incessant love for them', yet in the brief moment of return, Marcel did see his grandmother as a stranger. Could the grandmother have ever seen *him* as a photographer would? The telephone talk had changed Marcel: he understood a great deal more about the grandmother, and about their relationship as well: he loved her more than before and had got no pleasure from the freedom she had seemed to offer. The Marcel who entered the room was not the same as before, and for a moment he looked at her as a stranger. This could not have happened to the grandmother: her feelings for him were unalterable. Marcel's feelings are inherent in his youth: he is growing, changing, making mistakes, and his love for his grandmother is incommensurable with the love of an old person for a boy. She does not need any new knowledge about him; he goes on making discoveries about her both during her lifetime and after her death.

Proust probably did not invent Marcel's experience: it may well have happened to him when he returned from Fontaine-bleau. Some two years after that telephone talk his mother had

a serious operation for cancer, and had very likely looked old
and ill for some time before.

A photographic impression, as we know only too well from
Marcel, is entirely different from a memory 'since every casual
glance is an act of necromancy, each face that we love a mirror
of the past'. The 'photograph' that he took of his grandmother
in which she looked an old and common woman, will no more
live in him than the 'snapshots' he took of Venice, of Balbec, of
Combray: what will continue to disturb him is the experience
of looking at her as a stranger would, of *taking* that photograph.

The experience of the death of the grandmother, we know
from surviving chapter headings, was in the third volume of the
original version. In the final version Proust moved it back
hundreds of pages, and greatly expanded it. We know from
biographical sources that it was the death of his own mother
he was describing, just as it was with his mother that he had
the telephone talk. That the structural changes were a great
gain, as Mr Painter says, there can be little doubt. I want to
dwell only on two aspects of those important chapters. A
memory of the grandmother came back to Marcel on his second
visit to Balbec, a year after her death. It was on the night of his
arrival, and just as on his first night there three years earlier, he
was suffering a complete physical collapse. As he bent down to
undo his boots the grandmother came back to him, and 'saved
me from barrenness of spirit . . . I had just perceived, in my
memory, bending over my weariness, the tender, preoccupied,
dejected face of my gandmother, as she had been on that first
evening of our arrival.'

The Proust who was writing this was not the same as the one
who, perhaps a decade earlier, had begun the book. As we have
seen, according to the original plan there were to have been
only four involuntary memories: the madeleine, and the three
memories at the Guermantes party, yet in the final version,
before we get to this involuntary memory of the grandmother,
Marcel has given us many others. From the first memory which
he added to the definitive version (the one brought back by the
fusty smell of the lavatory in the Champs-Elysées) these involuntary memories become more complex, more like other
people's, no longer miraculous (as the Guermantes memories

are). But what is special about the memory of the grandmother is that it brought him only pain: no comfort, no joy. 'Suddenly my breath failed me, I felt my heart turn to stone. I had just remembered that for week after week I had forgotten to write to my grandmother', and as the grandmother became once again a living reality to him, his heart swelled to breaking point, for now he knew that he 'had lost her for ever'.[36]

The memory of the grandmother does not make Marcel feel that his past contains the material of a work of art, does not make him think about art at all. Proust had already created a work of art, he had even got the Prix Goncourt; he no longer regarded such an achievement as the ultimate aim of life, as he had done when he conceived the original version. He talks now not of art, but of the ultimate refuge: 'And I ask nothing better of God, if a paradise exists, than to be able, there, to knock upon that wall the three little raps which my grandmother would know among a thousand, and to which she would reply with those other raps which said: "Don't be alarmed, little mouse, I know you are impatient, but I am just coming", and that he would let me remain with her throughout eternity which would not be too long for us.'[37]

Proust had longed for a central idea which would make life meaningful in spite of all its contradictions: the cruelty, the bitter disappointments of friendship and sexual love, the agony of guilt. But he could not believe in a deity. Instead he searched for perfection. 'And even in my most carnal desires . . . I might have recognized as their primary motive an idea, an idea for which I would have laid down my life, at the innermost core of which, as in my dreams while I sat reading all afternoon in the garden at Combray, lay the thought of perfection.'[38]

Just as Proust had begun to add 'fresh personalities' to Swann, Charlus, the grandmother, so he did to Marcel. The young Proust had stated plainly in *Jean Santeuil* 'that no simplest occurrence of the past can be felt by others as it is by us, that we cannot enter into their way of feeling, nor they into ours'. When Marcel, who is not a homosexual, overhears and overlooks so much of the lives of homosexuals, we know it is a literary device, that in the art of the impossible literary devices are something we have to put up with.

Proust, like Tolstoy, when asked to explain why he did this or that in his writings, often gave very superficial answers. Such is Proust's advice to Gide: 'You can tell everything, but only on condition that you never say "I".' But there is a passage in Gide's *Journal* which is important: 'He [Proust] said that he bitterly regretted the "irresolution" which had led him – in the hope of bolstering up the heterosexual part of his book – to transpose into *L'Ombre des jeunes filles en fleurs* every gracious, tender, and delightful emotion which he had experienced in homosexual relationships, with the result that it was only the grotesque and abject aspects that were left for *Sodome*' (*Journal, 1889–1939*, pp. 692–4). In his regrets, his evaluation of what he had done, he is no different from other mortals: what seemed right to him when he began the book looked different years later; what matters to us are the facts: he had translated a homosexual affair into a heterosexual one. Proust tells us that 'In reality every reader is, while he is reading, the reader of his own self. The writer's work is merely a kind of optical instrument which he offers to the reader to enable him to discern what, without this book, he would perhaps never have perceived in himself.[39] He had very good reasons, at the time he conceived Marcel, for making him heterosexual. By so doing he was giving the normal reader the glass he could use. He would have got away with this had he not blurred the glass in the later volumes.

We know when it happened. In the original version the love story of Marcel and Albertine was, as Mr Painter says, far too meagre. Then, when Proust was correcting the proofs of *Swann's Way*, Agostinelli turned up and asked Proust for a job. He had been Proust's chauffeur for a short time in 1907, but Proust had not seen him for five years, during which the whole of the original version had been written. Agostinelli had with him his wife or, rather as it later turned out, his mistress. Proust took him on as his secretary, and there began, in January 1913, one of the two great loves of Proust's life, the other being his innocent boyhood love for Marie de Benardaky, as he stated shortly before his death. Proust kept Agostinelli a prisoner in his flat, but in the spring of 1914 he ran away, and was killed in a flying accident. Proust put aside what he was doing and, in

1915, wrote the bulk of the first draft of the Marcel–Albertine love story.

When we read of Marcel's jealousy of Albertine we are greatly puzzled. It remains for us, if we are honest, 'a spectacle without rhyme or reason' until we focus our attention on what Proust reveals to us about the jealousy of homosexuals. There are two types of homosexual, he tells us in the *Cities of the Plain*.[40] In the eyes of one kind 'women would have no existence apart from conversation, flirtation, love not of the heart but of the head'. In this kind, jealousy is kindled only by their friend's love for another man, 'which alone seems to their lovers a betrayal', for if the friends practise love for a woman they do it only with the thought of eventual marriage, and get so little pleasure from it that it cannot distress their male lover. The second sort are capable of loving both sexes, and it is they who 'often inspire jealousy by their love affairs with women. For in the relations which they have with her, they play, for the woman who loves her own sex, the part of another woman, and she offers them at the same time more or less what they find in other men, so that the jealous friend suffers from the feeling that he whom he loves is riveted to her who is to him almost a man, and at the same time feels his beloved almost escape him because, to these women, he is something which the lover himself cannot conceive, a sort of woman.'

In the original version Marcel can be compared to a man who, himself deaf to music, by chance gets to know a real musician; and the period being one when music is flourishing his friend the musician introduces him to many others. Being both an intellectual and a student of the human heart, he learns a lot about the nature of musicians, and finds he can write about them, although he remains deaf to music. The Marcel of the early volumes is very interesting about homosexuals, but he is 'deaf' to their experiences. In the later volumes he ceases to be deaf: in fact he reveals a knowledge which cannot be obtained by an intelligent observer.

Proust knows how difficult his book has become. 'A book may be too learned, too obscure for the simple reader, and thus be only offering him a blurred glass with which he cannot read. But other peculiarities (like inversion) might make it necessary for the reader to read in a certain way in order to read well; the author must not take offence at that but must, on the contrary, leave the reader the greatest liberty and say to him, "Try whether you see better with this, with that, or with another glass".' Nearly every important character turns out to be a homosexual. One day Marcel asked Gilberte who the young man was with whom he had seen her walking along the Avenue des Champs-Elysées. The answer, it was Léa, in male attire.[41] But Léa was a well-known lesbian! Charlus insinuates that even Swann 'whose hostility to that sort of thing' had always been notorious, had been a homosexual 'long ago, in his school-days'.[42] The Marcel who reports all this is not a man who has matured, and discovered evil. We do not find a mature Tolstoy in the *Kreutzer Sonata*: Proust, like Tolstoy, has become obsessed.

Proust was well aware that the reader would see similarities between Marcel's love for Albertine and Swann's for Odette, so he stressed the differences. 'I had received a blessing and a curse which Swann had not known . . .': Swann had been so jealous of Odette because at that time he saw her only occasionally; and even had difficulty, on certain days, in gaining admission to her. 'I, on the contrary, while I was so jealous of Albertine, more fortunate than Swann, had had her with me in my own house.'[43]

And there are other contrasts. Of course Odette and Albertine are very different people, so that the two stories were bound to be different; it is Swann's and Marcel's peculiar love and suffering which reveal the same fingerprints. Proust goes on: 'For nothing is ever repeated exactly, and the most analogous lives which, thanks to the kinship of the persons and the similarity of the circumstances, we may select in order to represent them as symmetrical remain in many respects opposite.'

Assuming that he originally intended to represent Swann's and Marcel's love stories as symmetrical, they are in many respects opposite, but not because of the differences *he* points out to us. Swann's love is the work of Proust's imagination, a translation of an experience at a great distance of time. Marcel's, as George Painter says, has the stamp of 'immediate experience'. But as usual Proust helps us: 'The facts of life have no meaning for the artist, they are to him merely an opportunity for exposing the naked blaze of his genius ... Only, after the rising tide of genius, which sweeps over and submerges a man's life, when the brain begins to tire, gradually the balance is upset, and like a river that resumes its course after the counter-flow of a spring tide, it is life that once more takes the upper hand.'[44] Gradually the balance was upset, and while his imagination was adding new personalities to Swann and Charlus, life took the upper hand in Marcel's love story.

More puzzling than anything else is the effect on Marcel of his memory of Montjouvain. As soon as he heard that Albertine knew Mlle Vinteuil, 'an image stirred in my heart', the memory of watching, at Combray, through a window, Mlle Vinteuil encouraging her lesbian lover to spit at her dead father's por-trait; 'and striking, like an Avenger, in order to inaugurate for me a novel, terrible and merited existence, ... but for those who had done no more, have thought that they were doing no more than look on at a curious and entertaining spectacle, like myself, alas, on that afternoon long ago at Montjouvain, con-cealed by a bush where (as when I complacently listened to an account of Swann's love affair), I had perilously allowed to expand within myself the fatal road, destined to cause me suffering, of Knowledge.'[45] Once again we are compelled to change the glass, and Proust encourages us to do so. He saw again 'the room at Montjouvain where she [the lover] was falling into the arms of Mlle Vinteuil with that laugh in which she gave utterance to the strange sounds of her enjoyment. For, with a girl as 'pretty as Albertine, was it possible that Mlle Vinteuil, having the desires she had, had not asked her to gratify them?' Marcel had earlier decided to part with Alber-tine, and had told his mother that he was not going to marry Albertine and would soon stop seeing her, but now, as he imagined her as Mlle Vinteuil's lover, he decided that 'it is absolutely necessary that I marry Albertine'.[46]

We know from *Jean Santeuil* that Proust had influenced his mother, had made her more tolerant of shady people because they were kind to her son. But her moral values did not alter.[47] Though she tolerated her son's vicious friends and no longer felt that he was damned irretrievably, she could never have tolerated the vice of homosexuality in him. What a profound truth there is in Marcel's statement that after the grandmother's death the mother became like her, afraid to influence him in the wrong direction, 'so spoiling what she believed to be my happiness. She could not even bring herself to forbid me to keep Albertine for the time being in our house' while she was away from home; but had she known of Albertine's friendship with Mlle Vinteuil, 'this would have been to my mother an insurmountable obstacle'.[48] But now, having discovered that Albertine knew Mlle Vinteuil and feeling sure that she must be a lesbian, he changes his mind and tells his mother that he is going to marry her! To the very end, Proust was condemned to belong to the 'sons without a mother, to whom they are obliged to lie all her life long and even in the hour when they close her dying eyes'.[49] But it was not only in real life that Proust could not tell his mother the truth, he could not do so in imagination.

It is no use our pretending that this, and many other actions in the novel are not difficult to understand. Proust was well aware of this, and is constantly at our elbow. Talking of the unusual character of Jupien, he says: 'Art extracted from the most familiar reality does indeed exist and its domain is perhaps the largest of any. But it is no less true that a strong interest, not to say beauty, may be found in actions inspired by a cast of mind so remote from anything that we feel, from anything that we believe, that we cannot ever succeed in understanding them, that they are displayed before our eyes like a spectacle without rhyme or reason. What could be more poetic than Xerxes, son of Darius, ordering the sea to be scourged with rods of iron for having engulfed his fleet?'[50]

But actions may be interesting and still remain alien: Dostoyevsky's preoccupation with murder made him 'very alien' to Marcel.[51] Is Marcel's preoccupation with Mlle Vinteuil alien to us? When Marcel tells us that the evil he had learned by chance as a boy at Combray, watching Mlle Vinteuil and her lover, came 'as a punishment, as a retribution (who can tell?) for my having allowed my grandmother to die, perhaps',[52] the glass he has given us is much too blurred.

Compare this to Tolstoy's statement, a few months before his death, to his friend Biryukov that he was suffering from his terrible sin of seducing, in his youth, the girl Masha, who was then driven out of his aunt's house and 'ruined'. The lives that Tolstoy and Proust lived in their imagination were far more real to them than reality. But in *The Cities of the Plain* we are only at the beginning of Proust's concern with Mlle Vinteuil.

We read that 'Mlle Vinteuil had only acted in a spirit of Sadism, which did not excuse her, but it gave me a certain consolation to think so later on. She must indeed have realized, I told myself, at the moment when she and her friend had profaned her father's photograph, that what they were doing was merely morbidity, silliness, and not the true and joyous wickedness which she would have liked to feel. The idea that it was merely a pretence of wickedness spoiled her pleasure.'[53] On the other hand, the same idea must then have diminished her grief. ' "It was not I," she must have told herself, "I was out of my mind: I myself mean to pray for my father's soul, not to despair of his forgiveness." ' So Marcel Proust, who had profaned his mother's picture for the sake of sexual enjoyment (perhaps because he could not otherwise free himself of her disapproval) must have come to believe that he was not wicked. But still not satisfied, he says: 'I would have liked to be able to put it into her mind. I am sure that I would have done her good and that I should have been able to re-establish between her and the memory of her father a pleasant channel of communication.' And just as Mlle Vinteuil's lesbian lover saved the most important works of the old musician and gave them to the world, so Proust's lover Agostinelli helped him to erect a monument to his grandmother–mother. She does not die in *A la Recherche*: now that she has ceased to be the lover–mother she lives on.

Not less difficult for Proust than to add to Marcel the new personality of the man with so much knowledge of homosexuality, was to turn the Marcel of the numberless strata of memories into Marcel the writer.

That Proust should have written the three Guermantes memories, which were to show him that his past contained the material for a work of art, soon after he conceived the beginning

10*

of the novel is not at all surprising. Before Tolstoy married he began a novel about a happy marriage between a Pierre and a Natasha, and after all the many changes that *War and Peace* underwent that was its end. Tolstoy had dreamt for years of a happy marriage; he was thirty-four, a toothless ageing man, when he achieved it. Of achieving a work of art he had no need to dream: it had happened to him when he was still a youth. Proust dreamt and believed that he had it in him to write a great work of art, but years of hard labour had failed to produce it, and he was an ageing man when he conceived his novel.

In the original plan Marcel would in the end discover his vocation, and that he was ready to start on a work of art; that is he would reach the state Proust was in when he began *A la Recherche* in 1909. An ingenious and artificial plan. It seems to us that the Marcel of *Swann's Way*, as he lives in his memories through sleepless nights is, like the soliloquising Hamlet, talking to himself, not to us. When *Within a Budding Grove*, the earliest part of the final version, appeared in 1918, the first additional pages indicated that Proust was abandoning his plan that Marcel should live in his memories until he discovers his vocation in the end. Instead Marcel is writing the book. This is not admitted at once. Scott Moncrieff, who did not know how the novel had developed, refers openly to 'the reader': 'But who, the reader has been asking, was the Marquis de Norpois.' But in French it is simply: ' "Disons pour finir qui était le Marquis de Norpois.'[54] Proust was not yet quite ready to abandon the pretence that Marcel was still a long way from discovering his vocation and writing a book. Later, in *The Guermantes Way*, the translator again inserts 'as the reader will learn'; but Proust still avoids the word 'reader'. But the strongest proof that Proust had in reality abandoned the original plan is the insertion of more and more involuntary memories. There is a new one of the boy Marcel. Then there are the memories of Doncières, Rivebelle, and Combray, memories of youth, and these make it necessary for Marcel to give excuses why he did not discover his vocation then and there. Proust is like an architect who has planned a remarkable house, his first, with one pillar in the entrance (the madeleine) and three at the exit (the memories at the last Guermantes party), finds the house too small for him and, no longer doubting that he is a good architect, begins to build on. For a time he continues to keep an eye on the original design, and so do we; but by and by he refers less and less to his plan, and we judge the additional rooms and note their superiority to the old ones. The memories they contain, of Doncières, Rivebelle, and Combray, are superior to the madeleine and the three Guermantes memories. They do not depend as much on chance as on Marcel's state of mind, on the fact of his being alone in the house, with time on his hands. There are no exaggerated joys in these memories of youth, no revelations: they are much more complex experiences than the madeleine and the three Guermantes memories, and they are more like other people's involuntary memories.

When 'life has taken the upper hand' we see what is going on in this invalid who has been living for years in a cork-lined room. So that Marcel could live in his imagination, it was necessary that Albertine should have gone out. It was all right for Françoise to come in to light the fire, but Albertine deprived him of the delights of solitude. When he was alone, and Françoise threw a handful of twigs on the fire, the scent brought him back the memory of himself 'poring over a book, now at Combray, now at Doncières'. But it was not only identical sensations, the scent of twigs now and in past moments, which re-created in him the boy, the youth, that he had once been. A change of weather had the same affect: 'Communicating doors, long barred, opened themselves in my brain. The life of certain towns, the gaiety of certain expeditions resumed their place in my consciousness. All athrob in harmony with the vibrating string, I would have sacrificed my dull life in the past, and all my life to come, erased with the india rubber of habit, for one of these special, unique moments.'[55]

Proust carefully revised the book up to the end of *The Guermantes Way*, but after that, Marcel is sometimes a writer, sometimes has still to discover his vocation. In *The Cities of the Plain*[56] Proust makes his reader say '... allow me, gentle author (laissez moi, Monsieur l'auteur), to waste another moment of your time in telling you that it is a pity that, young as you were (or as your hero was, if he be not yourself) you had already so feeble a memory that you could not recall the name of a lady whom you knew quite well'. And in *The Captive*[57] we read 'As soon as she [Albertine] was able to speak she said: "My – " or "My dearest – " followed by my Christian name, which, if we give the narrator the same name as the author of this book, would be "My Marcel", or "My dearest Marcel".' But later we find Marcel telling Albertine: ' "I am not a novelist." '[58] Marcel says that when he was trying to recall Venice, Balbec, Combray, with 'uniform memory' he failed. The memory of habit, he tells us, does not contain our past, but even 'a change in the weather is sufficient to create the world and oneself anew'.[59] But how did his spirits stand up to his ill-health? He answers that our sense of well-being 'is caused not so much by our sound health as by the unemployed surplus of our strength, by diminishing our activity. The activity with which I was overflowing and which I kept constantly charged as I lay in bed, made me spring from side to side, with a leaping heart, like a machine which, prevented from moving in space, rotates on its own axis.'[60] This is Marcel Proust at work during the long years.

What makes the confusion worse confounded are Proust's many generalizations about the nature of memories throughout *A la Recherche*, and in the end repeated in *Time Regained*. Let us take only one example. In *The Guermantes Way* we read: 'But between one another of the memories that had now come to me in turn of Combray, of Doncières and of Rivebelle, I was conscious at the moment of more than a distance in time, of the distance that there would be between two separate universes the material elements in which were not the same.'[61]

This is given as a new discovery by Marcel in *Time Regained*. Where were these generalizations first written, in the middle volumes or in *Time Regained*? Or were they written simultaneously and, if so, when between 1909 and 1922? In the middle volumes they come with an expanding experience of involuntary memories, the experience of a man who is working on them: a writer. And like the memories themselves, the generalizations are truer, and at the same time more complex, in the earlier than in the last volume. In *Time Regained* the many generalizations appear as a *deus ex machina*, in a matter of hours, as do the three involuntary memories at the Guermantes party. But there are also in *Time Regained* generalizations which were clearly made when the original plan was conceived, and may well have been present in the lost last volume of the original version. For example there is a statement in *Time Regained* which could only have been made very soon after he had conceived the original plan of the book: that involuntary memories had come back to him only three or four times.[62] But there are dozens of them throughout *A la Recherche*! We now know that he continued to make changes in *Time Regained* as late as 1918, but clearly he never revised it finally. *Time Regained* is like a cave, inhabited over a long period, in which there are to be found bones, jars, ornaments, and tools long out of use side by side with those of recent date and some even which are still being used.

The felicity brought to Proust by the three memories at the Guermantes party made him search for the cause, and 'I began to divine as I compared these diverse happy impressions, diverse yet with this in common, that I experienced them at the present moment and at the same time in the context of a distant moment, so that the past was made to encroach upon the present and I was made to doubt whether I was in the one or the other'.[63] This could easily have been written in 1909, at the very beginning of the conception of the plan, for, as we know, two of these three memories he had already described in the *Prologue* and *By Way of Sainte-Beuve*, and just such involuntary memories are to be found in *Jean Santeuil*.

Such experiences are described by many autobiographers: De Quincey, Aksakov. I have given many examples of such experiences of my own in *A Collection of Moments*. Their main features are greatly increased intensity of sensations, and the stretching of time. When Proust maintains, of his Guermantes memories, that time in them was not the ordinary time, he is saying no more than many others have said, though his expression: 'a fragment of time in its pure state' is not enlightening.

The sensations, and unusual sense of time, of a past moment may be preserved either in a memory, or in a record made at the time in a diary or letter, but we do *not* find them in our memories of habit, of the background of our life. We may be nostalgic about a habit, but emotions are always part of the memory of a moment. A study of autobiographies, especially of childhood, shows that this experience of sensations and of time in the memory of a moment is universal. Autobiographers whom nobody would accuse of sentimentality, and who dislike exaggeration, like Aksakov and De Quincey, express their feelings about recollected sensations in superlatives. But more striking in such a memory of a moment is the feeling of stretched time. Darwin remembered that when he fell off a wall (he was nine years old) the number of thoughts that went through his head in the short period of the fall was surprisingly large. Dostoyevsky remembered the experience of a few minutes becoming an eternity while he believed he was going to be executed. I happened to read a remarkable example in an article in the *Radio Times* about David Jenkins, the 400 metre runner. I had never heard of him before. His race lasts only three-quarters of a minute, and he remembers, he says, moments from many of his races; 'an instant when I first saw someone's back, or when a rival came alongside, and my reaction'.

Each of these examples is of a very disturbing moment, a moment of fear or shock. David Jenkins had once a very frightening experience, when he had already gained a reputation as a runner: he fell and was injured in a race, and had to withdraw. Clearly every race is for him fraught with anxiety and fear. Not everyone lays down memories at such moments, but David Jenkins does, and later, living in his memories, he finds that much happened in those three-quarters of a minute.

Marcel tells of the great joy brought to him by the Guermantes memories, and of finding that his past was alive. For a moment his sensations and his feeling of time are in 'a pure state'. In his memory of the railway carriage when the train halted, a whiff of smoke, the sensation of great heat relieved by the cool smell of a forest background and a row of trees, bring him great joy, but, as he reminds us in the moment of re-living the memory, he had found them tedious both to observe and to describe.[64] More than that: go back to the beginning of that chapter and you will find a disturbing moment: looking at those same trees he said to himself 'If ever I thought of myself as a poet, I know

now that I am not one'. Or take the memory of the starched napkin which brought him back the sea at Balbec, and go back to the experience itself, when he tried to dry himself on a starched unyielding towel with the sea stretched out before him, and you will find that that morning followed on a night of despair, when he wanted to die. It is in memories which contain disturbance, fear, suffering, that our sensations and time are special.

How do we regain lost time and lost traumatic sensations? Would we find such past moments in our diary or letters? A person may be an excellent diarist, and returning to his diary after many years may be delighted to find many things he had forgotten: clothes, food, the weather, friends he met, fleeting feelings, things he heard and said. But not even an adult, let alone a child, can deal with a traumatic experience immediately after it happens, especially if he is a poet. An excellent example is Dostoyevsky's experience of having only a few minutes left to live. He wrote that very day to his brother, but did not 'embody' (his word) the memory: years later he recollected his emotions and recorded in *The Idiot* his experience of those few minutes becoming 'an endless term'. We only regain 'lost time', a past moment, when its emotion is transfused into the present moment. Like poetry, it is recollected in tranquillity. It is the emotions of a disturbance, a shock, which give intensity to our sensations and change time into 'an endless term'. To Richard II, it was only in prison, inactive, without hope, that 'thoughts became minutes'.

Proust learned everything through suffering. Some critics tell us that Proust, De Quincey, Dostoyevsky, were in love with suffering. They were nothing of the sort: they could not avoid it. 'Brief though our life may be, it is only while suffering that we see certain things which at other times are hidden from us'; and 'Perhaps only for a few great geniuses does this movement of thought exist all the time, uncontingent upon the agitation of personal grief'.[65] But to Proust, as to all poets, the road lay through suffering: for twenty years his only moments of inspiration were involuntary memories, not the new creations of imagination. 'A man born with sensibility but without imagination might, in spite of this deficiency, be able to write

admirable novels. It may be that, for the creation of a work of
literature, imagination and sensibility are interchangeable
qualities.' It was not till 1909 that he conceived a work of the
imagination: his previous writings, valuable as they are, are
not works of art. Some critics maintain that his great purpose in
life was to create a work of art. This may have been true before
he began *A la Recherche*, but after the 'rising tide of genius' swept
over and submerged him, new purposes beckoned to him. This
is what he says in *The Captive*: 'Grief penetrates into us and
forces us out of painful curiosity to penetrate other people.
Whence emerge truths which we feel that we have no right to
keep hidden, so much so that a dying atheist who has discovered them, certain of his own extinction, indifferent to
fame, will nevertheless devote his last hours on earth to an
attempt to make them known.'[66]

To think that Proust felt this overwhelming urge to communicate his discoveries, that the thousands of pages of *Jean
Santeuil* and *A la Recherche* are chequered with experiences of
involuntary memories, and yet he never exhausted his vast
knowledge of their nature!

As an example let us take the memory of the train journey as
he gave it in the Prologue to *By Way of Sainte-Beuve*. 'I strove to
draw impressions from the passing landscape. I wrote about the
little country churchyard while it was passing before my eyes.
I noted down the bright bars of sunlight on the trees, the way-
side flowers like those in *Le Lys dans la Vallée*.' Proust goes on to
say that when he tried to conjure up that day, 'I could never
manage it', but one day 'when at lunch, not long ago, I let my
spoon fall on my plate' – it made the same kind of noise as the
hammer of the linesmen tapping on the wheels of the train
which had halted – 'The burning blinded hour when the noise
rang out instantly came back to me and all that day in its
poetry . . .' 'except for the country churchyard, the trees
streaked with light, and the Balzacian flowers, gained by
deliberate observation and lost from the poetic resurrection':
in fact everything except what he had been trying to write
about at the time. Of course Marcel's memory differs from
Proust's, because Marcel is not a writer. But what is truly
amazing in Marcel Proust's real experience is that the deliberate

observations, the effort to write down impressions, did not come
back to him. My own and other writers' experience of memories
show that what one makes – a poem, a story – never comes back
involuntarily: nor do dreams, as if they too are things one
makes. There is nothing amateurish in Proust's study of the
nature of memories, as there is in Tolstoy's generalizations on
history, medical science, even literature.

Writing of Vinteuil the musician[67] Proust says: 'Each artist
seems thus to be the native of an unknown country, which he
has himself forgotten, different from that from which will
emerge, making for the earth, another great artist. When all is
said, Vinteuil in his latest works, seemed to have drawn nearer
to that unknown country. The atmosphere was no longer the
same as in the sonata, the questioning phrases became more
pressing, more uneasy, the answers more mysterious; . . .
Vinteuil's last compositions were the most profound. Now no
programme, no subject supplied any intellectual basis for judgment' – one more fragment of Proust's great confession. And
again: 'the art of a Vinteuil, like that of an Elstir, makes the
man himself apparent'. Two motives were wrestling together:
'A wrestling match of energies only, to tell the truth; for if these
creatures attacked one another, it was rid of their physical
bodies, of their appearance, of their names, and finding in me an
inward spectator, himself indifferent also to their names, and to
all details, interested only in their immaterial and dynamic com-
bat, and following with passion its sonorous changes. In the
end the joyous motive was left triumphant . . . I might be sure
that this new tone of joy, this appeal to a super-terrestrial joy,
was a thing that I would never forget . . . But should I be able,
ever, to realize it?' He compares the musical phrase to his
impressions 'of the steeples of Martinville, or of a line of trees
near Balbec'. No mention now of the madeleine or the Guermantes memories! It was such a long time since he had erected
those pillars that they seemed unimportant.

It is after describing this super-terrestrial joy that he goes on
to tell us that the artist's daughter was not really wicked, only
morbid and silly, that 'a pleasant channel of communication'
between her and the memory of her father could be re-
established; and that he himself, in whom Mlle Vinteuil

revived afresh his jealousy of Albertine, would never cease to hear the strange appeal of the music 'as the promise and proof that there existed something other, realizable no doubt by art, than the nullity that I had found in all my pleasures and in love itself, and that if my life seemed to me so empty, at least there were still regions unexplored'.[68]

Proust could have said of *A la Recherche* what Tolstoy said of *War and Peace*, that it was not a novel: it was what the writer wanted to say, and the only way he could say it. He might have been writing of *A la Recherche* when he analysed Marcel's experience of hearing, for the first time, the Vinteuil sonata, played by Mme Swann: 'But often one listens and hears nothing . . . Probably what is wanting, the first time, is not comprehension but memory . . . great works of art do not begin by giving us all their best. In Vinteuil's sonata the beauties that one discovers at once are those also of which one most soon grows tired, and for the same reason no doubt, namely that they are less different from what one already knows. But when those first apparitions have withdrawn, there is left for our enjoyment some passage which its composition, too new and strange to offer anything but confusion to our mind, had made indistinguishable and so preserved intact; . . . this comes to us last of all. But this also must be the last that we shall relinquish. And we shall love it longer than the rest because we have taken longer to get to love it.'[69]

# CONCLUSIONS

AKSAKOV's *Family Chronicle* was received with joy not only by ordinary readers but by great writers as different as Tolstoy and Herzen. Soon after its appearance, Tolstoy wrote in a paper called *Molva* that he did not share the opinion of those who judge 'these magnificent pages of S. T. Aksakov's as inventions of the imagination', they were painted from nature, and one need only judge 'the excellence of the painter's brush, and how well he has put on the shadows'. Later, when *Years of Childhood* appeared, he was even more enthusiastic. If De Quincey's memories of childhood and boyhood, and that fragment the *Original Confessions*, had not been scattered in so many journals, I believe he would have been known and loved in this country as well as Aksakov was in Russia.

At a distance of some forty years after experiencing the breathing of life into my own growing years by involuntary memories, I turned to autobiographers to compare my experience with others'. Many of my generalizations were confirmed, others enlarged: it was a rich harvest.

Why did I choose Aksakov and De Quincey? Why reject, for example, the invaluable autobiographies of Edwin Muir and Stendhal (*The Life of Henry Brulard*)? One reason was that the latter are not works of art. Edwin Muir's autobiography ceases to be a work of art when continued into his adult life. Stendhal's book, which ends with the boy at eighteen, suffers from the deliberate intention *not* to make it a work of art: a great novelist, he seemed to distrust art in autobiography, as if it impaired the truth. That is exactly the flaw in the old Tolstoy's memories given to Biryukov. Aksakov says plainly of *Years of Childhood* that though he was not capable of invention he intended to write a work of art; and there can be little doubt that that was

De Quincey's intention too: he himself claimed for the *Confessions* and the *Suspiria* (and only for these) that they were works of art in conception.

What makes Aksakov's and De Quincey's autobiographies paradigms is that we know the whole process of their recovery of the past. Lifelong men of letters, they yet succeeded only late in life in recovering and breathing life into their childhood and boyhood. Psychologists ought to study what Aksakov and De Quincey, with their great self-knowledge, still did not know about themselves at the age of sixty, the all-important memories which had lived beneath the threshold of consciousness for so long and would be recovered at last.

Mashinsky, Aksakov's biographer, has collected many interesting facts about him. He says that the only valid criticism of his work has been that his peasants are all alike (except for his *dyadka* Yevseitch), that they are done in contour only, that to writers who belonged to the nobility the peasants were 'a grey mass'. But this is not the reason why Aksakov's peasants are 'grey'. Mashinsky appears to have forgotten Turgenev's and Tolstoy's peasants: every one is a person in his own right. In De Quincey, people he loved most, who most profoundly affected his life, are done only 'in contour': his sister Elisabeth, Ann of Oxford Street, his wife Margaret. We do not see them, we hardly hear them, they rarely act. Even Kate Wordsworth we only know from a poem by her father. Tolstoy's, Proust's, Dickens's imaginations are teeming with characters, and what is special about them is that in the imagination of the novelist they live independent lives.

Aksakov was a better husband, father, and friend than Tolstoy, but only people who had a great effect on him in his growing years lived in his imagination; of others whom he knew and liked he could write memoirs, like De Quincey, not works of art.

My reasons for choosing Tolstoy and Proust, among novelists, were partly personal: they had mattered to me in maturity far more than, for example, Dickens and Stendhal. I read Tolstoy in my school days, but he did not matter to me then nearly as much as Pushkin, Turgenev, Ibsen, and, above all, Dostoyevsky, or later Goethe, when I was quite at home in German. From my thirties onwards I found myself moving away from Dostoyevsky to Tolstoy. The more I read and reread Tolstoy's memories and thinly disguised autobiographical writings the more I marvelled at his 'translation' into fiction. He could have said, as Goethe did, that every thing he wrote was 'a fragment of a great confession'.

What first brought me to Proust was my interest in involuntary memories. This or that scene in *A la Recherche* made an impression on me, but his material, the society he described, his language, did not attract me. But I began to be interested in Proust himself, and then in the contradictions in the nature of the Narrator and the ambiguities in this theme of involuntary memories; and the mumbo-jumbo that critics wrote about him puzzled me more and more. There came a time when I read the whole of *A la Recherche* like a thriller, following up clues.

Suppose that the second original volume had been lost, as the third was, and that neither *Jean Santeuil* nor *By Way of Sainte-Beuve* had ever seen the light of day; suppose that the only evidence that Proust made great changes in the original version came from a comparison of the chapter headings of the three volumes, which were printed opposite the title page of *Swann's Way* in 1913, with those of the definitive version, would it have been possible to clear up the contradictions and ambiguities in the definitive version? Undoubtedly. Given a reader who paid heed to Proust's efforts to help us to understand his book, and who had had some experiences of involuntary memories so that they did not appear to him miraculous, and used his common sense, he would have asked the right questions, and the right answers would have followed. If he had asked himself whether the memory of the dead grandmother could have come back to Marcel involuntarily where it occurs in the original version, in the third volume, *Time Regained*, he would have been bound to doubt it. Why did not Marcel discover then and there that his past contained the material of a work of art; why did this not happen until he experienced the three miraculous joyful Guermantes memories? And can one imagine Proust, when describing those three involuntary memories, not referring to the involuntary memory of the grandmother, so important and yet so different: full of pain, not joy.

In the original version, as I have shown, Marcel could not have experienced an involuntary memory before the end of his active life, until as an ageing man, the madeleine brought him back childhood; and then after years of living in his memories – an indefinite period – the memories at the Guermantes party made him realize that he was ready to write a book. In the definitive version the grandmother memory comes back involuntarily in *Cities of the Plain* and it has been preceded by Marcel's other involuntary memories; moreover in that book Marcel already talks openly of his 'reader': he is a writer, and is regaining lost time.

Once it became clear to me that the whole of Proust's writings is a single book 'im werden' I got more and more fascinated by his mind and his great disabilities. Was there ever a great novelist who found it harder to conceive a novel? It reminded me of my surprise when I first came to the Cavendish Laboratory and learnt, on good authority, that the two great experimentalists, J. J. Thomson and Rutherford, were 'no good with their hands'. The obstacles a genius can overcome are as astonishing as his achievements.

But often tired of Marcel's and Albertine's love story, I returned to Shakespeare: what were they, compared to Antony and Cleopatra, which now struck me as the eighth wonder? Sometimes a scene between that mad Charlus and Marcel struck me as a remarkable feat, but then I would remember the relationship between that tragic madman Saul and David, and put Proust aside. But I returned, and slowly became more and more captivated by Proust's wonderful mind, as much a scientist's as an artist's, and by his long search. If Proust had been able to conceive novels as easily as Dickens and Dostoyevsky he would have started a new novel after the original version was completed. But he did not have that gift, and anyway he was clearly not content with the second and third volumes as they stood. That he had the courage to abandon his original plan was as much due to necessity as to the seriousness with which he had approached his work from its earliest beginnings. To revise *Time Regained* was an impossible task: he had been depositing ideas for a decade; and during that period he had changed both as man and artist much more than

Tolstoy did in the decade between *War and Peace* and *Anna Karenina*. But I still regret, for the sake of its readers, that *A la Recherche* is so very very long.

Aksakov, De Quincey, Tolstoy, Proust, all had great self-knowledge, and their weaknesses, shame, guilt, grew in their minds to gigantic size; but so did their delights in life, and gratitude.

All these writers had in common the need for solitude. Aksakov and Tolstoy found it in their field sports, and spent most of their lives close to nature. Proust found it in locking himself up in a room for years. De Quincey, like Wordsworth, was a great walker, in fact he claimed that it was an antidote to opium. He says in the *Suspiria*: 'No man ever will unfold the capacities of his own intellect who does not at least checker his life with solitude.'

But the most fundamental trait of all these four writers is seriousness. Professor Pascal says that for an autobiography to be significant not only as information but as a literary work 'the first condition is the seriousness of the author, the seriousness of his personality and of his intention in writing. And the overriding problem is that of truth.'

Needless to say 'seriousness' does not exclude humour, satire, even comedy; but it does mean that there is no deliberate lying. Since no great artist-autobiographer claims factual truth, the lying consists in manufacturing emotions and beliefs. If the autobiographer does this he gives himself away. Suppose De Quincey, by nature a deeply religious child (a gift which did not grow with years) had manufactured religious feelings in the *Confessions*: we would hear the false tones. But what of the novelist, who is free to invent, and who creates characters who have lives independent of him?

During Levin's visit to Anna, his first and last, the talk turns on modern French art and Vorkuyev accuses 'the artist of realism pushed to coarseness'. Levin's opinion is that 'In the fact that they no longer lie they see poetry.' Anna agrees; 'But perhaps it is always like that – they build their conceptions out of thought-up, conventional forms, and later – after they have made all the possible combinations and got bored with them – they begin to think up forms that are more natural,

and just.' Both Anna and Levin speak authoritatively: Tolstoy
has endowed them with the nature of real artists. Realism,
factual truth, is often combined by the novelist with manufactured thoughts and feelings, and is as far removed from
profound truth as from poetry. What then makes us say that
Tolstoy and Proust are compulsive pursuers of truth?

In our growing years we are affected by books as by people:
it is what they do to us that forms our judgement. But in
maturity the first sign to us that a writer is dealing in truth is
the freedom he gives us to form our own judgement. With all
his great admiration and love for Tolstoy, Chekhov felt free,
when rereading *The Kreutzer Sonata*, to say that it was ridiculous. However much one cares for Proust one surely must say
the same of what he does with his Saint-Loup: this golden
youth not only reveals in the later volumes an extraordinary
viciousness, but we discover that he is also a homosexual. So
what, in retrospect, are we to make of his scamper round the
walls of the restaurant in such a great hurry to bring Marcel
an overcoat when he felt chilly? When Saint-Loup came
'bounding towards' him, Marcel's pleasure lay in recognizing
that the cause was not only in Saint-Loup's own nature, 'but
even more in that which by birth and upbringing he had
inherited from his race'.[1] Proust destroys the character out of a
bitter resentment against his own earlier adoration of the
French aristocracy: he sacrifices art to truth – the truth about
himself. A Tolstoy, a Proust could have so easily obscured the
truth, as many great and not so great novelists have done.

To Tolstoy, even in his last years when he was decrying his
greatest creations, the need to tell the truth in art was compulsive. And Proust says of the dying atheist and the truths he
discovers: certain of his own extinction, indifferent to fame, he
still nevertheless devotes his last hours on earth to an attempt
to make them known.

# Notes to Proust

The references to *A la Recherche du Temps Perdu* (*ALR*) are to the
Chatto English and Pléïade French editions, in that order; and to
the English editions of *By Way of Sainte-Beuve* (*Contre Sainte-Beuve –
SB*) and *Jean Santeuil* (*JS*). I have only given references to allusions
or quotations of significance. The volume titles of the two editions
of *ALR* are as follows:

| | |
|---|---|
| 1. *Swann's Way.* Part I | 1. *Du Coté de chez Swann* |
| 2. *Swann's Way.* Part II | *A l'Ombre des jeunes filles en* |
| 3. *Within a Budding Grove.* Part I | *fleur* |
| 4. *Within a Budding Grove.* Part II | |
| | |
| 5. *The Guermantes Way.* Part I | 2. *Le Coté de Guermantes* |
| 6. *The Guermantes Way.* Part II | *Sodome et Gomorrhe* |
| 7. *Cities of the Plain.* Part I | |
| 8. *Cities of the Plain.* Part II | |
| | |
| 9. *The Captive.* Part I | 3. *La Prisonnière* |
| 10. *The Captive.* Part II | *La Fugitive* |
| 11. *The Sweet Cheat Gone* | *Le Temps retrouvé* |
| 12. *Time Regained* | |

## The conception of *A la Recherche*

| | |
|---|---|
| 1. *JS*, x | 8. *JS*, 96 |
| 2. *JS*, 85 | 9. *JS*, 96 |
| 3. *JS*, 85 | 10. *SB* |
| 4. *JS*. 95 | 11. *ALR*, 1.58; 1.45 |
| 5. *JS*, 95 | 12. *SB* |
| 6. *JS*, 133 | 13. *ALR*, 1.58; 1.45 |
| 7. *ALR*, 4.309; 1.922 | 14. *ALR*, 1.59; 1.45 |

15. *ALR*, 1.9; 1.9
16. *ALR*, 1.6; 1.6
17. *ALR*, 12.223; 3.867
18. *ALR*, 12.225; 3.868
19. *ALR*, 12.225; 3.868

## Swann's Way

1. *JS*, 83
2. *JS*, 83
3. *JS*, 36
4. *JS*, 37
5. *JS*, 215
6. *JS*, 217
7. *JS*, 207
8. *JS*, 71
9. *ALR*, 12.387; 3.986
10. *JS*, 723
11. *JS*, 725
12. *JS*, 726
13. *JS*, 27
14. *JS*, 30
15. *ALR*, 1.41; 1.32
16. *ALR*, 1.38; 1.30
17. Painter, vol. 1, 325
18. *ALR*, 1.230; 1.167
19. *ALR*, 1.207; 1.151
20. *ALR*, 9.96; 3.79
21. *JS*, 38
22. *JS*, 738
23. *JS*, 732
24. *ALR*, 7.20; 2.615
25. *JS*, 285
26. *ALR*, 1.12; 1.11
27. *ALR*, 4.61; 1.746
28. *ALR*, 12.342; 3.954
29. *JS*, 50
30. *JS*, 60
31. *ALR*, 1.153; 1.113
32. *ALR*, 1.223; 1.162
33. *ALR*, 1.225; 1.164
34. *ALR*, 12.255; 3.890
35. *ALR*, 1.165; 1.122
36. *ALR*, 1.256; 1.186
37. *ALR*, 2.225; 1.379
38. *ALR*, 1.267; 1.193
39. *ALR*, 2.25; 1.236
40. *JS*, 49
41. *ALR*, 2.288; 1.427

## The Addition of New Personalities

1. *ALR*, 3.90; 1.492
2. *ALR*, 3.148; 1.532
3. *ALR*, 3.368–9; 1.685
4. *ALR*, 12.283; 3.910
5. *JS*, 579ff.
6. *ALR*, 2.29; 1.239
7. *ALR*, 1.38; 1.30
8. *ALR*, 3.2; 1.432
9. *ALR*, 8.305; 2.1075
10. *ALR*, 3.198; 1.567
11. *ALR*, 11.243; 3.591
12. *ALR*, 7.106; 2.676
13. *ALR*, 7.108–9; 2.678
14. *ALR*, 12.271; 3.901
15. *ALR*, 7.125; 2.690
16. *ALR*, 7.143; 2.703
17. *ALR*, 7.4; 2.603
18. *ALR*, 8.78; 2.910
19. *ALR*, 10.135; 3.306
20. *ALR*, 8.283; 2.1059
21. *ALR*, 10.50; 3.243
22. *ALR*, 10.151; 3.317
23. *ALR*, 8.304; 2.1075
24. *ALR*, 12.143; 3.805

25. *ALR*, 11.110; 3.495
26. *ALR*, 12.213; 3.859
27. *ALR*, 12.256; 3.891
28. *ALR*, 12.221; 3.865
29. *ALR*, 1.12; 1.11
30. *ALR*, 1.27; 1.22
31. *ALR*, 3.343; 1.667
32. *ALR*, 3.344; 1.668
33. *ALR*, 5.179; 2.135
34. *ALR*, 12.263; 3.896
35. *ALR*, 5.188; 2.141
36. *ALR*, 7.220; 2.758
37. *ALR*, 7.227; 2.763
38. *ALR*, 5.53; 2.46
39. *ALR*, 12.283; 3.911
40. *ALR*, 7.31; 2.622
41. *ALR*, 11.378; 3.695 n.
42. *ALR*, 10.126; 3.299
43. *ALR*, 11.114; 3.498
44. *ALR*, 4.209; 1.851
45. *ALR*, 8.362; 2.1115
46. *ALR*, 8.384; 2.1131
47. *JS*, 733

48. *ALR*, 9.7–8; 3.14
49. *ALR*, 7.20; 2.615
50. *ALR*, 9.54; 3.47
51. *ALR*, 10.239; 3.379
52. *ALR*, 8.362; 2.1115
53. *ALR*, 10.76–7; 3.262–3
54. *ALR*, 3.6; 1.434
55. *ALR*, 9.24; 3.25
56. *ALR*, 7.71; 2.651
57. *ALR*, 9.91; 3.75
58. *ALR*, 10.239; 3.379
59. *ALR*, 6.49; 2.345
60. *ALR*, 9.25; 3.26
61. *ALR*, 6.123; 2.398
62. *ALR*, 12.234; 3.875
63. *ALR*, 12.229; 3.871
64. *ALR*, 12.225; 3.868
65. *ALR*, 12.264; 3.897
66. *ALR*, 9.192; 3.146 n.
67. *ALR*, 10.69ff.; 3.257ff.
68. *ALR*, 10.77; 3.263
69. *ALR*, 3.143; 1.529

## Conclusions

1. *ALR*, 6.145; 2.413

# Select Bibliography

## AKSAKOV

AKSAKOV, S. T. *Collected Works*, 4 vols, Moscow 1955 (in Russian) –
*Years of Childhood; A Russian Gentleman; A Russian Schoolboy*,
trans. J. D. Duff, Oxford 1915–17.
MASHINSKY, S. *Aksakov: Life and Works*, Moscow 1961 (in Russian).

## DE QUINCEY

DE QUINCEY, T. *Collected Works*, ed. David Masson, Black 1889–90.
ELWIN, M. Confessions of an English Opium Eater *in both the
Revised and the Original Texts with its Sequels* Suspiria de Pro-
fundis *and* The English Mail-Coach, Macdonald 1956.
SACKVILLE-WEST, E. *De Quincey's Recollections of the Lake Poets*,
1948.
*A Flame in Sunlight: The Life and Works of Thomas de Quincey*,
Cassell 1936.
(ed.) *Confessions of an English Opium-Eater together with Selections
from the Autobiography of Thomas de Quincey*, Cresset 1950.

## TOLSTOY

TOLSTOY, L. N. *The Jubilee Edition*, 90 vols, Moscow 1928 (in
Russian).
*Centenary Edition*, trans. Aylmer and Louise Maude, Oxford 1928.
BAYLEY, J. *Tolstoy and the Novel*, Chatto 1966.
BIRYUKOV, P. *Biography of L. N. Tolstoy*, 4 vols, Berlin 1921 (in
Russian).
*Leo Tolstoy*, Heinemann 1906.
*Tolstoy's Love Letters with a study on the autobiographical elements in
Tolstoy's work*, trans. S. S. Koteliansky and Virginia Woolf,
Hogarth 1923.
CHRISTIAN, R. J. *Tolstoy's 'War and Peace'*, Oxford, Clarendon
Press 1962.

GOLDENWEISER, A. B. *Talks with Tolstoy*, trans. S. S. Koteliansky, Hogarth 1923.

KUZMINSKAYA, T. *Tolstoy as I knew him; My Life at Home and at Yasnaya Polyana*, Macmillan, New York 1948.

SHKLOVSKY, V. *Leo Tolstoy*, Moscow 1963 (in Russian).

SUKHOTIN–TOLSTOY, T. *The Tolstoy Home*, trans. A. Brown, Harvill 1950.

TOLSTOY, S. *Tolstoy Remembered by His Son*, trans. M. Budberg, Weidenfeld 1961.

*Tolstoy and the Russian Critics*, 2 vols, Moscow 1960 (in Russian).

TROYAT, H. *Tolstoy*, trans. Nancy Amphoux, W. H. Allen 1968.

## PROUST

PROUST, M. *A la Recherche du Temps Perdu*, 3 vols, Bibliothèque de la Pléiade, Gallimard 1954.

*Les Plaisirs et les Jours*, Gallimard 1924.

*By Way of Sainte-Beuve (Contre Sainte-Beuve)*, trans. Sylvia Townsend Warner, Chatto 1958.

*Jean Santeuil*, trans. G. Hopkins with a Preface by A. Maurois, Weidenfeld 1955.

*Remembrance of Things Past (A la Recherche du Temps Perdu)*, trans. C. K. Scott Moncrieff, Chatto; vol. 12, *Time Regained*, trans. Stephen Hudson, Chatto 1931; trans. Andreas Mayor, Chatto 1970.

FEUILLERAT, A. *Comment Marcel Proust a composé son roman*, Yale 1934.

MAUROIS, A. *The Quest for Proust*, trans. G. Hopkins, 1950.

PAINTER, G. D. *Marcel Proust, A Biography*, vol. 1, Chatto 1959; vol. 2, Chatto 1965.

## OTHERS

FORSTER, J. *Life of Dickens*, 1872–4.

MUIR, EDWIN. *An Autobiography*, Hogarth 1954.

PASCAL, R. *Design and Truth in Autobiography*, Routledge 1960.

STENDHAL. *The Life of Henry Brulard*, trans. J. Stewart and B. C. J. G. Knight, Merlin 1958.

# Index